The Child in the Electric Chair

The Child in the Electric Chair

The Execution of George Junius Stinney Jr. and the Making of a Tragedy in the American South

Eli Faber Foreword by Carol Berkin

THE UNIVERSITY OF
SOUTH CAROLINA PRESS

© 2021 University of South Carolina

Published by the University of South Carolina Press
Columbia, South Carolina 29208

www.uscpress.com

Manufactured in the United States of America

30 29 28 27 26 25 24 23 22 21
10 9 8 7 6 5 4 3 2 1

Library of Congress Cataloging-in-Publication Data
can be found at http://catalog.loc.gov/.

ISBN: 978-1-64336-194-9 (hardcover)
ISBN: 978-1-64336-195-6 (ebook)

In Honor of
Carol Ruth Berkin
Scholar, Teacher, Friend Extraordinaire

In Memory of
Gail Kotler
Brave, Compassionate, Wise
Daniel A. Sarot
"He Never Gave Up"

I give special thanks again, again, and again to my wife, Lani,
for her undaunted love and support. Her help and constant friendship
have made all the difference in my life and in the life of this project.

Justice: Justice shalt thou pursue.

Deuteronomy, 16:20

Contents

Illustrations

Acknowledgments

Lani Faber knew her husband's wishes well. She made a list of all those who Eli would have wanted thanked in his acknowledgments. This list includes Robert Alderman, descendent of the Alderman family who founded Alcolu and whose friendship opened many of the doors of Alcolu's residents to the author. It also includes Eli's longtime friends, Barry Latzer and Avi Mendelowitz, who provided much-needed legal information and advice about criminal law procedures. Ben Krull and Peter Freedman read the book as it progressed, offering suggestions about organization and style, while Tom Litwick, Ken Moran, Louis Lainer, and Lydia Rosner listened with patience and encouragement as Eli thought through thorny issues of analysis and structure. Scott Chen kept Eli's computer operating smoothly, ensuring that cyberdemons neither invaded nor carried manuscript pages off into cyberspace; the New York Public Library staff provided Eli with a home away from home during the long years of research and writing. Thanks also go to the anonymous peer reviewers whose careful reading of the draft manuscript provided critical editorial suggestions that guided both Eli's editor and Carol Berkin in producing the final version of the book. Lani Faber is especially grateful to Dr. Alice Zervoudakis and her staff at Memorial Sloan Kettering, whose herculean efforts gave Eli the time he needed to finish eight chapters of the manuscript.

Carol Berkin joins Lani Faber in thanking Cecelia Hartsell for doing the arduous work of compiling an index and all the staff at the University of South Carolina Press whose admirable skill turned the manuscript into a printed book. Finally, we both thank Ehren Foley, editor extraordinaire, for his enthusiasm for the project and his steadfast belief in its importance. In Ehren, Eli would have surely found his kindred spirit.

Foreword

Eli Faber and I met in graduate school, during the tumultuous years of antiwar protest, the rise of the Black Panthers, Students for a Democratic Society (SDS), and the occupation of college campus buildings by angry students. The friendship that quickly emerged between us was a bit of a surprise to us both—I was a proud lefty, quick to form my political opinions, always ready to join a picket line or a march in Washington, emotionally committed to that vision of a perfected world that defined much of my generation; Eli was intellectually though not actively engaged with all the same issues of the day, but he was maddeningly willing to see the complexities and ambiguities of our nation's political life. Yet, even in these early years, I recognized that Eli was that rare person, a man both honorable and sincere, a thoughtful man who did not wear his deep empathy for others on his sleeve or shout his intense commitment to justice from any rooftop. Luckily for me, our friendship lasted over fifty years.

When, a decade ago, Eli told me he was working on a book about South Carolina's 1944 execution of a young African American boy, I had misgivings. Historian and subject seemed a bad fit: Eli's roots were in Queens, New York, and he had lived a life untouched by violence or by the deep racial hatred that I, who grew up in Alabama in the 1940s and 50s, knew all too well. Could he make the necessary connection to the residents of small-town South Carolina, Black or White, he planned to interview? Would he understand the culture of the rural South? I needn't have feared. The people he interviewed in Alcolu and Stinney's aging siblings saw in Eli what I had seen so many years before: his sincere interest in understanding events and the people who were caught up in them. Eli knew how to listen—and thus they talked.

Eli worked on this book patiently. He scoured South Carolina archives and newspapers for accounts of the murder of the two young girls and the trial and execution of George Junius Stinney Jr. He interviewed eyewitnesses and poured over the interviews collected by another scholar years ago. Eli contacted Stinney family members, who were at first reluctant to share their memories with him but soon warmed to the project. He carefully and deeply read the literature on Jim Crow, lynching, and life in the mill towns of the South. Throughout these years, he labored to understand the motives and the actions of the men and women involved in Stinney's brief life and capture the cultural and social context in which the tragedy played out. As he at last began to write *The Child in the Electric Chair,* Eli confessed to me that the most difficult part of this project was coming to terms with the fact that he would never truly know the guilt or innocence of this fourteen-year-old boy who was convicted of murder. Yet he never doubted that Stinney's story must be told.

In the Fall of 2019, Eli called me with the terrible news: He had been diagnosed with pancreatic cancer that February. Through all the chemo treatments, the doctor visits, and a bout with the COVID-19 virus, Eli continued to work on the book. He was not afraid of what lay ahead for him; he was only fearful that he would not have time to finish telling George Junius Stinney Jr.'s story.

In January 2020, when he knew he was losing his battle with cancer, he called me with a request: Would I use his notes to write the final chapter, edit the manuscript, find a publisher, and see the book through to publication? I agreed. By the end of April, Eli was gone.

I kept my promise. I kept it not merely as an act of friendship—which it was—but also because, as I read the manuscript, I knew Eli had been right. I had in my keeping an important story that needed to be shared. In the current era of rising racism and the challenge to it by Black Lives Matter activists, our nation must finally reckon its past if it hopes to justly shape its future. I believe George Junius Stinney Jr.'s story can help us grapple with this task. Eli Faber wrote this book because he believed it too.

Note on Sources

Writing about the life of George Junius Stinney Jr. and the times in which he lived has been a project requiring many years of gestation, not least because of the scarcity of original sources that historians regularly rely upon. No written accounts or memoirs by individuals who participated in the case or who were otherwise present at the time are known to exist, save for the recollections of an individual who was sixteen years old in 1944, the year of the dual murders of two young girls in the village of Alcolu, South Carolina, and the execution of fourteen-year-old George Stinney, which ensued only eighty-three days later. Contemporary newspaper accounts are few in number; investigative reporting by journalists is entirely nonexistent, in contrast to the mountain of coverage that a death sentence imposed upon a fourteen-year-old would actually happen, were such an event at all possible in today's world. Above all, there is no transcript of Stinney's trial because there was no appeal of the case to higher courts.

Interviews with individuals present in 1944 in Alcolu, South Carolina, have therefore been a source of inestimable importance in the effort to reconstruct what occurred and why. Paramount among these have been the interviews with Robert Lewis Alderman, a fourth-generation member of the family that established Alcolu, who has devoted much of his time and energy to preserving the history of the beloved village where he spent his early years. By opening many doors for interviews with other residents of Alcolu, both past and present, Alderman in effect functioned as the "village elder" who made the interviewing process feasible. I am indebted to him for his confidence in my efforts to comprehend the life and times of George Junius Stinney Jr. as well as to the gracious and welcoming receptions I received from the parties I was recommended to interview, and to the individuals whom I found on my own who were willing to speak with me. In many cases, they opened their homes to me for my interviews with them.

Interviews with three of George Stinney's immediate family members were crucial for comprehending much and for adding many poignant details: his brother, Charles Stinney, the youngest member of the family; Katherine Stinney Robinson, the oldest of his two sisters; and her daughter, Norma Jean Robinson. All who read about and contemplate George Stinney's life and times should be deeply grateful to them for their willingness to share their painful recollections of the catastrophe that engulfed their family in March 1944, which affected their lives forever after.

In January 2014, Katherine Stinney Robinson and Charles Stinney, together with their sister, Amie Ruffner, provided extensive additional information about what they witnessed and heard almost seventy years before on March 24–25, 1944, when they testified under oath before a special court that convened in Sumter, South Carolina, to determine whether their brother had received a fair and impartial trial. This unusual proceeding is described here in the epilogue, but the testimony of the three siblings is woven earlier into the account of what transpired on those two fateful days in their family's life.

Many of these living sources pale in comparison to the significance of a set of seven interviews conducted in 1983, thirty-nine years after George Stinney's execution, by David I. Bruck, an eminent criminal lawyer widely known for his work representing indigent clients who have been sentenced to death. In several instances, Bruck has pleaded their cases before the US Supreme Court. In 1985, Bruck published an article in the opinions section of the *Washington Post* in which he argued against provisions in twenty-six states that allowed juveniles under the age of eighteen to be sentenced to death. The shocking example of George Stinney provided Bruck with powerful ammunition. While preparing his essay, he was able to interview key participants and observers who were present in Alcolu in 1944, whose recollections go far in addressing the absence of in-depth newspaper reports and, especially, the absence of a transcript of the trial. The seven were the older sister of one of the two murder victims; the state constable who arrested Stinney; the son of the county's sheriff, who, at the age of seventeen, witnessed the execution; a member of the enraged crowd clamoring to lynch him; the member of a well-known family in the village, who attempted to see Stinney in the jail in which he was held after his arrest, posing a distinct threat to his life; one of Stinney's court-appointed defense attorneys; and, perhaps most important of all, the foreman of the jury that found him guilty after only ten minutes of deliberation. The transcripts of these invaluable

interviews are part of the David I. Bruck Collection in the South Caroliniana Library of the University of South Carolina. So far as is known, they
have escaped the attention of the many interested parties who have been
drawn to the case of George Stinney in the aftermath of his tragic end, as
well as to the violent deaths of the two young girls who were murdered in
Alcolu on March 24, 1944.

Several of the individuals whom Bruck interviewed in 1983 had no
hesitation in freely using the "N" word. As ugly as it is, as unacceptable
as it is in decent society, the entire word has been spelled out when citing
their statements in order to preserve the authenticity of their voices, as
well as the sentiments that lay behind their utterances. The same policy
has been applied when citing original sources in other locations, notably
in chapter 4 ("Postponing a Lynching"). The goal throughout has been to
adhere with fidelity to what has been a part of our history that ought not
to be softened.

Chapter 1
June 16, 1944

Don't really remember that much. . . . I
remember wanted to get out of there. I wanted
to get out of there bad.

Lt. James E. Gamble recalling the
execution of George Stinney Jr.

June 16, 1944. Friday—the day of the week for executions in the State of South Carolina.

In France, American forces maintained their momentum ten days after the landings on D-Day, pushing forward against the German army and toward the port of Cherbourg. Across the south of England, rockets carrying bombs, hailed by Germany as its "secret weapon," rained down from the skies for the first time; they were so new that the press called them "robot bombers." On the other side of the world in the Pacific, the Marines gained a half mile in savage fighting on the island of Saipan, while B-29 Superfortress bombers attacked the Japanese mainland for the first time, hitting Japan's steel-manufacturing center. And in Washington, DC, southern senators assailed the Fair Employment Practices Committee, while the House rejected proposals affecting funding for several Cabinet departments.[1]

In Columbia, the capital of South Carolina, Governor Olin DeWitt Johnston continued to hone his plans for winning his race for the US Senate. The campaign, in which the contenders debated each other in successive appearances across the state, had commenced two days before. Johnston's decision to run would seal the fate of the fourteen-year-old African American youth, who on the morning of the sixteenth awaited execution on death row a few miles away in the state penitentiary. South Carolina juries had twice before condemned fourteen-year-old boys to death, but in neither case was that sentence carried out. This time, it would be. George Junius Stinney Jr. would thus become the youngest person executed during the twentieth century in the United States of America.[2]

Less than three months before, on March 24, a double murder had been committed in a small village in Clarendon County, approximately fifty miles southeast of Columbia. Two young White girls—one eleven years old, the other seven—had been found bludgeoned to death; and Stinney, an African American, had quickly been arrested on suspicion of having murdered them. Fury surged in the village in the hours after the arrest, and there was talk of taking care of the matter without time wasted on a trial, but the lynching had been averted. The case against Stinney proceeded according to what were then the prevailing norms of the legal system.[3]

Two local physicians conducted examinations of the corpses and submitted their findings to a coroner's jury, which then ruled the two girls had indeed been murdered. Because the county's criminal court was not scheduled to meet for another three months, a special term was convened in late April to try the accused for the murder of the older of the two girls. The court met on April 24, disposed first of seven lesser criminal cases, and then, in the climax of the special session, turned to the trial of the fourteen-year-old. A jury was empaneled and heard the prosecution's case and then a plea for mercy from the two court appointed defense attorneys. The jury deliberated for less than ten minutes; the verdict they delivered was guilty. The presiding judge pronounced the sentence of death and directed that it be administered on June 16.

George Stinney was transported to the state's penitentiary in Columbia and housed on Tier F, the prison's most isolated and secure section. Tier F housed five other men, one of whom was scheduled for electrocution on the same morning as Stinney. In the weeks leading to the day of execution, Tier F's inmates were said to spend much of their time reading the Bible and singing hymns. It was said that one of the five older prisoners gave the boy a Bible, which he reportedly read a great deal of the time.[4]

A photographer in the prison's administration department took two pictures of every person who entered the institution to serve time there—or to be electrocuted. The two photographs of George Stinney underscore his youthfulness. He is dressed in black-and-white-striped prison clothing that hung loosely on his thin body. His childlike face

George Stinney Jr., 1944. Dept. of Corrections, Central Correctional Institution, Record of Prisoners Awaiting Execution. Inmate George Stinney, File #260. South Carolina Department of Archives and History.

belies his age of fourteen. In the profile view snapped by the photographer, Stinney's right shoulder is so slight that it suggests the possibility that he had not yet reached puberty. He stood only five feet, one inch, tall and he weighed only ninety-five pounds. His slight size would figure gruesomely during his execution.[5]

Following the state's execution protocol, on the morning of June 7, the prison's authorities removed Stinney and the second inmate scheduled for electrocution from Tier F and transferred them to the death house. This was a small brick building that contained two rooms: the execution chamber, a small space that held the electric chair, and an adjoining room with six cells secured by heavy bars. This had been the site of all executions since 1912, when South Carolina replaced hanging with the electric chair. Four days after the transfer, several of Stinney's relatives visited him in his death-house cell. This may have been the only occasion since his arrest at the end of March that the boy saw members of his family. The prison's White chaplain, as well as an African American chaplain, visited him and his condemned fellow inmate regularly. On at least one occasion, the White chaplain reported finding the two condemned men reading Bibles and singing hymns. Both of them assured him that, "spiritually," they were ready to die. The chairman of the State Pardon and Parole Board also visited Stinney and later announced that he could find no reason to recommend to the governor that the boy's sentence be commuted to life in prison. Pleas to spare his life had been arriving at the governor's office from all over South Carolina as well as from other states, but the petitions, letters, and telegrams apparently had little, if any, effect upon the Pardon and Parole Board member. In the end, they did not dissuade the governor from carrying out the death sentence either.[6]

Three days before the death penalty was to be administered, the penitentiary's captain of the guard, charged with supervising all preparations for the double execution, entered the death house and obtained what one newspaper characterized as a "full confession" from Stinney:

> Which one did you kill first? . . .
> The smaller girl. . . .
> Then I hit the big one.
> What did you hit them with?
> A piece of iron. . . .[7]

On the day before his execution, two chaplains again visited the condemned child. That night, the governor of the state reportedly also visited. According to newspaper accounts, Stinney slept soundly on that final night. At some point on the morning of the execution, the two chaplains visited with him one last time, and later reported that he had been entirely calm. At 7:00 a.m., a half hour before the time set for his electrocution, the sheriff of Clarendon County entered the death house and conducted his own final interview:

> George, you know that you have only a few moments to live, don't you?
> Yes[,] sir.
> Well, are you guilty of the crime for which you were convicted?
> Yes, sir.

Did any officer from the time that you were arrested up until
now take advantage of you, threaten you, or punish you in any way?
No, sir.
Was there anyone else with you when this crime was committed?
No, sir.
Was there anyone else connected with or know anything about it?
No, sir. . . .
Well, good-bye[,] George.
Good-bye[,] Sheriff.[8]

The captain of the guard scheduled Stinney's death first. At 7:30
a.m., a procession known as the execution escort formed up in the cell
room and Stinney and four guards proceeded to the adjoining chamber in which the electric chair waited. Wearing socks but no shoes, the
boy walked with his Bible tucked under his arm. About fifty witnesses
crowded into the public section of the execution room, approximately
forty of them from Clarendon County, the scene of the double murder.
In addition to the county's sheriff, the witnesses included the fathers
of the two young murder victims, two visibly agitated undergraduate
young women from a criminology class at nearby Allen University, and
James E. Gamble, the sheriff's seventeen-year-old son. Thirty-nine years
later, by then a seasoned law-enforcement officer himself, James Gamble
described his reaction to what he witnessed in the execution chamber.
He admitted he "wanted to get out of there bad."[9]

As the procession entered, the witnesses began to whisper audibly,
causing the prison's superintendent to bang his cane on the room's con-
crete floor, commanding silence. With order restored, the assistant captain of the guard asked the youth if he wished to say anything. "No sir,"
Stinney replied. One of the attending chaplains asked, "You don't want
to say anything about what you did?" Again, Stinney replied, "No sir."
At that, another of the chaplains who had visited Stinney twice the day
before, as well as early on the morning of the execution, was heard to
murmur in a subdued voice, "The way of the transgressor is hard."[10]

Stinney sat in the chair and the guards proceeded to strap him in, but
his small size made it difficult to affix the electrode to his right leg. When
that problem was at last resolved, the state electrician turned on the current, sending 2,400 volts of electricity surging through Stinney's body.
The mask covering his face was too large, and it fell off after the electricity
began to flow, revealing that his eyes were wide open. Two more jolts of

electricity were administered. Three minutes and forty-five seconds after the state electrician had first turned on the current, the penitentiary's physician pronounced George Junius Stinney Jr. dead.[11]

As was so often the case, the impact of electrocution on Stinney's body was neither neat nor clean. "When they shot the juice to him," recalled Lieutenant James E. Gamble in 1983, "his head went up and the mask came off of his face, and I remember that saliva and all was coming out of his mouth, and tears from his eyes, and there was an odor that I really couldn't describe. . . but I hope I never smell such an odor again."[12]

Electrocutions in the South Carolina State Penitentiary frequently left the body of the deceased too hot to touch; the corpses had to be carried quickly to a cooling trough filled with water. George Stinney's small, lifeless body, frozen rigidly in an upright position was unstrapped, lifted from the electric chair, and removed from the death chamber. It was severely damaged; electrocutions often did that—and not only in South Carolina. Sixty years later, the older of his two sisters recalled in a radio interview, "I remember going to the funeral. I couldn't believe what they had done to that little boy. I'll never forget the way he looked." Ten years after that, his other sister elaborated that the body had been scorched, seared, and burned; its skin had turned the color of blue.[13]

But George Stinney's sisters were not the only ones who many later years described the havoc wreaked upon the human frame. Half a century later, the sole surviving sibling of one of the two murdered girls remembered vividly that the back of her sister's head had been smashed and that the other victim had been beaten in the face.[14]

Bitter memories of this double murder and the execution that followed thus endured for decades, not only in the memories of the three families directly affected, but also in the minds of current as well as former residents of Clarendon County. Two generations later, those who had been there in 1944 could still describe the events of that spring. More than sixty years had passed, but one woman would say on her death bed in 2008 that Stinney had threatened her and several young friends as they walked by his family's neighborhood. He had, she said, aggressively warned them to get out and never return. Another, a man who was ordinarily calm and low-key, instantaneously flushed beet red when asked about the possibility that Stinney might have been innocent. Yet another, a vein throbbing in his forehead, his face turning to stone, could grimly clench his jaws as he declared with conviction, "He killed those girls."[15]

STATE PENITENTIARY
COLUMBIA, SOUTH CAROLINA

To   R. E. Wells   Clerk of the Court of General Sessions

    of   Clarendon   County:

We do hereby certify that   George Stinney, Jr.   was

duly electrocuted on   Friday   the 16th day of   June 1944   ~~192~~

in accordance with law and in execution of the judgment pronounced against him at the

  April 24, 1944 ~~192~~   term of the Court of General Sessions of   Clarendon

County, ~~which judgment, on appeal, was affirmed by the Supreme Court, and which~~

~~date was fixed for the electrocution by the Governor in accordance with law.~~

    Witness our hands this the   16th   day of   June 1944   ~~192~~

                                   J. D. Walson
                                   Superintendent of State Penitentiary

                              M. W. Cheatham M. D.
                                   Physician of State Penitentiary

    The following persons were present and acted as witnesses:

J. E. Danull Sheriff   *Lee Burke*
Ben O. Thames   *Donald Padgett*
J. S. Pinnicke   *Clyde Bonner*
Preston B. Halls   *K. E. Stiles*
J. R. Boone   *Vernon Ivy*
Raymond Kirvinsen   *Jos E. Bates*

Certification of Execution for George Stinney Jr.,
Clarendon County, Court of General Sessions, Indictment File of George Stiney. Series L14095, Indictment
#1853.
- -

But whether or not Stinney had, in fact, killed these girls, one won-
ders how it was possible in the middle of the twentieth century, in the
United States of America, that a fourteen-year-old child could have been
sent to the electric chair. Race was clearly at the heart of the matter. Angry men had gathered to lynch the boy on the afternoon of the day of his
arrest; and on the day of his trial, some planned to seize him and kill him

if the jury did not find him guilty. And if the jury did find him guilty but recommended mercy, they still planned to put him to death—their way.

But unanswered questions remain: Why was a fourteen-year-old brought to trial in an adult criminal court? Could a defense based on mental incompetence, whether because of mental retardation or insanity, have been presented? What part did the NAACP, an organization that had successfully won appeals after unfair court proceedings against African Americans, going up even as far as the US Supreme Court, play in this instance? Why did so many White people in the South Carolina of 1944, at a time when racial tensions were rising sharply in the state, dare to petition the governor to commute the death sentence? Above all, was George Junius Stinney Jr. guilty of the crime he was put to death for?

For that matter, how had it come to pass that the boy convicted for murder and the two even younger victims were in the same place at the same time? What drew their three families to the same small village, intertwining the fates of the three children?

The little place in which they resided, the stage upon which the three youngsters began their journeys toward their violent ends, provided conditions that made possible the terrible events that engulfed them less than three months before George Junius Stinney Jr. perished in the electric chair. It is to the unusual community of Alcolu in Clarendon County that we must therefore first turn our attention.

Chapter 2
A Company Town

Surrounded by educational and religious
influences, Alcolu is perhaps the most moral
mill town in the State. . . . No one, black
or white is allowed to "loaf" around Alcolu.
The town authorities soon put him on the go.

Clarendon County Directory, 1900

George Stinney Jr. and his family made their home in the small, unincorporated village of Alcolu, South Carolina. It was located in the township of Plowdon Mill, in Clarendon County, approximately fifty miles southeast of Stinney's cell in the state penitentiary.[1]

Alcolu was hardly a quintessentially Norman Rockwell kind of small American town, with a town green at its heart. Although both its churches were painted white and one had an elegant steeple, the din and clang of the lumber mill that sat at Alcolu's center were louder than the peal of the church bells. The air was filled with clouds of sawdust rising from the tons of logs being cut and shaped into boards, flooring, and ceilings for the construction industry, and with the soot from the fires that powered the mill machinery. This soot posed such a constant fire hazard that the town's entire population was required to participate in periodic fire drills. The traffic on a national railroad line, with tracks that ran through the village near the homes of both White and Black residents, added to the thrum of background noise.[2]

And yet, despite its noise, dust-laden air, and unpaved streets covered in soot, the village was seen by its residents as a place of stability and harmony. Alcolu townspeople considered it a safe and lovely community, one in which the best Christian values undergirded daily life and provided the ethical and moral framework for their relationships. Many men and women, now in their sixties, seventies, and even eighties, look back with nostalgia and great affection upon their years as children in Alcolu before the grisly murders in 1944. As one of them wrote at a reunion in 2006:

> Alcolu. . . it never was big, except to a child. . . . Kids roamed freely through backyards and fields, playing til dark without fear. . . . Meetings at the community center where food was plenty and scrumptious, where all the village met together . . . together . . . the best word for the village. . . . This little village, these special times, and these wonderful people. . . .[3]
>
> "Everything that went on in that community included everybody" recalled a woman at the reunion. "I mean it was just like one big family of people. . . ."[4]

It was even a place where the relentless humiliations and daily cruelties meted out by the South's Jim Crow way of life were not as pronounced and were not as extreme as elsewhere. True, the norms of segregation governed relations between the races and a racial hierarchy consigned African Americans to the bottom. And, true, as one White informant admitted, Alcolu had its share of White racists. But hostility to Black residents could be a matter of degree, and, by most standards, Alcolu's was moderate. Many years after his brother's execution, Charles Stinney reflected that, until things unraveled after the murder of two White girls, overt tension between the races did not exist.[5]

The lumber mill at the village's center not only dominated the landscape, but it also explained why Alcolu existed at all. This was, pure and simple, a company town, created in the mid-1880s, by a family named the Aldermans. When George Stinney was electrocuted, the Aldermans still controlled the town; in fact, they owned both the mill and every other structure in the village. The founder of this milling enterprise, David Wells Alderman, had grown up on a farm in North Carolina. As a young man he tried, unsuccessfully, to run a business dealing in "general merchandise." Failing this, in 1881 he emigrated from North Carolina to South Carolina with his wife and children, settling first in Marion County—roughly sixty-five miles from the site of the future Alcolu. Here, in the town of Mullins, he established his first lumber company. Alderman was smart enough to realize that South Carolina presented greater opportunities in this industry. In 1884, a promotional publication in the Charleston *News and Courier*, one of the state's leading newspapers, touted these advantages in South Carolina. Since 1880, it boasted, "In manufactures, in lumber and naval stores the growth of the State is nothing less than marvellous [*sic*]." Indeed, the production of lumber and the turpentine extracted from pine trees exceeded the output of the state's quickly growing textile-mill industry by more than half a million dollars.[6]

Alderman's decision to uproot his family and establish a lumber mill in South Carolina belonged to a larger contemporary context. Whether knowingly or unknowingly, whether by choice or by chance, he was participating in the drive after the Civil War known as the New South movement. This movement was committed to moving the region out of its extreme dependence on agriculture by a focus on industrialization. Although industry in the South continued to lag well behind its exponential growth in the North and the West after the Civil War, it did begin to grow at the end of the 1870s. Northern and English financiers began to invest in the region, channeling capital into the development of ports, railroads, iron, coal, tobacco, and lumber mills. Southerners, too, played an important role in creating a "New South" when they began the development of South Carolina's cotton mills.[7]

Family tradition does not record why David W. Alderman abandoned Mullins after only four years. Perhaps it was because little in the way of land was available for sale in Marion County. The land that did come on the market sold for an average of eight dollars an acre. In Clarendon County, South Carolina, on the other hand, thirty-eight thousand acres were available, at prices that ranged from three to six dollars an acre. A considerable amount of this land was not "plough land," but "Fair timber." The county seal reflected this mix by featuring "Lumber and Agriculture" in its upper-left quadrant. Most important of all, much of Clarendon County was swampland where stands of valuable tupelo, yellow pine, and cypress grew prolifically in the boggy soil.[8]

In addition to swamps, timber, and an ample supply of land at low prices, Clarendon offered ambitious men like Alderman other advantages. There were two locomotives used for transporting lumber here while logging companies in the state's other timbered counties still relied on horses. And Clarendon had a large population of impoverished African American farmers trapped by the Southern credit system that reduced most of the agricultural population to debt peonage. As the booster who wrote the *News and Courier*'s section on Clarendon County reported: "The stores, the Lien law, &c. keep the darkies under a heavy load-some rare exceptions of course. . . . Condition of colored farmers as landowners and tenants? Poor indeed. . . . Are colored farmers making progress, saving money and acquiring lands? No! This meant that Black labor was readily available for the back-breaking work required at logging camps, as well as highly dangerous tasks inside the sawmills."

The Clarendon booster also pointed out that the county was a healthy place to live, its inhabitants warmly welcomed newcomers, and they were committed to education. Best of all, the correspondent reminded its readers, "We have an abundance of good timber, such as pine, cypress, walnut, &c. Many hard woods are to be found on the margin of the Santee and Black Rivers."[9]

Alderman, attracted by all these virtues of Clarendon County, put down stakes within its borders in Plowden Mill Township, named for a family that settled in the area in the late 1700s and established several mills over the course of the nineteenth century. In fact, a Plowden would serve as one of two court-appointed defense attorneys in George Stinney's trial in 1944. When an existing mill nearby went into bankruptcy, Alderman acquired it. He moved his family to its location, established his company, expanded the mill, and began to create a village around it. He called this mill village Alcolu, coining the name, according to family lore, from three elements: "Al" as in Alderman; "Co" is in Colwell, the surname of his partner at the time; and "Lu" as in Lula, his eldest child.[10]

Alderman soon constructed his own railroad, laying track from Alcolu to the Black River, erecting bridges wherever necessary, and securing rights-of-way across lands he did not yet own. The railroad not only carried employees to the swamps to fell and haul trees, but it also carried passengers from the village to and from other locations beside the Black River. It was along unused tracks of the Alcolu Railroad, not far from the lumber mill, that Betty June Binnicker and Mary Emma Thames would be brutally murdered—the murder instrument, according to one version, was a railroad-track spike.[11]

The village grew. By the early twentieth century, it contained fifty-five buildings, including the mill complex, sheds servicing the Alcolu Railroad, a company store, several warehouses, an office building, a chapel constructed around 1890, and the small houses the D. W. Alderman & Sons Company constructed and rented to its employees. Churches and schools, separate ones, of course, for Whites and Blacks, had not yet been constructed; they would be added later.[12]

When David Alderman died in 1921, he reportedly owned in excess of 100,000 acres, not only in Clarendon but also in several adjoining counties where his company had logging operations. His acclaim had spread, and he had become a figure of consequence in the county's civic life. He served on the three-man committee that in 1908 built the elegant and imposing county courthouse in which George Stinney would stand trial for his life thirty-six years later.[13]

In the years that followed Alderman's death in 1921, Alcolu successfully weathered the buffeting the lumber industry in the South took over the course of the next twenty years. The opening of the Panama Canal in 1915 brought competition from the Northwest to markets in the East, and overcutting reduced the timber supply in states like South Carolina. By the end of the 1920s, the Aldermans owned one of only two surviving mills in Clarendon County. The other mill failed during the Great Depression. The Alderman enterprise, however, did not escape the Depression unscathed; it was forced to lay off a reported six hundred employees in 1931. Yet D. W. Alderman & Sons Company managed to emerge from the Depression as a still-viable concern. Its railroad, however, did not. The company ceased to operate the Alcolu Railroad in 1936. Unfortunately, it did not remove the tracks, so that, in their seclusion, these served as the scene of the double murder in 1944, and they may have supplied the implement allegedly used to kill the two White victims.[14]

- - - - - - - - - - -

By 1940, the fully mature company town of Alcolu contained 185 small houses rented to the company's employees and to a handful of other inhabitants who were not its employees. Five larger houses were owned by their occupants. There were two churches: one White, one Black, and two elementary schools (again, one White and one Black). The town had a boardinghouse for visiting businessmen, which also housed unmarried, White, female schoolteachers, two baseball fields (one for Whites, one for Blacks), tennis courts, a children's playground, a gasoline-filling station, a restaurant, a barber shop, a community center, and an auditorium above the company store, all of which had been added at various points in the past. The auditorium presented plays, movies, and held communal activities such as school graduations and an annual Christmas party where company-supplied gifts were distributed to the village's White children. (African American children received the same gifts at their homes in door-to-door distributions by members of the White community.) It was in the auditorium that the villagers, both White and Black, gathered to listen to the radio broadcast of President Roosevelt's speech following the attack on Pearl Harbor. Three physicians from Manning visited every day between Monday and Friday, using a room in the company store as an office for examinations, while a barber, also from Manning, cut hair several nights during the week.[15]

Alcolu had its own currency. Like the housing rented to workers, the company store, the churches and schools, and a community auditorium, currencies like this were a frequent feature of life in company towns. In most of these towns, the employees received their salaries in coins called "babbitt," made of a metal alloy named for its inventor, one Isaac Babbitt. Babbitt coinage helped get around the problems created by a shortage of US currency in rural areas and remote towns. But babbit had one major disadvantage: it could only be used for purchases in the company store. The result was that employees faced monopolistic conditions. Alcolu was different; here, the company did not assert this form of control over its workers. The Aldermans paid their employees in US currency. Only advances for purchases at the company store were given in babbitt, in coins that ranged in value from one cent to a dollar. Babbitt advances were then subtracted from the cash in the pay envelopes distributed every two weeks at the mill.[16]

In 1940, the village's population stood at 770, of whom 431 were African Americans. Its 191 households were, in the main, nuclear families, but there were also extended families, often with an elderly mother, a cousin, or a son-in-law. Many households also included boarders, often permanent town residents who had been renters since at least 1935. In fact, many of the people living in Alcolu had been in the village since 1935. They brought a sense of continuity and stability unusual in an industry more typically characterized by a transient workforce.[17]

The American company town could be either a hellish, exploitive place or a utopia. If the many elderly informants today are to be believed, Alcolu fell into the latter category. Almost 75 percent of the White heads of households who were present in 1940 had been there in 1935. The proportion was even higher among African Americans. Even though the 1930s were years of mass migration by African Americans out of the South, 81 percent of Black household heads in Alcolu in 1940 had resided in the village in 1935.[18]

Of the three families devastated by the 1944 murders, only Mary Emma Thames's had been in Alcolu since then. With only seven years of

education, her father, Oliver Ben Thames, supported his family by working as a sawyer.[19]

The Binnicker and Stinney families arrived in Alcolu sometime after
April 1940, the month when that year's national census was recorded.
Their arrival coincided with an increase in the mill's labor force as the
company shifted to wartime production. John Binnicker, who, like
Thames had gone to school through the seventh grade, had moved from
neighboring Orangeburg County with his wife, five children, and a son-
in-law. His motive for uprooting his family may have been the hope of
a higher salary. As a foreman in a lumber mill in Orangeburg, he had
earned $720 in 1939; in Alcolu's mill, foremen averaged $1,403 that year.
But once in Alcolu, it is unclear what Binnicker did. He may have worked
as a logging foreman, which would require him to be in logging camps
during the week, or he might have been employed as a night watchman
at the mill.[20]

The Stinneys had come to Alcolu from Pinewood, a village approximately fourteen miles to the northwest in next-door Sumter County.
George Junius Stinney Sr. had completed the fourth grade, and this
placed him squarely in the middle of Black male heads of households in
Alcolu. His firstborn child, George Jr. outpaced him; he was in the seventh grade at the time of the murders. This fact was driven home to the
jury and to the public at the time of George's trial, no doubt suggesting
that he possessed normal intelligence and therefore knew the difference
between right and wrong. Why Stinney Sr. together with his wife and
their four young children, left Pinewood is unknown. He may have chosen to do so because, during his years as a debt-ridden sharecropper, he
had some experience with mill work. He had, in fact, supplemented his
income by working as a laborer in a Pinewood sawmill, earning a meager
$208 over the course of fifty-two weeks in 1939. This salary reflected the
extremely low wages common to the South Carolina lumbering industry.
But, in that same year in Alcolu, African American laborers averaged almost $11 a week. Once he made the move to Alcolu, Stinney worked as a
laborer in the mill, unloading logs and feeding them into the processing
machinery.[21]

The Alcolu mill was unique in other ways. Here, a small number of African Americans were employed as skilled workers. This went against the
prevailing assumption held by southern Whites that Blacks were incapable of performing skilled work or handling and working with machinery.
As Gunnar Myrdal reported in 1944, "Defensive beliefs were constantly

growing among the Whites in the South that the Negro was inefficient, unreliable, and incompetent to work with machinery." Furthermore, he wrote, "[t]he beliefs that Negroes get sleepy when working with machines and that they, on the whole, lack mechanical aptitudes, serve a need for justification of being kept out of industry. The beliefs of their general unreliability, their inborn lack of aptitude for sustained mental activity, and, particularly, their lower intelligence, help to justify their vocational segregation and to excuse the barriers against promotion of Negroes to skilled and supervisory positions."[22]

The lumbering industry shared these dismissive stereotypes, as one of its national publications in 1890 made clear: "A saw mill requires a large number of laborers of different grades of intelligence to work side by side, the bulk of whom in the South must of necessity be negroes. This has made it difficult to secure first class white labor . . . the sawyer, the edger man and a few of the other important workmen being white, and the balance negroes."[23]

These attitudes still prevailed in 1940. But in Alcolu, a Black man named George Stinney worked with cranes. In fact, since 1903, the Alderman company operated on the assumption that African Americans could work with machinery.[24]

The Alderman company's belief that African Americans could work with machinery extended at least as far back as 1903. David W. Alderman employed Black men as engineers on the Alcolu Railroad. Although this was not unique in the lumber industry, Alderman went further than all others in South Carolina, with only one other exception, when he inaugurated the practice of having Black engineers run trains carrying not only logs but also passengers. The idea that African Americans were now in charge of trains that transported Whites clearly violated Jim Crow norms, and in 1903, the Brotherhood of Locomotive Engineers protested Alderman's practice to the state railroad commission. They insisted that Black engineers were "not competent, in our estimation." They also warned that fatalities or injuries, caused by the "lack of knowledge of the engines [Black men] may be intrusted with" would discredit not only all engineers but South Carolina's railroad commissioners as well. The Railroad Commission doubted its authority to issue a desist order to the Aldermans; instead, they referred the matter to the state legislature who took no action at all. And the matter ended there.[25]

Despite the presence of Black engineers of the Alcolu line, Alcolu was still a Southern community in the Jim Crow era. Here, the usual features of Jim Crow life existed: segregated housing, churches, and schools; lower pay for Blacks; less financial support for the education of African American children; and no social contact between the races, except among preadolescent children. These were conditions of life that institutionalized what sociologist John Dollard, in his classic 1937 study of life in a Deep South small town, termed the "lower-caste status" assigned to African Americans in a hierarchical social system that defined caste membership by race.[26]

The two populations, Black and White, lived in broadly—though not exclusively—separate sections of the village. White families found homes near the mill complex, along today's Highway 521 and Hotel Street, where the company had maintained a hotel for visiting clients and salesmen until it burned down in 1937. The Binnickers and Thameses lived in adjoining houses on Hotel Street. The Aldermans lived in this neighborhood too, one that housed the company's offices, the company store, the filling station, the community center, the two buildings of the White school, the church at which White residents worshiped, and the depot of the Atlantic Coast Line Railroad. Many African American families, but by no means all, also lived near the mill complex, but about one-third of a mile from the White community on the other side of the company's railroad tracks. Most of the houses in the Black section of town clustered along Camp, East Chapel, and West Chapel streets. The Green Hill Baptist Church, where Alcolu's Black residents worshiped, sat on a short street, aptly named Church Street. The Stinney home was a short walk from the church and from the two school buildings for African American children. As fate would have it, their house stood right next to the company's railroad tracks.[27]

Both White and Black employees lived in small wooden houses rented to them by the company. These houses, ranging from three to seven rooms for Whites and two to seven rooms for African Americans, were constructed all on one level. They had no basements, but most had a front porch and some, like the Stinney home, had a rear porch as well. Water and electricity were included in the monthly rental fee. A small piece of land on the side and in the rear of these houses allowed residents to plant a small garden and to keep a few farm animals such as chickens, cows, and pigs. The Stinney family had a small vegetable garden and kept chickens, and a cow named Lizzie. This cow, as well as the family's back porch, would figure in the events surrounding the two murders.[28]

According to a key informant, the monthly rent charged on a house depended on its size. In 1940, White employees paid an average of $8.86 a month. This figure included eight Whites who comprised a small salaried elite (defined here as earning more than $2,000 in 1939); the remaining sixty-two White renters paid an average of $7.25. African Americans families, who occupied much smaller quarters, paid on average $2.84. The Stinney house, for example, had only three rooms. If an African American employee were unmarried, he was relegated to what one White informant called a "shanty." Shanties were tiny in size and had no kitchen; cooking was done outside "on the ground." No rent was charged for these shanties.[29]

Size was not the only thing that distinguished White homes from Black ones. According to some recollections, the houses rented to White employees were usually painted either gray or White; Black homes were not painted at all. And there were other, more serious differences based on race, including the company's attitude toward educational needs. Since the company preferred to pay all the expenses for the village schools rather than accept county funding, it was free to set both policies and budgets for their segregated educational system. And, according to a highly knowledgeable White informant, the company did not think it was necessary to provide African American students with the same support as White ones. In 1940, six teachers taught the seven grades in the school for White children; the seven grades in the school for Black children had only three teachers. Upon graduation from seventh grade, White students who graduated from seventh grade could continue their educations by traveling to the high school in Manning in a school bus provided by the company; no bus for African American students was provided so that they could continue their education through tenth grade in the Manning Training School.[30]

The company's educational practices mirrored practices in the larger county and in the South at large. The disparities were—and are—shocking; in 1930–31, Clarendon County spent an average of $68.61 on White students and only $5.33 on Black students. In another example, one that ultimately had national consequences, Black children in Summerton, a town in Clarendon County approximately fifteen miles south of Alcolu, were denied bus service and were thus forced to walk great distances to school. On rainy days, some had to cross flooded streets in boats. One of their school buildings did not have indoor toilets, forcing the six hundred children who attended the school to rely on two outhouses. Yet another had no drinking faucets; water was carried in buckets from a nearby home. In 1947, a Black resident of Summerton brought an unsuccessful court action against these conditions. This would set in motion a train of events that led two years later to *Briggs v. Elliott*, the first lawsuit in the South to challenge discriminatory practices in education. Eventually, the case became one of the five cases the US Supreme Court bundled together in its 1954 landmark decision, *Brown v. Board of Education*.[31]

Even terms of address were based on race, both in Alcolu and across the South. Alcolu's White children learned at an early age to call adult whites "Mr." and "Miz," but they prefaced the first name of Blacks with "Uncle" and "Aunt." White adults addressed Blacks by first name, but Blacks added a "Mr." and "Mrs." when speaking to White men and women. Black men were also allowed to refer to White men as "Boss." Violating this racial protocol was dangerous. The dilemma arose when a White person addressed an African American with professional status; it was apparently more acceptable to call a highly respected schoolteacher or principal "Professor" than to address him as "Mister."[32]

Income differences in Alcolu also reflected, and reinforced, the racial divide. In 1939, the average annual salary for White employees was $948; it was $451 for African Americans. Whites with the job title "laborer" earned, on average, $666; African Americans, $446. In 1944, the year of the murders in Alcolu, the average salary received by White employees was still significantly greater than that earned by Black employees. This was also the case in 1945 and 1946.[33]

Finally, although Black and White men worked together in the mill, the two races did not mingle socially. To be sure, Whites occasionally attended a service in the Black church, and Blacks occasionally prayed in the White church, sitting separately in the balcony. In baseball, the village's leading form of public entertainment, they did not play together. Separation of the races even extended to separate ball fields. However, Whites did love to attend the games played by Black ballplayers at their field. These games were fast and furious; the action was hotter than anything the White players ever produced. Any interracial play to be found in Alcolu was among children, but it ceased at adolescence when teenagers went their separate ways. To judge from President Jimmy Carter's memoir about his childhood in Plains, Georgia, this was a familiar pattern in the South. Most of Carter's childhood playmates were African

Americans. By the age of fourteen, however, all of his interracial ties had been severed.[34]

However, there are significant indications that caste lines in Alcolu were not as rigid as elsewhere, that a milder form of Jim Crow existed in Alcolu—and not simply because African American railroad engineers transported White passengers. Perhaps it was for this reason that, between 1935 and 1940, a higher percentage of Blacks remained in the village than Whites. To begin with, Blacks in Alcolu had permanent, rather than seasonal, employment and a small number of held positions as skilled workers. The average African American salary in Alcolu was significantly higher than all incomes, White or Black, across the South. And though White men did earn more than Black men, Black women earned higher salaries than most White women. In addition, the company's generosity crossed color lines. It paid for medical treatment for Blacks as well as Whites, and it distributed the same fruit baskets and gifts to Black children as to White ones. Finally, although residential segregation existed it was not as pervasive as in many other southern communities. In John Dollard's "Southerntown," for example, virtually every African American lived in a seedy, rundown, unpaved section that was literally on the other side of the tracks. In Alcolu, many Blacks and Whites lived in proximity to one another, in two adjoining areas of the village. Alcolu's housing pattern more closely resembled Charleston than other southern towns and cities. There, as Roy Wilkins, the assistant executive secretary of the NAACP, observed six days before George Stinney's execution, Whites and Blacks lived on the same streets, sometimes next door to one another.[35]

— — — — — — — — — —

In the years before murder came to Alcolu, the village was a self-contained community made up of families of hardworking men and women and their children living comfortably in safe surroundings. The social stability and order that enveloped them owed much to the Alderman family's control and direction of every aspect of village life, including religion, education, medical care, and even to help during times of personal crisis.

Paul Repton Alderman Sr. who headed D. W. Alderman & Sons Company between 1932 and 1946, exemplified the family's authority. He was born in 1881, the second son of the founder. When his older brother died, Paul took over the company presidency. He was a tall, imposing figure who often rode through the village astride an equally imposing horse, surveying and inspecting everything in his domain. On Sunday mornings, he could be found, presiding over the service at the White Baptist church, examining the congregants as they entered from the vantage point of his chair placed next to the communion table. After everyone was seated, he left this chair and took his place among the worshipers; only then did the service commence. Even Alcolu children were aware of his commanding presence; many apparently loved him. On the day of his sudden death in 1946, an eleven-year-old wrote in her diary: "Mr. Paul died. I cried." The son of one of the village's pastors remembered Paul Alderman as a man whose approval was difficult to win:

> My first paid job in a church was in Alcolu. . . . I remember having to clean out the furnace one time. . . . But to clean the inside of the fire box required getting inside of the furnace. I thought I had done a good job and everything seemed to be just fine. One Saturday morning though Mr. Paul Alderman came into the church while I was cleaning and gave me a dressing down about the furnace. I remember that he said I had burned out the grates of the furnace with my carelessness. I couldn't believe what I was hearing. I had built very few fires in the furnace and had done my best to keep the ashes removed.[36]

If Paul R. Alderman Sr. symbolized authority, rigor, and discipline, Ben Geer Alderman, his nephew, personified gentleness and kindness, or the benevolent side of the Alderman family's leadership. Ben Alderman lacked his uncle's commanding presence; he was a short, stocky, unimpressive-looking man. Ben was born in 1907, did his undergraduate work at Davidson College and then went on to Harvard Business School. During the early 1940s, he put his business training to work as the company's treasurer. His reputation for kindliness and accessibility led village inhabitants to come to him with their problems, to turn to him for advice. Apparently, African Americans felt comfortable approaching him for help. George's mother is said to have gone to Ben Alderman for advice on handling her son. Many years later, one resident of Alcolu recalled Alderman's account of Mrs. Stinney's visit: "The boy's mother had went to Mr. Alderman and said couldn't they do something about him because she couldn't rule him. He wouldn't pay her no attention, he wouldn't pay his daddy no attention neither . . . He'd do whatever he wanted to do, steal whatever he wanted to steal . . . and he just wouldn't listen to his momma and daddy at all."[37]

The boy who wouldn't listen was George Stinney, Jr. That he was a source of acute concern to his parents may have become even clearer on Thursday, March 23, 1944, the day before the two murders. In school that day, he allegedly stabbed and injured another child with a pair of scissors. There is, however, no way of knowing whether news of this incident reached Ben Alderman at the time.[38]

The Aldermans enforced strict standards of behavior: they would not tolerate alcoholism, fighting, or what many informants characterize in general terms as "troublemaking." Employees guilty of drinking or brawling in the logging camps could be fined three to five dollars. The proceeds went to the village's African American church. Anyone guilty of a third infraction was fired. The company owners also embraced neatness and encouraged pride in well-maintained homes and yards. Toward this end, they employed a permanent crew of carpenters to ensure the upkeep of the houses, both inside and out, and a yard crew to keep all public areas mowed and cleared of debris. For a time, the company awarded ten dollars every month to the family with the cleanest, most attractive front yard.[39]

Those who could not or would not comply with the standards the Aldermans insisted upon were fired. This forced the offending employee and his family to leave the village, since a company house was no longer available to him. As one informant commented several times, with a wry smile, although with no hint of disapproval: "The Aldermans ruled the nest. There wasn't no use to tell them what to do." On another occasion, he explained similarly: "They ran it with an iron hand. Whatever they said was gospel. . . . Don't argue with me." However, another individual reminisced critically: "Back then, the Aldermans, they didn't pay you nothing. My brother worked in the mill—dollar and a quarter a day for ten hours' hard work. He was a lumber inspector. Other people got about 90 cents a day. And they were going to cut wages 25 cents a day. Paul Alderman said if anyone don't like it, turn in your badge. My brother is the only one who walked up and said you can have mine."[40]

There were, on the other hand, two important areas in which the Aldermans did not impose their authority. They did not require employees to attend church, much less a Baptist church, and they did not attempt to influence employees' political choices. Alcolu did not have a mayor or a town council—the Aldermans made all of the decisions normally handled by locally elected officials—but its White inhabitants were qualified to vote in county, state, and federal elections. The Aldermans applied no pressure to shape their choices at the ballot box.

The Aldermans' firm control—some might call it authoritarianism— was coupled with benevolence and generosity toward employees and their families. They provided an array of social services, offering assistance when an individual was injured in an accident, when children lost a parent, or when a person faced a personal crisis. They built, oversaw, and financially supported the village's churches and schools. They arranged with the three visiting physicians from Manning to hold daily office hours in the company store, rent free, on Mondays through Fridays and villagers paid only 50 cents per visit. The company took care of all expenses when an employee was injured in the mill or when a family couldn't afford medical expenses. It provided food for the families of employees who were ill and could not work. These practices could be dismissed as gestures meant to buy the loyalty of the company's workforce, but elderly, former residents of the village believed the wellspring of Alderman generosity was the family's deeply held religious convictions. Informant after informant pointed to the Aldermans' commitment to what they describe as the Christian beliefs and values so evident in their daily lives. It was for this reason that Tyler Wyman, a high school principal who spent his youth in Alcolu, rose spontaneously at the 2006 reunion of former and present-day Alcolu residents and declared that the village "was as close to a Christian town as you can get. It was a utopia—a Christian utopia." Another described the village as a "Little Heaven" where the Aldermans set an example of integrity and upright living that influenced all its residents. But whatever the source of their benevolence, it goes far to explain why George Stinney, Jr., would believe the officers who arrested him when they said he could count on help from Mr. Alderman if he told them what they wanted to hear. This prompted the fourteen-year-old to begin what they subsequently testified was his confession.[41]

— — — — — — — — — — — —

A company town that offered permanent employment and housing to both African Americans and Whites; a village that contained abandoned railroad tracks that were hidden from view; and a community headed by a family whose name could be used as a lure to pry a confession from an accused youngster: all of these factors figured in the tragedy that occurred in Alcolu in late March 1944. But there was at least one additional feature of life in the village that played a part in the background to the murders, namely, the freedom that children enjoyed to move about on their own, to roam and ramble where they wished without fear. From the perspective of many American parents in the late twentieth and early twenty-first centuries, this latitude to wander about without the supervision of an adult or an older sibling, a freedom enjoyed by children in many American towns and villages in the first half of the twentieth century, must seem nothing short of astonishing. In the end, however, it proved deadly in Alcolu.[42]

The children of Alcolu were not free of responsibilities, of course. After school, even the younger children had house chores to complete. In their teen years, some had part-time jobs during the school year and full-time jobs during the summer. But there was also ample time for fun, as well as the opportunity to roam on one's own or with friends. The childhood years of Francis Batson, recounted by him in a memoir written for his children, offer a window into this freedom. Batson was five years old when his family moved to Alcolu in 1933. His father, Paul Batson, served as the village's White pastor and as the pastor in the Baptist church in neighboring Sumter County. Despite the prestige and influence that his position brought, Paul's salary was well below what the company store manager earned; in fact, he earned less than a well-paid saw filer and only several hundred dollars more than the company's bookkeeper. This modest income for a family with five children meant hand-me-downs and homemade clothing were a regular part of Francis Batson's childhood. He recalled wearing a suit previously worn by three of his brothers and shirts cut by his mother from a flour sack. Much like his clothing, Francis's play reflected the family's modest standard of living. The first bicycle he owned and shared with one of his brothers was a hand-me-down, the gift of one of Pastor Batson's Sumter County parishioners. His fishing rods were homemade, with only strings and hooks dangling at their ends. For cowboys-and-Indians games, he and his friends made the cowboy pistols from clothespins filched from their mothers and put together homemade bows and arrows for the Indians. Baseball, the favorite sport in Alcolu, also required resourcefulness. Few children had gloves, and the Batson boys shared a used one given to them by their wealthy neighbor, Mrs. Robert Alderman. Bats were made from tree limbs, and balls were often fashioned from pieces of saved string wrapped around a stone or piece of metal and then bound up with Black tape—when it was to be had.[43]

Yet if Francis Batson readily joined in team sports like baseball, basketball, and football and played games like cowboys and Indians with friends, he also loved to roam about the countryside, alone, on his bicycle. It was on one of these solo rides, in the middle of March 1944, that the sixteen-year-old Francis encountered George Stinney Jr. who accosted him and knocked him off his bike into a ditch.[44]

The young girls of Alcolu were equally free to roam the area around their village. "We were free to go everywhere," recalled Mary Ellen Bilton many years later, her voice rising emphatically: *You didn't worry.*" Thus it was that, on the afternoon of March 24, 1944, eleven-year-old Betty June Binnicker and eight-year-old Mary Emma Thames set out on a bicycle, Betty June peddling, Mary Emma sitting on the handlebars, to pick flowers along the village's railroad tracks.

It was a ride from which they never returned.

POSTSCRIPT. The D. W. Alderman & Sons Company dissolved in 1947. Irreconcilable differences among the stockholders, all sixteen of whom were members of the Alderman family, led to the sale of the company's mill assets to the Williams Furniture Company. Extensive landholdings outside Alcolu were divided among members of the family.[45]

Chapter 3
March 24–25, 1944

A fear began to grip the little community.
For some who remembered the events of those
dreadful days, that fear continued for months
and years to come. Sadness continues for all.

Robert Lewis Alderman,
"Sad Days in the Little Village," 2004

The weather conspired with murder on Friday, March 24, 1944. It dawned cloudy and cold, the temperature in the low 40s. The winter and early spring of 1944 had been unusually wet in the Clarendon County region, but, despite the morning clouds, this particular Friday was a dry one. As the day wore on, it warmed to the low 70s and unfolded into a perfect afternoon for an after-school bicycle ride.[1]

Betty June Binnicker's twenty-three-year-old married sister oversaw her that day; their mother worked ten miles away in Sumter making chenille bedspreads. When Betty June returned from school, she asked permission to go bicycle riding with her next-door neighbor, Mary Emma Thames. Her older sister readily assented: "They'd always done it, and of course I felt it was alright for them to do it." And why not; the pervasive sense of safety allowed children in Alcolu to be away from home on their own. The two girls set out on a single bicycle shortly after 3:00 in the afternoon—Betty June, with straight, dark-brown hair and dark-brown eyes peddling; and Mary Emma, a curly redhead with freckles, perched on the handlebars. They carried a pair of scissors to cut maypops, a purple wildflower that grows on a vine. The flower's name came from its greenish fruit, about the size of a chicken's egg, that made a popping sound when children stomped on it. According to one recollection many years later, the flowers were intended for a service in the village's White

Baptist church. As the two friends rode past homes in the village where Whites resided, they reportedly invited other young girls to join them. At least this is how several women now in their seventies recalled the events of that afternoon, each adding somberly that she could have been a third victim of the murderous violence that ensued.[2]

Since maypops were known to grow along rail lines, the two girls headed away from their adjoining houses and pedaled toward the town's Black section on the other side of the company's abandoned railroad tracks. As they arrived here, they encountered George Stinney together with Amie, the youngest of his two sisters. The two Stinney children were tending the family's cow, Lizzie.[3]

A half-century later on the fiftieth anniversary of her brother's execution, Katherine Robinson, the older of Stinney's two sisters, recounted that George and Amie had gone out to tend the family's cow, and then they returned home together. Twenty years later in early 2014, almost a full seventy years after the events of 1944, both Katherine and her younger sister, Amie Ruffner, provided greater detail. Under oath, they testified that George, together with seven-year-old Amie, had taken Lizzie from her shed behind their house and led her across the train tracks to a spot within sight of the house. While they sat on the grass watching their cow graze, two young White girls appeared, pushing a bicycle—a plausible memory, since riding a bicycle over the track ties would have been difficult if not impossible. The girls stopped to ask if the Stinneys knew where maypops could be found. Nine-year-old Katherine was inside the house and therefore did not see the encounter, but the Stinney house was close enough to the tracks for her to hear the girls' question. Amie testified that she did not recognize these White girls. As far as she knew, the two had never been to the Black section of the village before. Still, she and George answered that maypops were to be found close by, growing along the tracks.[4]

The two girls continued on their way in search of the flowers while George and Amie, leading Lizzie, eventually recrossed the tracks and returned to their yard. George filled a pail with water for the cow and led Lizzie back to her shed. Their chore complete, the two children went into the house and, together with Katherine, waited for their mother and brother Charles to come back from shopping at the company store. According to the testimony of the two sisters, Mrs. Stinney ran a strict household, and she expected to find her children at home when she returned. Unlike other parents, they declared, their mother *never* permitted her children to be away on their own. George, they therefore implied, had not wandered off down the railroad tracks after returning Lizzie to her shed. Later, the Stinney family went together to a neighborhood party. They had not yet learned that the two White girls were missing from their homes.[5]

For the Stinney sisters, Katherine and Amie, it was just a normal day. But, in the section of Alcolu where the two girls lived, the day was anything but ordinary. As the afternoon waned, Betty June and Mary Emma failed to return home. Betty June's mother returned from Sumter around 4:30 and immediately felt something was wrong. It was unlike her daughter to leave home and not come back within half an hour. Mrs. Binnicker and her older daughter began to search for the missing girl, but, when they could not find her, the worried mother notified the sheriff's office in Manning. By nightfall, the news that the two children were missing spread through Alcolu. More than a hundred village residents, both Black and White, joined the search party led by Ben G. Alderman.

George Stinney Sr. and George Jr. had joined the search when word of the missing girls had reached the neighborhood party. As the night dragged on, volunteers from the Lions Club in Sumter County and the Masons in Manning also arrived. After receiving a phone call around 10 p.m., assistant Deputy Sheriff Henry S. Newman of the Clarendon County sheriff's office in Manning arrived to assist as well. Joanne Poe, nine years old at the time, sensed that something was terribly wrong. Disregarding her mother's orders to go to sleep, she stole out of her bed and watched from the window of her room. She especially remembered many years later how the men's flashlights repeatedly bobbed up and down in the darkness and how the two fathers repeatedly shouted out the names of their missing children. Like her, others recalled the frightening vigil of that night for the remainder of the lives. More than sixty years later, one wrote of "[l]iving in terror when two little lives were snatched from us in a terrible deed. Suffering through the night as the search was made, the horrible truth seen in the dawn. Death . . . and violence, a generation before its time, forever marring childhood memories."[6]

There were hundreds of nooks and crannies to check within the village. Were the girls in the depot of the Atlantic Coast Line Railroad? Had they slipped into an empty room at the boardinghouse and hidden there, afraid to face their parents because they had stayed out late? Were they in the auditorium above the general store? Would they be found in the yards where milled lumber was stacked high or somewhere on the

Lumber mill complex in Alcolu.

----

grounds of the sprawling lumber mill? Could they have fallen into the sizable log pond on the mill grounds? Or could they be in any of the small buildings where the company stored chemicals? Perhaps searchers also made their way down the pitch-dark path that led to Cooter Creek, a nearby swampy area outside Alcolu, where village boys swam in waters alive with moccasins and alligators. Could they have floundered in the marshy ground or, worse, fallen into the water of Cooter Creek and drowned? As the hours dragged by, there was no response to the girls' shouted names. There was no sign of Betty June or Mary Emma.[7]

Sixteen-year-old Francis Batson joined a search party in the company of two adults. At 3:00 a.m., the men told him to return to the parsonage where his family lived and to go to sleep. Francis did as he was told, but once at home, he found he that could not calm down. He left the house and rejoined the two men. Eventually the three searchers began to make their way down the unused tracks of the company railroad, near the African American church. Batson was the first to spot the little bicycle; it was lying in a ditch filled with water. Scrambling down into the ditch, he discovered the lifeless bodies of the missing girls under their bicycle. The bicycle had been partially dismantled, its front wheel removed; brush had been piled on top. Apparently, the murderer had been capable of acting with coolness, deliberateness, and a calm presence of mind.[8]

A grisly sight greeted the searchers when they removed the brush and the bicycle: the heads and faces of the two children had been severely bludgeoned. As Lee Burke recounted thirty-nine years later, "Their brains [were] beat out . . . Their brains was a pulp. When the doctor examined their head, and touched it there, they just bulged out." The men that young Batson had accompanied immediately ordered him to return home again. They would bring the village the news of their terrible discovery. As word circulated in Alcolu, the belief that the small world of their community was safe and secure began to collapse. After this violent event, how would there ever again be trust among neighbors? How could children ever again roam freely in their village? As Robert Lewis Alderman would write many years later: "Fear continued for months and years to come."[9]

In the normal course of events, the county's sheriff would have arrived and headed the investigation to find the murderer or murderers, but Sheriff James E. Gamble appeared only briefly later that day in Alcolu. He had played no part in finding the killer, nor was he present during the detention and examination of George Stinney, Jr. His absence would soon after haunt him during his campaign for reelection. Instead, it fell to Deputy Sheriff Huger Newman, who had participated in the search for the missing children, to begin the investigation on the morning of March 25. Newman made no headway until Sidney J. Pratt, an officer in the state constabulary, arrived on the scene. Pratt had learned about the murders in a phone call that came, most likely, from one of the Aldermans. As he walked unpaved streets of Alcolu, Pratt encountered an African American resident and began to question him. In 1983, Pratt described that fateful meeting: "This is very important as far as I'm concerned—I met a colored man. I'll not divulge his name . . . He was very concerned about it. I asked him if he knew of anybody that would do such a thing. And his reply to me was, 'The meanest fellow in this community is a boy by the name of George Stinney.'"[10]

Although Pratt carried the name of his informant with him to the grave, his identity has been established with more than reasonable certainty. Even now, however, it is necessary to preserve his anonymity; accordingly, he is referred to here as John Doe.[11]

Pratt asked John Doe where Stinney resided. Although initially hesitant to say more, Doe at length pointed out the family's house. Pratt then found Deputy Sheriff Newman and shared with him what he had learned from John Doe. Newman gave the information little or no credence. The constable nevertheless persisted, saying to Newman, "All I'm asking you to do is to go with me." Newman agreed, and the two drove over to the Stinneys' house. After arriving there, Pratt walked around to the porch at the back of the house, went up several steps, positioned himself next to the door, and listened to a conversation underway inside between two male individuals. At length, he heard one say to the other, "Well, you will not tell on me."

What Constable Pratt overheard might well have been about nothing more than an innocuous childhood prank, but he found the statement decidedly suspicious. As he told his interviewer in 1983, "Well, that was enough for me to hold him and question him, and for me to start a sure enough investigation."

Pratt and Newman entered the house, where they found fourteen-year-old George Stinney together with a relative, nineteen-year-old John Green. The two law officers immediately detained George and John and transported them to the Clarendon County jail in Manning for questioning.

When they arrived at the two-story jailhouse, the lawmen separated their suspects, placing George upstairs and John on the lower floor. They proceeded to interrogate John, pressing him to explain what George was referring to when he said, "You will not tell on me." (Pratt did not explain how he and Newman concluded that it had been George who had spoken those words.) But, according to Pratt, John shed no light on what George had meant. After a short time, they released him.

The two officers then brought George downstairs and began to question him about the murders. At first, he resolutely maintained his innocence. Before long, however, Pratt changed tactics and said ominously to him,

> Well, apparently you're in deep trouble. And there's only one
> man that can help you.
> Do you know Mr. Alderman?

It was at the mention of "Mr. Alderman" and the thought that he might be of help that Stinney began to change his story. As Pratt recounted it, "Up until that point he was saying that he was innocent. . . .

When I got into the Alderman situation, that Mr. Alderman might be of some aid to him, then he said he wanted to see Mr. Alderman. And before we got through questioning and talking with him, he admitted that he was guilty and that he had killed the two little girls."[12]

When questioned next about what he had used to kill them, Stinney responded that it had been "a piece of pipe." Not a railroad spike, Pratt insisted when interviewed many years later, but rather "a piece of iron." However, at Stinney's trial for murder a month later, the prosecution identified the murder weapon as a railroad spike. During the trial, however, Stinney's court-appointed defense attorneys would never pick up on this contradiction; they would make no attempt to undermine Pratt's credibility.[13]

At the time—and for years thereafter—the widespread assumption among the white population was that Stinney spoke the truth when he confessed to Pratt and Newman that he had murdered Betty June Binnicker and Mary Emma Thames. However, there is a strong possibility that it was a false confession. Much is now known about the genesis of false confessions, including factors such as physical coercion, mental impairment, fear of violence, the threat of a harsh sentence, and the isolation of the suspect. More pertinent than any of these to the case of George Stinney Jr. is this repeated finding: no matter the age of the person who falsely confesses, often a point comes when the suspect concludes he has more to gain from confessing than continuing to maintain his innocence. Children, as well as some adults, thus falsely confess, especially when they are led to believe an admission of guilt will allow them to go home.[14]

If the circumstances surrounding George Stinney's confession are examined, then the possibility of just such a dynamic arises. There he was, alone in a jailhouse, devoid of any support—here was the element of isolation—and subjected to questioning by two officers of the law: he, a youngster—they, adults; he, Black—they, White. Both of the White men asking the questions were experienced lawmen. In fact, Deputy Sheriff Newman was still remembered almost forty years later as "a born bloodhound himself. . . . He could get you. He *would* get you." When Stinney was told that Mr. Alderman would help him if he told the truth, it becomes entirely plausible to imagine that George, expecting Mr. Alderman would arrange for him to go home to his family, his home, and his familiar surroundings, would weaken and give Pratt and Newman what they wanted.[15]

A second, dramatic confession was soon to come. Hoping Stinney could find and identify the murder weapon, Pratt and Newman took the boy back to the location where the bodies of the two girls had been found. According to Pratt's account, Stinney fished in the water that filled the ditch and on his second try pulled out "the pipe, the piece of metal that he stated he used in taking these little girls' lives." At that point, according to the constable, Stinney went on to make an explosive admission: he had sexually abused one of the girls. In Pratt's words: "He also admitted that he had sexually assaulted—he didn't use that word, but had 'fooled with' one of the little girls after he had hit them. I asked him some questions, enough to know that that was with her privates."[16]

An admission of "fooling with one of the girls" raised the specter of one of the most potent racist myths: that Black men craved to possess White women's bodies. This myth had grown since the 1890s, when a generation of free African Americans seemed, to White Southerners, to be far less controllable than their enslaved parents and grandparents. It was widely accepted by many White Southerners and had justified horrific lynchings, tortures, and the burning alive of the alleged offenders. Fear of this alleged Black lust was strengthened by lurid descriptions, bordering on pornography, of Black men waiting to ravish their White victims. It drew power from the labeling of African American men as "brutes," "fiends," and "beasts." This insistence on the predatory nature of Black males struck fear into White women, a fear that would be seen in pleas to the governor of South Carolina that clemency should not be granted to fourteen-year-old George Stinney. He should not have his sentence commuted to life imprisonment wrote one woman because

> The Negro question is getting to be a serious one right here in
> this town where I live it seems that the Negros are becoming more
> belligerent, I am one of thousands of women that have to work at
> night. I have to walk three blocks to the Bus or trolley, I leave my
> home at 11: o'clock at night, & there is so many Negros roaming the
> streets that I am in fear of my life there have been several attacks &
> attempts on White Women and girls here this year, so I ask you not
> to commute any of them to life. . . & that will put a stop to so many
> crime [*sic*] committed now.[17]

Deputy Newman and Constable Pratt left the murder scene with Stinney and took him to Manning. Here, they secured him in the county jail. Word of the arrest spread quickly, and Pratt was soon fielding questions in Manning's streets about rumors of a rape. Fearing the possibility of an attack upon the jail by a lynch mob, Pratt, Newman, and Sheriff James Gamble conveyed George fifteen miles north to the county jail in neighboring Sumter County. Here he remained, sequestered in secrecy, until his trial in Manning a month later.

The rumors of rape quickly destroyed the relative civility between the races that had long defined Alcolu. That civility proved to be a thin veneer; it crumbled when it was subjected to stress and pressure. As one of the self-admitted agitators clamoring for the lynching of George Stinney recounted in later years: "There was quite an upstir about it . . . When we found out that he went back and raped the girl twice . . . We were gonna lynch him. . . . He was gonna die. Another recollected that, "I went to the house and got my damn rifle and started to cracking on them, see. . . . Every nigger that was in the whole village that I'd come up on I was ready to kill . . . They all got scared [and stayed in their houses]" (Brackets in the original).[18]

– – – – – – – – – – – –

At some point during the day, Ben Alderman traveled the short distance from Alcolu to Manning and met with Stinney in the jailhouse. Afterward, he took steps to defuse the possibility of an attack on the boy while he was in custody. But trouble was brewing back in Alcolu. Men were gathering in front of the company office on Highway 521, calling for immediate action and voicing threats of violence against George's family. Alderman knew he had to get the Stinneys out of town. As one participant in the mob later recalled, Alderman told George Sr., "George you better leave." Then he added: "course he could have come back later on I reckon and have went back to work, but sentiments were so high, there was a lynchin [sic] mob there ready to do it. The Aldermans gave him till night [to leave Alcolu]. If he hadn't of, he wouldn't have got out, I don't reckon. I reckon we would have got him."[19]

Ben Alderman told the members of the Stinney family to leave Alcolu by six o'clock that evening. The hapless Stinneys immediately began to comply, and, as John Doe recalled in 2003, they took the precaution of leaving their home one by one. He remembered watching as, singly, they left their house, proceeding separately to the Atlantic Coast Line Railroad depot, on what doubtlessly must have been a lonely, furtive walk filled with terror for their safety and lives. At the station, the overwhelmed Stinneys caught the next train that would carry them the short distance north to Sumter. From Sumter, they made their way to Pinewood, the village where they had lived before their move to Alcolu. There they found refuge with Mrs. Stinney's mother.[20]

One critically important legal task remained for the authorities. Before the funerals of the murdered children could be held, the victims' bodies would have to be examined by a physician. A report about the likely cause of death would then have to be sent to the county coroner for presentation to a coroner's jury of six men; they, in turn would send their findings and recommendations to the county's prosecutor. The bodies were thus taken to Sumter, where, at two o'clock in the afternoon, Dr. C. R. F. Baker of Sumter and Dr. Asbury C. Bozard of Manning examined the body of Mary Emma Thames. Their report described in detail the brutal injuries to her head and face. And then: "They had been caused by blows from a round instrument about the size of the head of a hammer." There were no other bruises elsewhere on her body, except for a "brush wound" on the right forehead, no doubt caused by the branches that had been piled on top of the dismantled bicycle that covered the two bodies in the ditch. Crucially, they found no evidence of sexual molestation. *"There were no bruises or discoloration about the genitalia and the hymen was intact,"* they reported (italics added). Because the two doctors found no evidence of cyanosis of the mucus membranes, Mary Emma's death most likely occurred before her body was placed in the watery ditch where the search party found it.[21]

The examination of Betty June Binnicker's body a half hour later at two thirty p.m. showed similar evidence of blows to the head by a hammer-like object, which had punched two holes in her skull and caused several other cracks in it. The beating was so severe that the rear of the child's skull was "a mass of crushed bones." In her case, too, death was most likely caused by the beating to the head, though there were slight signs of cyanosis of the mucus membranes. There were no other bruises on the body, although there was slight swelling of the external genitalia, with a "slight bruise" on the right side. As with the younger child, the *"the hymen was intact"* (italics added).[22]

The doctors' findings that neither child had been raped contradicted Constable Pratt's account that Stinney confessed to sexually assaulting one of them. But the evidence Pratt and Deputy Sheriff Newman gave at the trial a month later was that the sexual assault was indeed rape— nothing less. The prosecution, for its part, should have had to deal with this astonishing difference between the doctors' report and the testimony of the two officers, but it did not.

Meanwhile in Alcolu, the events of that traumatic Saturday were not yet over. Rumors and reports about rape continued to swirl about. From her house across the street from the company's office building, Mary Ellen Taylor, just shy of fourteen years old, watched and listened to the agitated talk. "They wanted to hang him," she emphatically declared many years later. Another witness, an adult who participated in the angry discussions, described how "they said, what they all wanted to do was to get him and hang him right there under that big pine tree. They were going to hang him under that pine tree. . . ." The orderly company town that the Aldermans had created, with its meticulously maintained equilibrium between the races so essential for their company's prosperity, quickly began to unravel in the space of a few hours, as southern racial mores surged to the fore, threatening to overwhelm Alderman order, decency, and Christian ethics.[23]

South Carolina had not seen a verifiable lynching since 1934, but on the afternoon of Saturday, March 25, 1944, the village of Alcolu teetered precariously on the brink of the next one.[24]

Chapter 4
Postponing a Lynching

Every Negro in the South knows that he is
under a kind of sentence of death; he does
not know when his turn will come, it may
never come, but it may also be at any time.

John Dollard, *Caste and Class
in a Southern Town*, 1937

Overwhelmed by terror, shrieking uncontrollably, the thirty-seven-year-old woman bolted from the car that had taken her from Sumter County to her home in the Black neighborhood of Alcolu. Her route there would have taken her past the gathering crowd of White men milling about in front of the Alderman company's office. She was engulfed by panic and desperation, for, like all African Americans in the South, she lived in the shadow of imminent violence.

The woman was George Stinney's mother, and her cries were those of a woman who feared she would lose her child to an angry White mob eager to hang him. To these men, his lynching would be a justifiable act of swift and certain justice. More than sixty years later, Charles Stinney, now an elderly pastor living in Brooklyn, could still remember his mother's piercing cries. As he recounted the events of that March 1944 day to an interviewer, a stillness eddied around him, as he shared his memories in a quiet voice.[1]

- - - - - - - - - - - -

Almost four thousand individuals were lynched in the United States between 1880 and 1940, according to Gunnar Myrdal's landmark study of African Americans, published in the same year that George Stinney was almost added to their ranks. Four-fifths of the victims of these lynchings were Black. The occurred in almost every state in the nation throughout the nineteenth century, but they became identified as a particularly Southern phenomenon in the late 1800s. Between 1880 and 1940, the South accounted for 90 percent of them, and more than two-thirds of the remaining 10 percent occurred in Maryland, West Virginia, Ohio, Indiana, Illinois, and Kansas, six states that bordered the South. Although lynching decreased nationally from an annual average of around two hundred during the 1890s to slightly more than ten a year during the 1930s, the decrease was slower in the South. At the same time, the number of lynchings accompanied by torture and by mutilation after death grew.[2]

A lynch mob might shoot, hang, or burn their victim. In a small number of cases, they dragged the victim behind a moving vehicle. Death by shooting could be painless, although sometimes lynchers inflicted it so viciously that the body was torn to shreds by the hundreds of bullets fired into it. Death by burning, on a stake or on a pyre, was known to be agonizing. So too was death by hanging. A professional executioner would know to ensure that the death was instantaneous. He would position the noose's knot under the angle of the left jaw and make certain that the condemned fell from a height calculated according to his or her height, weight, age, and musculature so that the neck broke at the second or third vertebrae. However, accounts of Southern lynchings suggest there was little interest in mastering the art of the professional hangman; most descriptions of these murders focused on where the hanging took place—a tree limb, a telephone pole, a railroad trestle or a signal crossing.[3]

Death by lynching could involve gruesome tortures. Victims could be dragged behind a horse or a car. They could be beaten with clubs, sticks, or whips. They could be stabbed with sharpened staves. Blowtorches could be applied while the victim was alive, and mutilation could also occur before the victim died. In many cases, the violence done to the bodies of lynching victims continued after death, as the members of lynching parties mutilated the corpses, eager to carry off such souvenirs as fingers, toes, or ears, and sometimes even genitals or chunks of flesh.[4]

Between 1907, the year that Mrs. Stinney was born, and March 25, 1944, the day of her son's arrest, at least forty-nine verifiable lynchings had taken place in the state of South Carolina. In 1911, a seventeen-year-old accused of raping a White woman was hauled up a telephone pole, briefly suspended upside down, and then shot. Five years later, Anthony

Crawford, a prosperous African American farmer, was seized by men who thought he needed a lesson for acting "uppity" in conversation with a White cotton gin merchant. To defend himself against the hostile crowd, Crawford struck their leader in the head with a hammer. In retaliation, they hanged him from a tree and filled his body with their bullets. In 1926, when Mrs. Stinney was nineteen, news of the lynching of three members of the Lowman family in Aiken, South Carolina, spread not only through the state but also the nation. The Lowmans had been implicated in the shooting death of the county sheriff. At their first trial, the state supreme court ruled there was insufficient evidence for a conviction; at a second trial, the judge ordered one of the defendants freed. Before this could happen, a band of Ku Klux Klan members decided to take matters into their own hands. The Aiken sheriff allowed the Klan members to take the Lowmans from the jail and, as a crowd of a thousand spectators watched, the lynchers shot all three. Two died immediately, but twenty-seven-year-old Bertha Lowman clung to life. She crawled along the ground, begging for mercy that did not come. She died of wounds to her head and abdomen. Many South Carolinians were shocked by this execution, so much so that the governor thought it politic to denounce the event in his 1927 address to the legislature.

But few lynchings surpassed the savagery inflicted upon Claude Neal in nearby Florida in 1934. News of this barbarous event was so widespread that George Stinney's mother may well have known of it. Twenty-three-year-old Neal was arrested for allegedly raping and then murdering the daughter of one of his employers in Jackson County, Florida. Hoping to prevent violence, law officers moved Neal around to jails in various counties, and even took him across the state line to an Alabama jail. Despite these efforts, a band of men from Florida managed to kidnap him late at night from his jail cell in Brewton, Alabama. In a carefully planned and skillfully executed operation, the kidnappers returned with him to Jackson County in early the next morning and proceeded to plan his lynching for that night. Word of the upcoming lynching spread so quickly that the Associated Press was able to post a national news flash about it. The crowd that gathered to watch the hanging was estimated from several hundreds to as many as five thousand people from eleven states, and it included both women and children.

An investigator for the NAACP was later able to reconstruct what Claude Neal's tormenters did to him over a period of two hours. Citing eyewitnesses, he made the following report:

They cut off his penis. He was made to eat it. Then they cut off his testicles and made him eat them and say he liked it. . . . Then they sliced his sides and stomach with knives and every now and then somebody cut off a finger or toe. Red hot irons were used on the nigger to burn him from top to bottom. From time to time during the torture a rope would be tied around Neal's neck and he was pulled up over a limb and held there until he almost choked to death when he would be let down and the torture began all over again.

In the end, a car dragged Neal's corpse to the farmhouse where his alleged victim had resided. A smaller crowd assembled there, and some of its members proceeded to drive knives into his body. Others kicked the corpse; still others drove cars over it; and young children stabbed it with sharpened staves. And in the weeks that followed, souvenir hunters showed off their trophies: fingers and toes cut from Claude Neal's body.[5]

Neal had been lynched for raping and murdering a White female, which were the same crimes Amie Stinney's son now stood accused of ten years later. George's age was unlikely to stand in the way of his lynching; only two years earlier, a fourteen-year-old and a fifteen-year-old were murdered by a mob after a White girl accused them of attempted rape.[6]

The men who participated in lynchings, and the women and children who were often present as spectators, were universally described both by advocates of lynchings and those who opposed the practice as "a mob"; it was the label employed by newspaper reporters and editors, by outside observers, and by historians. Unlike "crowd," or even "lynching party," the word "mob" suggests wild, frenzied, and berserk behavior, uncontrollable rage, and riot. As one Georgia journalist who supported lynching complained in 1893: "The newspapers speak of lynchings as the act of a howling, yelling, demoniac mob." Roughly a decade later, Ray Stannard Baker, one of the Progressive era's leading investigative journalists, described a 1904 double lynching spurred by several gruesome murders in Statesboro, Georgia, as the work of a berserk mob. In the grip of uncontrolled hysteria, the lynchers stormed the court where the two suspects were being tried and seized them: "The mob was now thoroughly stirred; it ceased to hesitate; it was controlled wholly by its emotions." At the lynching site, some called for hanging the two African Americans, but a recitation of their alleged crimes "worked the mob into a frenzy of ferocity." Rather than hang them, the lynchers poured kerosene over them and burned them alive. "When the faggots were lighted," Baker wrote, "the crowd [*sic*] yelled wildly." Afterward, the participants went on a rampage for several days, randomly attacking Blacks in the community, brutally whipping many. Baker reflected upon the terror that followed lynchings:

> This is the law of the mob, that it never stops with the thing it sets out to do. It is exactly like any other manifestation of uncontrolled human passion—given license it takes more license, it releases that which is ugly, violent, revengeful, in the community. . . . I have often heard of a "quiet mob," "an orderly mob," which 'went about its business and hanged the nigger,' but in all the cases I have known about, and I made special inquiries upon this particular point, not one single mob stopped when the immediate work was done, unless under compulsion. Even good citizens of Statesboro will tell you that "the niggers got only what they deserved," and it was all right if the mob had only stopped there. But it did not stop there; it never does.[7]

Labeling lynchings as the work of frenzied mobs suggests they were instantaneous eruptions of rage. Yet many lynchings exhibited deliberateness and planning. Many occurred days after an alleged culprit had been captured, which was enough time for passions to have cooled. Many were publicly announced days in advance, either in newspapers or on signs like the one posted widely in 1916 in the city of Paris, Texas. It advertised what would prove to be a particularly brutal double lynching:

> Niggers Caught
> Black Brutes Who Killed
> Hodges Will Be Burned In The
> Fair Grounds
> Be On Hand

This advertisement brought some three thousand spectators to the event. In fact, special trains were sometimes chartered for this type of scheduled spectacle, making it possible for thousands to plan their attendance at the gatherings.[8]

Most newspaper articles equated "mob" with members of the lower classes of the community. "The mob," explained one Southerner in a 1904 issue of the *Atlantic Monthly*, "may be recruited from the worst element of the community, men of bad character and low intelligence." He added that, in cases of rape, "the less intelligent classes will long regard the mob as the rightful executioner." Ray Stannard Baker reinforced the generally accepted image of lynchers when he described the participants in a mob in Huntsville, Alabama, as illiterate laborers in the cotton mills, "men from the hills, the descendants of the 'poor white trash.'" A generation later, a lengthy report put out by the Southern Commission on the Study of Lynching concluded that loafing, drinking, and gambling laborers and tenants who were idle after crop cultivation was completed accounted for most of the summary executions in the South.[9]

Yet despite what newspapers and reformers claimed, mobs were not exclusively made up of working-class and poor Southerners. There are many contemporary accounts of lynchings in which "respectable" Whites appeared as participants. Sometimes their participation was crucial in persuading a law officer to turn over the African American in his custody. One sheriff explained that he could not protect his prisoner when confronted by a lynch mob because "the first half-a-dozen men standing there were leading citizens—businessmen, leaders of their church and the community—I just couldn't do it." In 1915, in Marietta, Georgia, members of the town's political and social elite planned and organized the kidnapping and hanging of a White man, Leo Frank. Frank may have been White, but the fact that he was a Northerner, a Jew, and an industrialist probably sealed his fate. Five years later, in Wharton, Texas, shopkeepers closed their businesses to join in a manhunt for four African Americans, who were ultimately captured and killed. The mob that murdered and dismembered Claude Neal in 1934 included "well dressed" men regarded as leading members of their communities. And in 1938, a Mississippi mob that included "planters [and] businessmen" burned a Black man to death on the same site where he allegedly murdered "a prominent white planter." Gunnar Myrdal was thus correct when he wrote: "Occasionally . . . the people of the middle and upper classes take part" in forming the mob.[10]

Lynchings, then, were a shared experience that cut across class lines in the South, despite the tensions that might otherwise exist between the prosperous and the poor. There was, in fact, little love lost between men of comfort and wealth and those who lived in poverty. As one poor South Carolinian bluntly put it in 1942: "All of us hated bankers and we hated merchants. We hated them because they had robbed us[—]

they should have been shot and should have shot them . . . We would have felt better about them if we had killed a few. . . ." For their part, middle- and upper-class Southerners showed their contempt for the poor and laboring classes by the host of insulting terms they applied to them: crackers, hillbillies, clay eaters, rednecks, peckerwoods, wool hats, trash, low-downers, and no-counts. In their eyes, these "crackers" were "just as bad as niggers." In 1998, the Pulitzer Prize–winning novelist and journalist Rick Bragg would write of generations of his family's crushing poverty in northeastern Alabama. During the Great Depression, Bragg wrote, wealthy Southerners did little to relieve the suffering of the poor. "Some," he declared, "even seemed to take sadistic pleasure in driving poorer Southerners, a class they had long distained, to even greater pain."[11]

Yet by the turn of the twentieth century, a détente had been reached between the South's rich and poor. For in the late nineteenth century, a Populist movement arose whose program included regulating banks, railroads, telegraphs, and other enterprises the poor believed worked to their disadvantage. This movement had threatened the social order, attempting to build a political coalition of poor Whites and Blacks. The Southern elite defeated this threat of class-based politics by formally institutionalizing segregation in law, by disenfranchising Blacks, and by stressing a shared racial superiority that encouraged a coalition of White Southerners of every class. Lynching added cement to this unity through the emotionally unforgettable experience of gathering and standing side by side to protect White society—especially White womanhood—from the ravages of Black men.[12]

It was surely no accident that lynching in the South reached its crescendo during the 1890s, in numbers that would never be duplicated again. As Arthur Roper explained in his extensive study of lynching: "Lynchings often serve as socializing forces within the white group. Not infrequently more unanimity can be had on a lynching than on any other subject. Lynchings tend to minimize social and class distinctions between white plantation owners and white tenants, mill owners and textile workers, Methodists and Baptists, and so forth. This prejudice against the Negro forms a common meeting place for whites. . . ."[13]

- - - - - - - - - - - -

White Southerners justified lynching with two primary arguments. First and foremost, White women had to be protected from the predatory sexuality of Black men. During the era of slavery, went the argument, rape had not been a problem, nor had it been a problem during the Civil War, despite White women's vulnerability as their husbands and other protectors went away to war. It was only after the war, as Reconstruction began, that Black males began to prey upon White females of all ages. The controls under slavery that had kept Black men in line were gone. Worse, all the talk of equality bandied about was exacerbating the aggressiveness and expectations of the now free Black population. The only protection for White women was the fear of lynching. In this predominantly rural society, White women could not be safely left alone in their homes; they could not travel the countryside freely. Under these circumstances, only the threat of lynching could prevent attacks.[14]

And if a rape did occur? It was intolerable to ask the victim to testify in open court against her attacker. Lynching spared women this humiliation and the ordeal of cross-examination as well. As one leading southern defender proclaimed in a Chautauqua address, sexual assault by Black males against White women was "the crime which always has and always will provoke lynching," for it provided "the most potential bulwark between the women of the South and such a carnival of crime as would infuriate the world and precipitate the annihilation of the negro race." In his view, "the mob is to-day the sternest, the strongest, and the most effective restraint that the age holds for the control of rape."[15]

As opponents of lynching relentlessly documented and even some supporters acknowledged, allegations of rape and attempted rape accounted for a minority of lynchings. As early as 1892, the African American journalist and Muckraker, Ida Wells-Barnett, found evidence that less than a third of lynchings were for rape. In 1904, Thomas Nelson Page, a prominent southern apologist for lynching, admitted that in recent years fewer than one-fourth of lynchings were for rape; the remaining three-fourths were for murder, attempted murder, and a variety of less serious offenses. Thirty years later, Arthur Raper reported that only one-sixth of the Blacks who were lynched between 1889 and 1930 had been accused of rape. In 1938, another opponent of lynching concurred that, between 1882 and 1937, less than one-sixth of the 3,657 lynchings of African Americans were for rape.[16]

Yet rape remained the raison d'etre for the practice of lynching, at least in the popular imagination. Southern defenders explained to Ray Stannard Baker that it was necessary to continue to lynch alleged murderers and other criminals, even White ones, because, to admit that these could be handled by a court of law would undermine the ready acceptance of lynching when a rape occurred. In Baker's examination of lynching in 1905: "It is with this crime [rape] that lynching begins; here and here only could the furious mob spirit break through the resisting wall of law and order. . . . But it is only because lynching for rape is excused that lynching for any other crime is ever attempted. If there were no lustful brutes to deal with, it would be easy to develop a public sentiment that would make any form of lynching impossible."[17]

The second major justification White Southerners offered for lynching was the defects they claimed abounded in the American system of criminal law and criminal procedure. These defects, they charged, prevented swift and certain justice. Too many delays were permitted; too many postponements were allowed. There were too many rights and loopholes for the accused: "Preemptory challenges, habeas corpus proceedings, writs of error, changes of venue, exceptions, appeals, new trials, respites, pardon, etc." As Justice Brewer of the US Supreme Court explained in an address at Yale Law School, "It is not to be wondered at that some communities have arisen in their wrath and have inflicted the summary punishment that machinery of the law has delayed, and which they feared it might delay among them, too." Even the Roman Catholic cardinal of Boston, generally an opponent of lynching, agreed with its defenders that the insanity defense provided an escape hatch for many murderers and rapists. A former associate justice of the supreme court of Alabama observed that . . . "the tardiness of the law in bringing criminals to justice. . . . Caused by too infrequent terms of the trial courts, and the legal duty imposed on the higher courts of reversing convictions for technical errors of law," served as a "plausible apology" for lynching. Another Southerner put it more bluntly: "[T]he ordinary procedure of the courts is too slow and orderly and decent to act as a deterrent to such a race [as the Blacks] . . . the only preventive of crime among them is a vengeance so swift and ghastly as to fill the soul with dread."[18]

Both justifications for lynching figured in the events at Alcolu on the day following the rapes and murders attributed to George Stinney. The men preparing to lynch Stinney firmly believed that assault by a Black male against White females must be dealt with in summary fashion. But the townspeople who opposed lynching argued that criminal law and criminal procedures had not yet proven to be slow or faulty. They succeeded in obtaining a reprieve for Stinney from mob violence, if only for the moment. The would-be lynchers did not consider this a defeat, but only a postponement. If the apparatus of the criminal justice system failed to deliver the justice that George Stinney deserved, they would see that appropriate action was taken.

This rescue of George Stinney from the lyncher's noose was not unusual. While there were 762 lynchings between 1915 and 1941, almost twice as many attempts—1,467—were thwarted. And the prevention of lynchings grew steadily more effective. In 1915, the ratio of lynchings to prevented lynchings was 73 percent to 27 percent; but between 1935 and 1941, the 11 percent of proposed lynchings stood in sharp contrast to the 89 percent that were averted. Thus, despite Mrs. Stinney's fears, the chances had been good that her son would escape death at the hands of a mob.[19]

Governors could play a decisive role in the prevention of lynching. Although they often stood by, or even voiced support for a lynching, there were those who were willing to risk their political careers by calling up state militias and national guards to thwart the mob's wishes. Although many county sheriffs stood by while lynch mobs stormed the jail or walked away when mobs seized their victims in public places, others took decisive action to protect those in their custody, moving the mob's targets to other counties or to state penitentiaries for what was called "Safekeeping."

Civil society's opposition to the blight of lynching also grew. Although some newspapers continued to print editorials that backed lynching, many denounced the practice. And private organizations like the Commission on Interracial Cooperation, the Southern Commission on the Study of Lynching, and the Association of Southern Women for the Prevention of Lynching, established in 1930 by Jesse Daniel Ames, worked to end lynching. Ames's organization went straight to the heart of the matter: "Women dare no longer allow themselves to be the cloak behind which those bent upon personal revenge and savagery commit acts of violence and lawlessness in the name of women. We repudiate this disgraceful claim for all time." Ames herself did not flinch from exposing and publicizing the worst excesses of the lynch mob: "It was the bestial excesses which characterized the mobs. Long and exciting man hunts with frequent use of bloodhounds preceded the capture of the victims; barbarous tortures of living men were inflicted; mutilation of the bodies were indulged in. Women and children were frequently present, not as onlookers but as frequent participants."[20]

Lynching's opponents appealed to decency, to morality, to the tenets of Christianity, to what civilization and civilized behavior presumed, and to the necessity for a society to uphold law and order, to rely upon its courts. A society that did otherwise could not call itself civilized. They were also willing to administer a heavy dose of cynical realism by underscoring the harmful economic consequences to a community of lynching. They pointed out that landowners suffered loses when their sharecroppers, tenant farmers, and laborers left permanently for other locations in the wake of the violence. Businessmen were also reminded that "disorder had a tendency to frighten away capital, stop immigration, and retard development generally."

As Ray Stannard Baker succinctly put it: "[G]ood business demands good order." Anthony Crawford's lynching in 1916 prompted *The State*, one of South Carolina's leading newspapers, to stress the economic cost of mob violence. It asked: "Shall the mob go into partnership with the boll weevil to drive labor from the farms and bankrupt this Southern country?" And, in 1920, in the aftermath of a brutal lynching he witnessed in Georgia, "A Southern White Man" warned in a newspaper essay as follows:

> It is alike injurious to the white people of the South who need
> the labor [of the Black population], and if the white people do not
> protect the helpless negro may we expect to have the negro serve us
> upon the farms or in the city? . . . . If the white people of the South
> permit men to go unpunished and allow verdicts of coroners' juries
> to be procured to whitewash their bloody murders and to terrorize
> this humble race how can we expect anything else than that rail-
> roads will be continually selling tickets to the colored people to go
> North, they feel like their very life depends on getting away.[21]

But the biggest challenge the opponents of lynching faced remained the allegation that the structure of criminal law and criminal procedure could not be trusted to render justice. They could only respond by assuring that justice could, and would, prevail. They went so far as to promise that an agreement could be reached between the authorities and the mob that could satisfy even the most inflamed public. As Jesse Daniel Ames noted in 1942, "Investigations have disclosed that in more than one prevented lynching a bargain was entered into between officers and would-be lynchers before the trial began in which the death penalty was promised as the price of the mob's dispersal."

Gunnar Myrdal noticed the same phenomenon, writing in the year that George Stinney was arrested that "Police and court officials promise to vigilante leaders that the accused Negro will receive a quick trial and the death penalty if he is not lynched."[22]

A bargain made with the angry men who had gathered to lynch George Stinney is precisely what occurred in Alcolu, although no assurance or pledge was given that he would be found guilty at trial. Thirty-nine years after the girls' murders, Roston Stukes, who described himself as one of the leaders of the crowd that had gathered to lynch Stinney, told his interviewer the deal that had been made:

> We were gonna lynch him. . . . He was gonna die. They made a deal with me—I was the head of it. Don't mind admitting it. . . . They made a deal with us: let them try him, and they'd guarantee us that we could see him, if he was convicted—they didn't say he'd be convicted—we could see him if he got the electric chair. . . . [Following Stinney's sentencing] they got the permit or whatever they had to have to see it done. . . . We went to Columbia [to the penitentiary]. . . . and we went in there and we seen it happen.[23]

Stukes did not identify who made this promise of ringside seats at the execution, but it is unlikely that it was Sheriff James Gamble, or Deputy Huger Newman, who was with Sheriff Gamble and Constable Sidney Pratt at the jail in Manning where they were holding George Stinney. Could it have been one or more of the Aldermans, the ultimate source of all authority in the village? What is certain is that the Aldermans intervened to prevent violence on at least two more occasions on that volatile day.

"Why didn't they hang him?" The question was posed thirty-nine years later during an interview with Lee Burke, who made the short trip from Alcolu to the jail in Manning with his gun. Burke responded:

> I'll tell you what happened. Ben Alderman was a so-called to be [sic] a Christian. Well, whenever they got ahold of the boy, he said to me, "Lee, they're gone with him now to the jail house." So I said to him, Well, 'I'm going. And I went back over to the jailhouse." [Sheriff]

Eddie Gamble was standing there in the jail yard, and he walked back into the jail when I walked up, and he went in there and he told Newman, his deputy, he said, "Now, Lee Burke is standing out there right there in the jail yard, standing right there, and he's got a .38 pistol in his belt," and he says, "he ain't hiding it." And, "I don't know what's gonna happen here. . . ." So the SLED officer Pratt, he come out and got in his car and took off from around the back with a boy. . . . Ben Alderman and the sheriff, Eddie Gamble and Huger Newman and all come out there and says, "Lee, now that wasn't the boy. They really haven't got him. They're sending that one home right now."[24]

The lie these three men told succeeded in preventing violence at the Clarendon County jailhouse; it allowed the officers to secretly transport Stinney to the safety of the Sumter County jail. Burke recalled that, on the ride back to Alcolu, he and Ben Alderman had this exchange:

When we came across Manning swamp, Ben started to crying. He said, "Lee," he says, "I've lied to you." And he says, "I hope you'll forgive me." He says, "That was the boy, that Pratt took out of here. And I'm sorry that I lied to you, but I lied to you, and I hope you'll forgive me." And he says, "Pratt is carrying him to Columbia [*sic*]. He's confessed to everything."

So I says, "Well, I reckon that's the right way for you to handle it. *But you should have never done that. Because it wouldn't have cost the state nothing. Everything would have been over in a short while.*" (Italics added.)

During the course of the same day in Alcolu, the Aldermans realized that a second attack needed to be prevented; this time the target was George Stinney's father. If the Aldermans had not ordered the Stinneys to leave Alcolu immediately, no one could have protected them. As Lee Burke told his interviewer years later, if Stinney and his family had not fled, "I reckon we would have got him."[25]

George Stinney and his father were thus safe—but only for the moment. As far as Roston Stokes and his friends were concerned, the lynching of George Stinney Jr. had merely been postponed. A month later, they would attend George's trial with weapons concealed in the pocketbooks of women spectators. If the fourteen-year-old was not sentenced to die in the electric chair, these men intended to seize him and kill him then and there. Their version of justice would be done. "The law knew it," Stukes said, "And that's why they made the deal with me, if we'd just hold off."[26]

Chapter 5
The Road to Trial

Their findings cancelled previous beliefs
that one of the children may have been
criminally assaulted.

Manning Times, March 29, 1944

Alcolu's profoundly shaken White inhabitants gathered on March 27, 1944, for the funerals of the two murdered children. Local teenagers had filled the village's Clarendon Baptist Church with flowers in preparation for this double funeral service. Pastor Batson officiated, assisted by two clergymen from towns and churches associated with the Binnicker and Thames families. Batson's text, taken from Romans, was "Vengeance is mine; I will repay, saith the Lord." Perhaps he selected it to counter any lingering plans to discover where the authorities were secretly holding George Stinney in order to lynch him. As Vermelle Tucker believed thirty-nine years later, the authorities kept moving Stinney from jail to jail because so many people in the Manning area were intent upon seizing him: "There was just so much hate in everybody at that time. All they wanted to do was to get their hands on him . . . It was just like—it was almost broadcasted. . . . I guess it's best that they didn't get ahold to him because too many people would be in trouble about it."[1]

George Stinney wasn't the only target of hatred. Animosity toward Alcolu's Black population continued to fester in the immediate aftermath of the murders. "Negroes were antagonized and some even abused," an African American newspaper in Atlanta later reported. Alcolu resident Lee Burke confirmed these attacks in an interview thirty-nine years later. As he remembered:

It just got to me, and I went to the house and got my damn rifle and started to cracking on them, see. . . . And every one of them that would come upon to me and say, 'Mr. Lee, well sir, you sure got him,' I'd hit him. Or kick him. [And if he's have opened his mouth] I'd have killed him right there. Every nigger that was in the whole village that I'd come up on I was ready to kill . . . They all got scared [and stayed in their houses]. (Brackets in the original.)[2]

Following the church service, the two children were laid separately to rest, Betty June Binnicker in the town in Orangeburg County where her maternal grandmother resided and from where her family had lived before moving to Alcolu; Mary Emma Thames in a cemetery in Manning.[3]

Two days after the funerals, a coroner's jury convened in the county seat of Manning to hear testimony about George Stinney's role in the murders. The jury members included two men who had been leaders in the call for George's lynching only five days earlier. According to the *Columbia Record*, the sole witness, Deputy Sheriff Henry S. Newman, had read a confession, allegedly signed by Stinney, that he had beaten the two girls to death. Since Newman was apparently silent about Stinney's other alleged admission that he had sexually molested one of his victims, the jury's finding was for murder only.[4]

Reporting in both the *Sumter Herald* and the *Manning Times* attempted to put to rest the rumors about rape. The *Herald* cited the findings of the two physicians who examined the girls' bodies that "The children were killed instantly and . . . the only indications of abuse were the wounds in their head which caused their deaths. Both newspapers concluded that "Their findings cancelled previous beliefs that one of the children may have been criminally assaulted."[5]

Less than four weeks later, Deputy Sheriff Newman, along with Constable Sidney Pratt, would tell a very different story when they testified against Stinney during his trial.

Because Clarendon was one of four counties in the Third Judicial Circuit, the coroner sent the inquest's results to Franklin McLeod, the third circuit's solicitor (that is, prosecutor). Solicitor McLeod could have chosen to send the case to Family Court, which handled matters involving juveniles, rather than to the Court of General Sessions for Clarendon County, where criminal matters were tried. Much hung on McLeod's choice: there would be no trial in Family Court and a guilty offender would be confined in a reformatory for a limited time or perhaps sent to a state prison; in General Sessions, on the other hand, Stinney would be tried for murder as an adult and, if found guilty, sentenced to death or, if the jury recommended mercy, to life imprisonment at hard labor.[6]

Could a child of fourteen be tried as an adult in a capital case? This was the question posed in the office of the South Carolina Attorney General on the day the Clarendon County coroner's jury conducted its inquest. The law, according to the attorney general, specified only that a defendant less than seven years of age could not be tried for a crime. Otherwise, South Carolina law established sixteen as the age of responsibility for a crime. Yet a number of provisions in the state's code of criminal procedure, such as in the chapter devoted to the Family Court in Charleston County, prescribed that a person between the ages of fourteen and sixteen could be charged and tried as an adult for a capital offense—and therefore receive the death penalty.[7]

McLeod quickly determined that George Stinney had passed the age of fourteen five months before, and he could therefore be tried for his life in a criminal court for adults. If asked, McLeod could cite precedents for his decision. In at least two previous cases, fourteen-year-olds had been tried in General Sessions courts and found guilty; both had been sentenced to death in the electric chair. In one case, however, the governor commuted the sentence to life imprisonment. In the other, no record of actual disposition exists.[8]

The question of mental competence remained, however. It too had been raised in the discussion with the attorney general. South Carolina law recognized that insanity mitigated guilt. As *The State*, the newspaper of record in Columbia, pointed out, "the jury has the responsibility of determining the degree of guilt," but "when insanity becomes an issue, the experts determine whether or not the defendant is insane. Ability to distinguish between right and wrong is also often a point in such trials."[9]

Below-normal intelligence did not matter in South Carolina law if an individual could distinguish between right and wrong. This was made clear in 1939 in a statement by a state judge sitting in a capital case. Both the press and several public officials took care to point out that George Stinney, who was in the seventh grade in school, had reached a level of schooling that few White or Black adults in Clarendon had attained. Deputy Sheriff Henry S. Newman, for example, had gone only as far as the fifth grade. In Alcolu, fully a third of White heads of households had less than seven years of schooling. Making it to the seventh grade, the highest grade in elementary school, apparently implied mental sufficiency and therefore, in the public's view, the ability to know right from wrong. Statements that Stinney was in the seventh grade were often accompanied by the comment that he was perfectly normal and, as the Superintendent of Education said, "above the average in intelligence." The *Columbia Record* reported that Stinney "seems intelligent beyond his 14 years," and, after the trial, a member of the State Pardon and Parole Board who met with him in his death house cell, would describe Stinney as "bright and well up in his school." Thirty-nine years later, Stinney's intelligence was a salient feature of the memories several interviewees had of him. Lee Burke remembered: "He was smart. He was smart in school. When he would go to school." Constable Sidney J. Pratt recalled that "there certainly was nothing about him to indicate that he was retarded in any way, shape or form." And Charles Plowden, one of Stinney's two court-appointed defense attorneys, described Stinney as "Just a typical boy. A little brighter than usual," a boy who "seemed to be perfectly normal."[10]

McLeod was thus convinced that legal precedent and the certainty that George Stinney was more than smart enough to tell right from wrong were solid grounds to refer the case to criminal court. His first step was to seek an indictment by a grand jury. Assuming an indictment would be brought, McLeod had also selected thirty-six potential trial jurors out of the pool of grand jurors for 1944 to sit in judgment in a special session of General Sessions Court. Both the grand jury's members asked to bring the indictment and the pool of jurors who would try the case mirrored the socioeconomic composition of the county's population in all but one key respect: all the men whose names were drawn appear to have been White, despite the fact that Whites were distinctly in the minority in Clarendon County.[11]

In the 1940s, Clarendon County was predominantly rural, so much so that when South Carolina's Research, Planning and Development Board ranked the state's forty-six counties according to the percentage of their populations that were urban in 1940, it omitted Clarendon entirely. Blacks predominated by a wide margin within this rural population. In fact, with a population that was more than 70 percent African American, Clarendon County ranked 44 out of 46 counties in the percentage of White residents. Not surprisingly, the county was not just predominantly Black, it was also poor. Despite the creation of the monumental Depression era Santee-Cooper waterways project that gave a small boost to the county economy, much of the population was impoverished. Evidence of this could be seen in state statistics: the county's assessed valuation in 1941 was the third-lowest among forty-six counties; in per capita taxes levied on property only one county ranked lower. This deep poverty was an inevitable result of the South's Jim Crow social system that relegated the majority of the Black population—and many Whites as well—to a marginal standard of living. An astonishing 69 percent of the county's farmers were tenants or sharecroppers who lived and worked on property belonging to landlords. Clarendon ranked fourth-highest among the state's forty-six counties in the percentage of its farmers who were landless, and thus, for the most part, trapped permanently within a web of rents charged by their landlords, low prices they received for their crops, and debts they owed to the landlords and local storekeepers who advanced them credit until the year's crops were brought to market. This tenant and sharecropping population was overwhelmingly Black. Only a little more than a quarter of the nearly four thousand farmers were White, and this included both men who owned their land as well as those who did not.[12]

Identifying the twenty-one grand jurors who were to determine if an indictment would be issued against George Stinney is fraught with difficulties. Nevertheless, the 1940 census can provide a rough picture of thirteen of this group. (The eight others could not be located, perhaps because they did not reside in Clarendon County in 1940.) Three of the thirteen were not locked into the county's overwhelmingly rural patterns of life, and they enjoyed much more education than was the rule. Two were from the town of Summerton; one, who had completed a year of college, was the proprietor of a grocery store who lived in a rented home; the other, the manager of a drug store, had completed four years of college and owned his own home. The third, a resident of the town of Gable who had also completed four years of college, was an electrician who wired houses and owned his own.[13]

The remaining identifiable members of the grand jury were all farmers, and thus closely resembled the majority of the county's White population. Four owned their farms and ranged in education from the fifth grade to two years of college. Two others rented their farms, and had completed, respectively, one and two years of high school. Yet another had gone as far as the eighth grade and lived in a home owned by his wife's grandmother. The two remaining grand jurors tied to the land were one of the two George W. Burkes who lived in Alcolu and J. E. Childers.[14]

Solicitor McLeod presented only two witnesses to the grand jury: Ben Alderman and Deputy Sheriff Newman. Because grand jury proceedings are secret there is no way to know what they told the twenty-one jurors, but a part of an account written by Newman is among the few papers in the case preserved in the South Carolina state archives. It captures what must have been the gist of his testimony:

> H S Newman being sworn says on friday March 24—1944 I was called to Alcolu S.C. near 10 oclock and told that two little girls was missing Bettie June Binnicker, other was Mary Ema Thames, when I got to Alcolu there was a searching party searching for them, and near 8 oclock saterday Morning I was notified that the Bodies had been found I went down to where the bodies were at. I found Mary Ema Thames, she was rite at the edge of the ditch with four or five wounds on her head, on the other side of the ditch the Binnicker girl, were laying there with 4 or 5 wounds in her head, the Bycicle which the little girls had were side of the little Binnicker girl[.]
>
> On information I received I arrested a boy by the name of George Stiney [sic], he then made a confession and told me where a A [sic] piece of iron about 15 inches long were, he said he put it in a ditch about 6 feet from the bycicle wheel which was lying in the ditch the piece of iron were found in water where he said it were at.
> (over) [The document breaks off here.][15]

The grand jury issued two True Bills indicting George Stinney for the murders of Betty June Binnicker and Mary Emma Thames. Like the coroner's jury, they made no mention of rape. It is thus likely that Newman did not reveal to the grand jury that Stinney had confessed to rape when he stood with Newman and Pratt at the ditch where the two murdered girls and their dismantled bicycle had been found.[16]

With indictments in hand, Solicitor McLeod could now move the case forward to trial in in the Clarendon County Court of General Sessions. However, the next term of this court was not scheduled to convene again until late in June. It was exactly this kind of delay that many Southerners cited as a justification for the swift and certain justice that lynching brought. The way around this situation was to schedule a special term of the court that would convene sooner than the end of June. Solicitor McLeod had planned for this. On the day of the coroner's inquest—even before he had presented the case to the grand jury—he announced that he and the County Attorney, John G. Dinkins, a fixture in Clarendon

Sheriff Newman's handwritten testimony. Clarendon County, Court of General Sessions, Indictment file of George Stinney. Series L14095, Indictment #1853. South Carolina Department of Archives and History.

County politics, were working to insure that this special session could be called. Thus, a week after the indictment came down, Solicitor McLeod formally petitioned the administrative judge of the Third Judicial Circuit to authorize a special term. Judge Philip Henry Stoll, who usually presided over the court during its spring session and who subsequently was to preside at Stinney's trial, agreed to McLeod's request, as did the

The State of South Carolina,

County of _Clarendon_

S. 28.—INDICTMENT FOR MURDER
THE STATE COMPANY, LAW PRINTERS, COLUMBIA, S. C.

At a Court of General Sessions, begun and holden in and for the County of _Clarendon_ in the State of South Carolina, at _Manning_ Court House, in the County and State aforesaid, on the _Fourth_ Monday of _April_ in the year of our Lord one thousand nine hundred and _forty four_

The Jurors of and for the County aforesaid, in the State aforesaid, upon their oath, Present:

That

George Stinney, Jr.,

on the _Twenty fourth_ day of _March_ in the year of our Lord one thousand nine hundred and _Forty four_ with force and arms, at _Manning_ in the County of _Clarendon_ and State of South Carolina, in and upon one _Mary Emma Thames_ feloniously, wilfully and of his malice aforethought, did make an assault, and that the said _George Stinney, Jr.,_ him the said _Mary Emma Thames_ then and there feloniously, wilfully and of his malice aforethought with _an iron Rod_ did _strike, beat, bruise_ and wound; giving to the said _Mary Emma Thames_ thereby in and upon the _Body_ of the said _Mary Emma Thames_

George Stinney indictments for the murders of Betty June Binnecker and Mary Emma Thames. Clarendon County, Court of General Sessions, Indictment file of George Stinney. Series L14095, Indictment #1853. South Carolina Department of Archives and History.

The State of South Carolina,
County of _Clarendon_

S. 28.—INDICTMENT FOR MURDER
THE STATE COMPANY, LAW PRINTERS, COLUMBIA, S. C.

At a Court of General Sessions, begun and holden in and for the County of _____ _Clarendon_ in the State of South Carolina, at _Manning_ Court House, in the County and State aforesaid, on the _Fourth_ Monday of _April_ in the year of our Lord one thousand nine hundred and _forty four_

The Jurors of and for the County aforesaid, in the State aforesaid, upon their oath, Present:

That _____

George Stinney, Jr.

on the _Twenty Fourth_ day of _March_ in the year of our Lord one thousand nine hundred and _forty four_ with force and arms, at _Manning_ in the County of _Clarendon_ and State of South Carolina, in and upon one _Betty June Binnicker_

feloniously, wilfully and of his malice aforethought, did make an assault, and that the said _____ _George Stinney, Jr._

him the said _Betty June Binnicker_ then and there feloniously, wilfully and of his malice aforethought with _Iron rod_ did _strike, beat, bruise_ and wound; giving to the said _Betty June Binnicker_ thereby in and upon the _body_ of him the said _Betty June Binnicker_

court's chief justice. April 24,exactly one month after the two murders, was fixed as the date for this special term of General Sessions to begin. McLeod's next and final decision was to prosecute Stinney only for the death of Betty June Binnecker, the older of the two murdered children. He intended to hold prosecution for the murder of Mary Emma Thames in abeyance.[17]

Although South Carolina did not yet have a public defender's office, the state provided representation for indigents like George Stinney. All member of the bar in each circuit were required to serve in that role if called upon. Few lawyers welcomed this obligation. As one elderly attorney in Sumter explained with a slight laugh when he was interviewed in 2008, members of the bar sought invisibility by leaving town or otherwise making themselves scarce when the court had to make such an appointment. James Warren Wideman of Manning and Charles Nelson Plowden of Summerton were not able to avoid the court's notice, and thus they were named as Stinney's defense team.[18]

Wideman, a man in his mid-fifties, was by far the more experienced of the two in matters of criminal law. As a young lawyer, he had frequently appeared in the Court of General Sessions as the defense attorney for accused criminals, sometimes by choice and sometimes by designation. In 1918, he began a political career, serving a four-year term in the state legislature. By the 1930's, he had entered the federal bureaucracy, working for the Bureau of Internal Revenue and later for the Department of Justice. But in 1937, he suffered a severe heart attack and returned to his farm in Manning. Three years later, he made a failed bid to reenter public life, running for the position of magistrate, the lowest level in the state's judiciary system. Now, in 1944, he was ready to campaign for this position once again, this time against three challengers. His political ambitions would make his performance as Stinney's defense attorney risky.[19]

Wideman's younger co-counsel, Charles Nelson Plowden, also had a great deal at stake because of his own political ambitions. In 1940, he had been elected to the lower house of the state legislature, but two years later, in his bid for a seat in the state senate, he was soundly defeated by fellow attorney John G. Dinkins, who he would now face in the courtroom as a member of the prosecution. Now, in 1944, he was hoping to regain a seat in the lower house and thus, like Wideman, he was not likely to welcome this appointment in a highly visible and volatile case.[20]

As two men hoping for comebacks in the upcoming summer primaries, neither Wideman nor Plowden was likely to relish the task before them in the Stinney case. Conducting an aggressive defense, or worse, a successful one, would not serve them well. Any misstep could imperil their chances for public office. As Lee Burke reflected thirty-nine years later, a move by Plowden for a change of venue for the trial would not sit well with the county's voters. "I don't imagine," Burke said, "he'd have been so popular around Clarendon County . . . he was just a young man starting out on a political career."[21]

The challenge facing this reluctant defense was a formidable one. Stinney had, after all, confessed to the murders for which he stood indicted. As Plowden told James E. Gamble in later years, "He was limited in his defense by the boy's confession, taking officers back to find the spike, etc. That's right hard to beat in court." How, then, were they to construct a defense in the face of George's confession—assuming they wished to mount a credible one?[22]

They could not argue that Stinney, who stood only 5 feet, 1 inch, in height and weighed only 95 pounds, lacked the physical strength to inflict the devastating head wounds the two murdered children had sustained. According to five highly experienced forensic pathologists who examined the reports of the two doctors who examined the bodies in 1944, an individual of Stinney's size *could* pierce and crush the skulls of two smaller children by striking their heads from above with a fourteen-inch railroad spike or a solid metal pipe a foot or so in length. As one of the pathologists explained: "Here we are talking about a spike probably just less than a pound . . . and an iron pipe would have even greater weight. Both, because they have some length, but particularly the rod, could be swung and thus the mass leveraged over a distance. . . . The mass of these objects are significant and it would not need to take a strong individual to crush a skull with them, akin to a young boy using a hammer or an early hominid using a rock to crush a skull."[23]

Perhaps, instead, an insanity defense would work. South Carolinians were familiar with defense cases argued in this fashion. The older residents of Clarendon County might have remembered a case in 1905 in which an African American man was sentenced to death for the murder of his wife's stepfather. The defendant offered no motive for this act during his trial and this led many people to believe he was mentally unsound. The governor issued a stay of execution and appointed a commission of five physicians to examine him. When these doctors reported that the convicted man was sane, his sentence of death by hanging was carried out. Perhaps Wideman himself recalled a 1909 case that dragged on for several years. In this instance, a defendant convicted and sentenced to death for murder moved for, and won, a jury trial to determine his sanity. When the jury found him sane, he appealed to the state Supreme Court; it upheld the finding that he was of sound mind. Judge Stoll, who was about to preside over Stinney's trial, would certainly have recalled this case, for he was the solicitor, and thus the prosecutor, of the Third Circuit at the time.[24]

Stinney's personal history could add weight to a plea of insanity. His parents reportedly could not control him, and he had exhibited instances of uncontrolled aggression. Only two weeks before the murders occurred, he had done the unthinkable in a Jim Crow world—he had forcibly pushed a sixteen-year-old White boy off his bicycle. His hostile behavior extended to Black children as well. On the day before the murders, he had injured another schoolmate using a scissors. The defense's strongest basis for an insanity plea—Stinney's alleged confession that he had raped one of the victims—may not have been known to his attorneys before the trial began. Until the trial, there had been no mention of rape, either by the coroner's jury or the grand jury. But at the trial, both Constable Pratt and Deputy Sheriff Newman would testify that he had made such a confession to them. The story these two lawmen would tell about *how* he had committed the rape would prove shocking in the extreme for it was bizarre by any standard of normal behavior. This alone would have provided ample grounds for a sanity determination. Their testimony may have come as a surprise to Wideman and Plowden, but they had the right to call for a sanity test after hearing what they had to say.[25]

And yet, despite the precedents, despite the available reports of Stinney's aggressive behavior, and despite his alleged confession of rape, the defense team never asked that his sanity be tested. Thirty-nine years later, Charles Plowden admitted that he and Wideman had been given ample time to prepare an insanity defense. "I was pitched right in," he told his interviewer. "He [presumably Judge Stoll] gave us time to prepare for it. But there wasn't any preparation."[26]

This question of why Stinney's sanity was not tested troubled many of the people who, after the trial, asked the governor to spare George's life. Had Stinney been given a mental exam or been observed in the state's asylum for the insane, asked one woman. Another insisted in her letter to the governor that "[a] child fourteen years old who could commit such a crime has a sick and perverted mind and should be treated as a sick child." The prestigious Acting Rector of St. Michael's, Charleston's venerable Episcopalian church, also wondered if Stinney's mental condition had been examined or whether a psychiatrist had been called in Stinney's defense. Surely, he wrote, the viciousness of the crime indicated "an unbalanced mind." But perhaps the most perceptive and sharpest observation came from Mrs. Emily D. Moorer of Greenwood, South Carolina, who saw, in Stinney's death sentence, clear evidence of racial injustice. "If the boy had been white," she wrote, "life imprisonment at most, or a long term in a reformatory or institution for mentally deficient criminals would have been the sentence."[27]

Perhaps most surprising of all, Stinney's attorneys apparently never considered shaping their defense around the issue of blood—or, rather, its absence. The savage injuries to the skills of Mary Emma Thames and Betty June Binnecker would have caused a veritable fountain of blood. That blood would have cascaded all over George Stinney. As one forensic pathologist explained in a letter:

> The skull is the casing for the human computer i.e. the brain it is extremely well profused with blood, the number of blows and areas would cause a blood bath on both girls, and the surroundings. Think of the killers arm and weapon as a pendulum. This would cause a cast off arched pattern of blood from top to bottom of the arch. The pants shoes, skirts of both the killer and the victims would be covered in cast off and contact splatter. The crime scene and clothing of both girls and boy would be a must proof connecting killer to victims, impossible to deny.[28]

Where, though, were Stinney's bloody clothing and shoes? Were there witnesses who saw him return home after the murders with blood on his body or clothing? These were questions that begged to be asked by the defense attorneys, but were not. It would be half a century later, on the fiftieth anniversary of her brother's execution, that one of Stinney's sisters first raised this issue. In a newspaper interview, Katherine Stinney Robinson pointed out the absence of blood on any of her brother's clothes on the day of the murder. In 1944, however, the only person who seemed to find the absence of blood troubling was George Stinney himself. He mentioned the mystery of the missing blood in a letter to his family, written from prison.[29]

– – – – – – – – – – – –

By April 12, all the necessary elements were in place for the trial of George Junius Stinney Jr. for his life. The grand jury had sent forward indictments for the murder of both children. The Third Judicial District's solicitor had decided to prosecute for the murder of the older one, to do so in a criminal court for adults, and to seek the death penalty. A date had been set for a special term of Clarendon County's Court of General

Sessions. Two attorneys for the defense had been appointed, and they had decided to have their client plead not guilty, despite his confession. The names of thirty-six prospective jurors had been selected from the county's rolls.

Yet not everybody in Clarendon County was mollified. Public sentiment had already found Stinney guilty. As one of Betty June Binnecker's sisters said sixty years later, "Everybody knew that he done—even before they had the trial they knew he done it." But what if the jury were to find him not guilty? Or, what if they were to find him guilty but recommend mercy, commuting his sentence to life imprisonment? Rumors circulated widely during the two weeks before the trial began that Stinney would be seized as he arrived at the courthouse, carried off, and lynched. Other rumors had it that, if he went to trial and was found not guilty, or if the jury found him guilty but recommended mercy, he would be shot dead on the spot, right there in the courtroom.

The air was rife with speculation that guns would be brought into the courthouse by members of the public. Anticipating trouble, Sheriff Gamble decided to post officers of the law at every door, with instructions to search most of the spectators seeking admission to the trial. Thirty-nine years later, Gamble's son, himself an experienced officer of the law, observed: "It was unusual back in those days to search people going into a courtroom. But my father had a deputy at each door, and they searched most of the people going into that courtroom that day on account of the feeling-there was talk that they were going [to] lynch the little boy, and this, that and the other . . . It was widely talked [about] in the community."[30]

Those like Roston Stukes and his friends, who may have planned either an eleventh-hour kidnapping and lynching or an assassination in the courtroom, purportedly found a way around the sheriff's diligent preparations; it was rumored that they would have the women who attended the trial bring guns in their handbags. Their assumption was that no officer of the law would subject ladies to a search. Thirty-nine years later, Constable Pratt would recall looking out from the witness stand on a courtroom packed with the women of Clarendon County.[31]

POSTSCRIPT. James Warren Wideman and Charles Nelson Plowden went on to win the public offices they would seek in the summer of 1944.

Chapter 6
Clarendon County Speaks

Trial was real crowded. Overflow crowd in
the hallways.

Lt. James E. Gamble

On the morning of April 21, Clarendon County's Court of General Sessions met in special session, Judge Philip Henry Stoll, presiding. The seventy-year-old Stoll had extensive experience with cases involving capital punishment. As solicitor for the Third Judicial Circuit between 1909 and 1917, he had prosecuted many cases of murder, rape, and assault with intent to ravish (the latter, like rape, a capital offense), as well as the full gamut of lesser felonies. He lost some of his capital prosecutions but won many others, with convicted defendants sent to the gallows or, beginning in 1912, to the electric chair. The State Legislature rewarded his services with an appointment as one of the Third Judicial Circuit judges and since then he had presided over Clarendon County's General Sessions in Manning every June. In most instances, the accused who appeared before him on indictments for murder pleaded guilty to manslaughter, and Judge Stoll had imposed sentences of imprisonment from two to twenty years. Even in those rarer cases, when defendants went to trial, the juries had returned verdicts of manslaughter. Most of these trials were short, although one that was "hard fought" did last for two days. Stinney's trial, which would last only one afternoon, was thus not unusual. What was unusual, however, was that alone of all the protagonists in the Stinney case, Judge Stoll appears to have had no pending political or career ambitions. In fact, he would retire from the bench two years later.[1]

Stoll called the court to order and proceeded, first, to dispose of cases less serious than Stinney's. The defendants in these cases pleaded guilty to offenses ranging from malicious mischief, to peeping-tom activity, burglary, larceny, and assault and battery with intent to kill. In what the *Manning Times* called "clearing the jail," Judge Stoll imposed sentences from incarceration in a reformatory to imprisonment for nine and a half years.[2]

With these cases out of the way, George Stinney was brought into court and seated in the dock. In the month since he had been taken into custody, Stinney had been utterly alone. There is no way to determine how much contact, if any, his family had been permitted with him in his Sumter County jail cell where he had been held since he was spirited out of the Clarendon County jail a month before. From the moment in the Clarendon jail when Deputy Sheriff Newman and Constable Pratt confronted him and elicited his confession, he was cut off from his own world, save, perhaps for contact with another Black prisoner who may have shared his cell. For all intents and purposes, George Stinney was a lone African American in a Jim Crow society, and those who now exerted complete control over his fate were White.[3]

George's isolation and friendlessness were reinforced by the very architecture of the court room he had entered. It was the third courthouse on this site, constructed in 1909 as a centerpiece of small-town Manning's modernization program that also included a new high school for Whites and the installation of pavement in the business district. David Wells Alderman of Alcolu had chaired the committee of prominent citizens who commissioned the creation of this stately new brick building, whose columns and adherence to balance and symmetry reflected the classical style. Several years after it was completed, the town added a traditional Confederate war memorial—a soldier standing heroically tall with his rifle—in front of the building. The courthouse exterior is much the same today as it was when the court held its first session in 1910, but the courtroom, which was fifty feet wide in 1944 is not, for the interior was reconstructed during the 1960s. The building's original blueprints permit one to envision how the fifty-foot- wide room appeared in 1944 at the time of the trial.[4]

This large second-floor room had maple wood floors and stained-glass windows. The beauty of these large, arched windows, three at the rear of the room and one at the front, is still evident, despite the building's renovation in 1960. The front window is preserved under indoor wooden shutters, its lime-green and gold panes glowing in the sunlight that streams through them when a court attendant draws back the shutters. The room was divided in two by a wooden railing that ran across

Clarendon County Courthouse in Manning,
South Carolina.

its width, separating the seating for the public from the judge's raised
podium. There were two jury boxes on either side of this podium, and,
facing the judge, were two long adjoining tables where the defense and
prosecution lawyers sat.[5]

There was also a witness box and a box in the rear of this section for
the defendant that resembled the dock in a British courtroom. Because
the back of the defendant's dock abutted the railing separating the room's
two sections, the prisoner did not sit next to his or her defense attorney.
Thus, George Stinney sat entirely alone, a fourteen-year-old dressed in
blue denim pants and a faded-blue shirt on public display. Members of
the large crowd in the courtroom remarked how calm he appeared to
be, how unfazed was his demeanor, but whether this was indifference or
incomprehension, they did not know. His composure would not break
until the moment he was sentenced to death, and then, only briefly.[6]

Had George Stinney looked behind him at the portion of the room
reserved for the public, he would have seen it packed with the men and
women eager to witness his trial. One newspaper put the attendance at
1,500. They filled every seat, they stood in the doorways, and they spilled
out onto the second-floor landing. A law-enforcement officer stood at
each door because of the rumors of violence that had circulated in the

days before the trial; still other officers sat among the spectators. Accord-ing to the recollections of Constable Sidney J. Pratt, the section occupied by members of the public was remarkable for the number of women who attended. He marveled thirty-nine years later that "the courtroom was full. Seemed like that there were more ladies, there were more females than males. At least every time I looked out all I saw was females that I knew, see." And contrary to the belief among many at the present day, there were African Americans in attendance. Since the courtroom did not include a Jim Crow balcony, it is impossible to say where, precisely, these Black spectators sat. Yet, they too had come to witness a case of great moment and to witness how White Clarendon County would speak.[7]

Judge Stoll began the proceedings. After the grand jury indictment for the murder of Betty June Binnicker had been read aloud, Stoll asked Stinney, "How will you be tried?" Obviously coached by his defense at-torneys, Stinney replied, "'By God and my country.'" It was an old, ritual formula, one used in England during the arraignment of those accused of crime. It was a dramatic detail readily recalled by the foreman of the jury thirty-nine years later.[8]

The court spent most of the morning on jury selection. There were thirty-six men in the *voir dire* panel and, like the identifiable members of the grand jury, the twenty-three who can be identified with reason-able certainty resembled the social and economic composition of the county—except for the fact that, once again, all of them were White. Three members of the panel from Alcolu were quickly dismissed. One prospective juror was rejected because he was intoxicated; another was dismissed because he opposed the death penalty. In the end, the solicitor struck four members of the panel, the defense eight; a jury was finally seated at 12:30 p.m. Judge Stoll then asked forty-five-year-old William Clarkson, the owner of a general store in Summerton, to serve as fore-man. Clarkson had no idea why the judge selected him but speculated when he was interviewed in 1983 that perhaps it was because Judge Stoll knew his family, particularly his father.[9]

The solicitor began the prosecution's case by entering into the record two statements attributed to the defendant. According to the first, the two girls had approached him and asked where they could find flowers. He told them to search farther into the woods. But when Mary Emma Thames fell into a ditch, he attempted to come to her assistance. It was then that she and Betty June Binnicker attacked him. He had only struck them "in self-defense."[10]

The second statement entered into the record was Stinney's alleged confession to Constable Pratt and Deputy Sheriff Newman. In this statement—as the two law officers would soon testify—Stinney confessed that he had followed the girls into the woods with explicit sexual intentions— or, in the words the lawmen attributed to him, "to 'get something.'" More interested in the older girl, he struck and fatally wounded the younger one in order "to 'get her out of the way.'" He then chased after the eleven-year-old, and, after catching her, struck her with the same spike he had used to beat the younger girl "into unconsciousness." He removed Betty June's body from the ditch into which she had fallen, in order to assault her but failed in this attempt. Shortly after, he tried once more to sexually assault her, but failed once more.[11]

Having entered these confessions into the record, the prosecution was ready to present its case. Solicitor McLeod called his witnesses to create a logical sequence of events: beginning with why the two young girls left their homes, to the discovery of their bodies the next morning, then to Stinney's arrest and confession, and finally to the examination performed on Betty June Binnicker's body.

The first witness was Mrs. T. J. Morris, Betty June's twenty-three-year-old sister. Mrs. Morris had been visiting in Alcolu and oversaw her younger sister while their mother was at her job in nearby Sumter. Thirty years later, the witness recalled being "scared to death," never having been in a courtroom before; she had no idea, she told her interviewer, about "what to expect." She had been so anxious that she remembered very little of what was said but she did inform the court that she had given Betty June permission to go bicycle riding with Mary Emma, and she had provided the two girls with a pair of scissors to cut flowers. During her testimony she identified the clothing her sister had worn, as well as the scissors, which had been found not far from Betty June's body. In 1983 she remembered that "they were barber shears, long pointed . . ." and that her sister had them with her when the two girls rode toward the Black section of Alcolu.[12]

Scott Lowder followed Mrs. Morris to the stand. This thirty-year-old resident had left high school after a year to work in the lumber mill as a saw filer. According to the newspaper reporter covering the trial for the *Manning Times*, Lowder claimed to have discovered the bodies of the two girls. From the witness box, he described the positions of the bodies in the ditch where they had been hidden and the condition of the bicycle they had been riding. Its front wheel, he testified, had been "torn from

Age 14 Height 5-1 Weight 95 Hair Negro Eyes Drk. Maroon

Complexion Black Build Small Occupation None

Religious Faith Baptist R. & W. 7th Grade M. S. W. Single

Residence Sumpter, S.C. (Shannon Town) Born Sumpter, County, S.C.

Maximum Sentence Expires Commutation Allowed Minimum Sen. Exp.
Under death sentence
Admitted April 27, 1944 G. T. L. Released

Remarks

Previous Record Bureau No. Prison No.

Nearest Relative George Stiney, Sr. Relationship Father

Address SUmter, S.C. (Shanton Town)

Prominent Scars Small scar top of right hand, base of forefinger; two spot scars
left shank, lower.

Department of Corrections records for George Stinney
noting his height, weight, and age. Department of
Corrections, Central Correctional Institution, Record
of Prisoners Awaiting Execution. Series S132004.
Inmate George Stinney, File #260. South Carolina
Department of Archives and History.

---

the frame" and then placed across the bodies that were partially under water in the ditch.[13]

Under American law, the prosecution in a criminal trial must prove guilt beyond a reasonable doubt; the defense, on the other hand, does not have the burden of proving innocence. The defense is only required to plant seeds of doubt in the minds of the jurors, for a jury may convict, in the time-honored formula, only if it believes that a defendant is guilty "beyond a reasonable doubt." Lowder's testimony gave the defense an opportunity to lay those seeds of doubt. Could the damage to the bicycle he described be attributed to George Stinney? At just over five feet tall and weighing only ninety-five pounds, did a child of his slight size have the strength to tear the front wheel off the frame of a bicycle? The opportunity to raise this doubt passed without any word from the defense.

Indeed, Stinney's attorneys did not rise to pose any question, at any subsequent moment during the trial, including in their summation before the case went to the jury.

Scott Lowder was followed in the witness stand by the prosecution's star witnesses, Deputy Sheriff Henry S. Newman and Constable Sidney J. Pratt. The newspaper reporter who covered the trial did not specify in which order they spoke, but he did describe their testimony as "almost identical." In what may have been the dramatic high point of the trial, Judge Stoll halted the proceedings to warn that the details the two lawmen were about to reveal might cause the women spectators to be overcome. He advised them to leave since the graphic testimony "would probably become more horrible." According to the newspaper reporter, Judge Stoll characterized the details about to be provided as "morbid." But a more accurate description would have been "lurid." Several women chose to depart, but the majority, proving more stalwart, remained. Along with everyone else in the courtroom, they were about to hear a tale of sexual depravity.

The testimony by Pratt and Newman followed, and expanded upon, the second confession the prosecution had entered into the court record. The stark details they provided while on the witness stand were not published by the newspapers. For unlike the details of brutal lynchings, details of sexual assault upon White women would be viewed as offensive to the reading public. But, from interviews in 1983 with the foreman of the jury, with Constable Pratt, and with Lee Burke who attended the trial, as well as through statements made by Governor Olin Johnston during the final week of George Stinney's life, those details were shared. Newman and Pratt testified that, when they took Stinney to the scene of the crime on Saturday, March 25, in order to retrieve the murder weapon, he revealed to them that he had sexually abused the older of the two girls. As Pratt recalled, "On the second feeling into the water, he came up with the pipe, the piece of metal that he stated that he used in taking these little girls' lives. He also admitted that he had sexually assaulted—he didn't use that word, but had 'fooled with' one of the little girls after he had hit them. I asked him some questions, enough to know that that was with her privates."[14]

But what exactly did Pratt mean in his account thirty-nine years later by "fooled with"? The phrase, after all, did not necessarily mean rape, although he did say that Stinney "sexually assaulted" his victim. Confusingly, the newspaper reporter who covered the trial wrote that Pratt and

Newman said on the stand that Stinney "admitted *attempted* assault" (italics added), and that, when he tried to assault Betty June Binnicker a second time, he again failed. Pratt's memory in 1983 was hardly infallible; he could not recall an important event in 1944 in which he played a central role. However, corroboration, as well as elaboration, of what he and Newman related in their testimony is provided by Governor Olin Johnston in public statements released to the press and in replies to petitioners who urged the governor to exercise clemency after Stinney was sentenced to death. Exactly one week before the execution, the governor met with Pratt who informed him Stinney had confessed to raping the older of the two girls, to doing so after she was already dead, and then returning shortly after in order to rape her remains a second time. As Johnston wrote on June 9 in several of his responses to letters and telegrams pleading for the boy's life: "I have just talked with the officer who made the arrest in this case. It may be interesting for you to know that Stinney killed the smaller girl to rape the larger one. Then he killed the larger girl and raped her dead body. Twenty minutes later he returned and attempted to rape her again but her body was too cold. All of this he admitted himself."[15]

Through the press, Johnston issued a public statement explaining why he would not commute Stinney's death sentence: "Pratt tells me that Stinney confessed to killing the younger of the girls near Alcolu to get her out of the way so that he could rape the older girl. . . . Stinney then told officers that he killed the older girl with a railway spike, and that he dragged her out of a swamp to rape her. Further, he said that he went back about 20 minutes later to the girl, and that she was so cold he desisted from his intention to rape her again."[16]

In 1983, the foreman of the jury provided an account that largely concurred with the story that Constable Pratt provided to the governor. William N. Clarkson remembered that the two lawmen had specified rape when they were on the stand. In his own words, "The nigger went back there and 'jazzed' the dead bodies, tried to 'jazz' the dead bodies and all like that. That was brought out at the trial, but was never put in print." ("To jazz" meant to engage in sexual intercourse.) Clarkson also defended the governor's stand on commuting the death sentence:

> If they [the petitioners who asked the governor to spare Stinney's life] had heard what we heard, I don't think anybody would have wanted to commute it. That was the most horriblest thing I ever

heard of, to happen in that community. He killed that littlest girl to get her out of the way first. Then raped the other one. Then killed her. That's what they said. That's what the lawman said he had confessed to him. He was just telling the judge, using the nigger's language, how long it took him to come [to ejaculate] and all like that. It was horrible. Then he went back and tried to rape her after, the dead body, [but] he couldn't make it that time.[17]

Lee Burke, another eyewitness to Newman and Pratt's testimony, confirmed, though only in broad terms, what the two law officers said about the initial rape and the later attempt upon the dead body. In his 1983 interview, he said, "They asked him, 'Did you rape them?' and he said, 'I sure did. Twice. Once before they'd been dead and once after they'd been dead.'"[18]

This much is clear: Newman and Pratt's graphic testimony dramatically altered the story of the murders of the two girls. Newman's testimony to the coroner's jury and the grand jury had never included any mention of rape or sexual assault, and there had been no allegations of rape by those two courts. What, then, had led the deputy sheriff and the state constable to now insist that George Stinney had confessed to rape and murder?

The answer of what occurred between the grand jury's indictment and the trial is long lost and buried. Yet, some speculation seems in order and that speculation revolves around the career ambitions of the men involved. In the spring of 1944, Newman faced the prospect of losing his position as Deputy Sheriff of Clarendon County, for, after twenty-four years in office, the man who gave Newman his job was in danger of losing his. Sheriff James E. Gamble's insistence on his independence in office had made an enemy of the powerful Mayor of Manning, who, in 1944, handpicked someone he hoped could unseat Gamble. Gamble planned to run on his record of convictions, and thus Newman had every incentive to assure that the Stinney jury returned a verdict of guilty. His own future, like Gamble's, may have been riding on it.[19]

But a powerful and effective performance at the trial could also fuel grander ambitions in Newman. Gamble, after all, could not take personal credit for bringing the murderer of the two White girls to justice. It was Newman who appeared on the scene that March and Newman who conducted the investigation. As one of the state capital's newspapers, the *Columbia Record*, later reported, "relatives of the girl victims credited one of the sheriff's deputies, H. S. Newman, cooperating with S. J. Pratt of the Governor's office with clearing the case . . ." And, in fact, three weeks after the Stinney trial concluded, Newman suddenly announced his resignation as deputy sheriff. The *Manning Times* carried this news in May, adding the speculation by Newman's friends that he would soon "offer for one of the important offices."[20]

Constable Sidney Pratt may also have seen political possibilities in the testimony that helped ensure Stinney's conviction. The thirty-eight-year-old college grad had been Chief Constable, but Olin Johnston had replaced him when he won the governor's office. Pratt found himself demoted and reassigned to a rural, backwater post in Clarendon County. His role in the trial may have provided the opportunity he needed to gain favor with the governor and repair the damage done to his career. The account he gave the governor in their private meeting may indeed have put Johnston in Pratt's debt, for it could be used effectively in defense of a refusal to commute Stinney's sentence to life imprisonment.[21]

Stinney's defense attorneys responded to the shocking new testimony of rape by permitting Newman and Pratt to step down from the witness box without cross-examination. They did not pose a single question to either of them. In a different environment, in a different time and place, intense and rapid-fire cross-examination might have chipped away at discrepancies in the lawmen's accounts and raised doubts in the minds of jurors.

Wideman and Plowden could have asked whether the lawmen searched for blood stained clothing and shoes in Stinney's house? They could have challenged the sequence of events in the two testimonies that suggested inconsistencies and contradictions. For example, how and where had Stinney encountered the girls? At the coroner's inquest, Newman had testified that Stinney said he came upon the two girls as they picked flowers near the lumber mill. But the newspapers reported that Stinney claimed he had followed them for about half a mile before making contact with them.[22]

They could have pointed out that the two confession Newman and Pratt attributed to Stinney were entirely contradictory. In his first statement, Stinney allegedly claimed the two girls attacked him as he sought to help Mary Emma Thames after she had fallen into a ditch; in other words, he had struck back at them in self-defense. But to whom had he made this confession? Why did the two officers reject it as untruthful and accept instead his second alleged statement that he followed the girls in order to "get something," twice attempting to rape Betty June Binnicker and murdering them both in the process?

They could have asked about the sequence of events at the scene of the crime. Had Stinney told Newman and Pratt that he killed the girls, raped one of them, left the bodies on the ground, returned twenty minutes later to attempt rape a second time, and only then methodically placed the bodies, the brush, and the bicycle in the ditch? Or had he confessed that he placed the two dead girls in the water-filled ditch after killing them, gathered brush to heap over them, placed the damaged bicycle on top, and then returned twenty minutes later, disassembled the entire pile, extracted Betty June's body in a second attempt to rape her, and then reassembled everything? Would Pratt and Newman have told consistent stories if the defense had asked these questions?

They could have asked what the murder weapon was, a railroad spike or an iron pipe or rod? In his handwritten account, Newman stated that the weapon was "a piece of iron about 15 inches long . . . the piece of iron were found in water where he said it were at." Yet at the coroner's inquest, he provided a different version, informing the panel that Stinney had signed a statement confessing to killing the girls "with a heavy railroad trestle spike." Five days before his execution, however, Stinney reportedly told the member of the State Board of Pardons who visited him in prison that he had used "an iron rod about 12 inches long and about as thick as his thumb." Newspaper reports varied, some citing the iron rod, others a railroad spike of varying lengths. Again, however, the defense did not probe for inconsistencies in the evidence that Pratt and Newman provided in their testimonies. They did not even challenge Newman's rival versions.[23]

The confusion over the murder weapon persisted over the years. Thirty-nine years after Stinney's execution, Pratt declared with certainty that Stinney had told them that the murder weapon was a piece of pipe. "I want to be absolutely correct about what I say," Pratt told the interviewer, "but I do not recall that it was a railroad spike. But it was a piece of iron . . . He, and Newman and I went to the scene . . . and on the second feeling into the water, he came up with a pipe, a piece of metal that he stated that he used in taking these girls' lives." By contrast, Lt. James E. Gamble Jr. was equally certain thirty-nine years later that a railroad spike had been used to kill the two victims. He told his interviewer that he and his father had visited Stinney in his jail cell in Sumter. As he recalled, "My father had taken a railroad spike, one of these spikes that you put the tracks in with . . . and he said that the little boy identified it was the spike that had killed the little girls."[24]

Although the defense team did not challenge the prosecution's star witnesses, the Solicitor realized that Pratt and Newman's testimony was problematic. It flew in the face of the physicians' report that the hymens of both girls were intact. The jury might wonder at this contradiction; and it was always possible that the defense might pick up the issue later on. The prosecution knew it was necessary to neutralize the medical report. Thus Dr. C. R. F. Baker was called to the stand. It was Baker, together with Dr. Asbury Bozard of Manning, who had examined the bodies. Unfortunately for Baker, the full burden of defending their report fell on him since Bozard was purportedly too ill to appear in court. Equally unfortunate was the fact that the *Manning Times* report on Baker's testimony tells us little. We know only that, at first, the doctor "failed to make a positive statement about whether the autopsy revealed the girls had been assaulted." But under questioning by the prosecution, Baker did, at last, concede "assault was possible." Farther than that he refused to go. The bodies, he explained, had been immersed in water overnight and this, he insisted, made it "difficult to determine possible assault."

The defense made no effort to cross-examine Dr. Baker. Thus, they lost the opportunity to ask what relevance overnight immersion in water would have to a discovery that both girls' hymens were intact. They also let slip by the chance to ask if the "slight edema" and "slight bruising" on Betty June's genitalia could have several causes—the simple act of peddling a bicycle harder than usual with a rider on its handlebars or perhaps a fall from the bicycle during an assault with a powerful weapon. The original medical report suggested that the brush piled on top of Mary Emma Thames might explain the bruise on her forehead; Stinney's lawyers could have asked Dr. Baker if this effort to hide the bodies could explain Betty June's injuries as well.

But with no challenge from the defense, the prosecution could be fairly confident that it had done its job. Dr. Baker's concession of a possible rape swept aside the critical point that the hymens of both girls were intact. It overshadowed the reporting a month before the coroner's jury met that there had been no rape, and it ignored the fact that neither the coroner's jury nor the grand jury has cited rape in their charges against George Stinney.

Dr. Baker's turnabout was not the first time a White physician had changed what he knew in a case involving alleged sexual attack of a White woman by a Black man. Eleven years earlier, in the sensational Scottsboro, Alabama, case, one of the physicians who examined the two women claiming rape privately informed the presiding judge that there was no truth to their allegations. But when the judge pleaded with him to testify to this, the doctor refused. If he did, he said, he could never return to his community or his practice there. He was young and only recently graduated from medical school, and he did not want to pull up stakes and begin a practice anew. Both Dr. Baker and young Dr. Bozard would face the same backlash if they continued to insist that rape had not occurred.[25]

With Dr. Baker's testimony, the prosecution had completed its case against George Stinney. It was now up to Stinney's attorneys to mount a defense. So far in the trial, Wideman and Plowden had been silent. They had not cross-examined the prosecution's witnesses and they had made no attempt to cast doubt on the testimonies by Pratt and Newman. What could they argue on behalf of a client who had, it seemed, confessed to both murder and rape?

The defense had several options. They could call rebuttal witnesses, including people who could place the defendant someplace other than the murder scene. But they did not. Many years later, Stinney's sisters would testify they had been with him the entire day, in their home or in the pasture when he took Lizzie, the family's cow, to graze. Roston Stukes, a man who had after all agitated for Stinney's lynching, nevertheless supported the women's memory in his 1983 interview. Stukes said that the boy had been tending cows when Betty June and Mary Emma were killed. They could still put doubts in the minds of the jury by pointing to the discrepancy about where George was when he first encountered the two girls as they looked for maypops. Had he immediately followed them down the tracks into the woods? Had he spotted them from a perch nearby after they had entered the woods? They could have called witnesses who could attest that there was no blood on Stinney's body or his clothing in the hours after the murders. And they could have raised the question: had the law officers found any bloodied shoes and clothing in the Stinney household? They could raise doubts about the ability of a person as slight as Stinney to tear off the front wheel of the bicycle. They did none of these things. Nor did they raise a challenge to the truthfulness of the two officers of the law considering the postmortem examination performed by the doctors.[26]

They had one other option. Even if they conceded Stinney had committed rape and murder, they could propose a verdict of guilty by reason of insanity. They could strengthen this plea by putting witnesses on the stand or presenting affidavits about previous unstable behavior on Stinney's part. The principal of George's school had, after all, reported that he had attacked another student with a pair of scissors the day before the murders. And many expert witnesses might have testified about the psychiatric implications of raping a dead body. Yet no amended plea was proposed.

Wideman and Plowden had, in effect, offered no defense case at all. Thirty-nine years later, Charles Nelson Plowden, the surviving member of the defense team, offered this explanation for the poor defense of George Stinney: "We didn't have much to go on." A claim of insanity was not possible, he said, because Stinney "seemed perfectly normal. Don't know why he did it. Never could figure. Wasn't no need for psych. exam" —a remarkable statement in view of the testimony that Stinney had twice attempted to rape a corpse. In his interview, the foreman of the jury sympathized with Plowden's plight. "I guess he done the best he could with what he had to go with . . . I think Mr. Plowden done the best he could. Nobody could have done him [Stinney] any good I don't believe." The "best he could" was to plead in the defense summation, that the jury grant their client mercy because of his age. With this plea, they implicitly conceded that their client was guilty of the crime.[27]

In 1983, Plowden told his interviewer that he did not think the death penalty should have been inflicted. Instead, Stinney should have been given life. After all these years, he added, he still regretted "to see something like that happen & not be able to prevent it," although he remained convinced he had done the best he could to defend George Stinney. "My heart was in it," he insisted, "The fact is it made me very emotional & I made a strong plea."[28]

Solicitor Franklin McLeod's summation can be reconstructed from a handwritten list on a sheet of yellow, legal-sized paper preserved in the files of the case in the South Carolina state archives. That list begins with the word "Age," doubly underscored, suggesting that he intended to undermine the defense plea for mercy. Next on the list were the words "Went to Dance," underscored three times. The large size of the letters— the largest on the list—together with the emphatic underlining indicates that the prosecution meant to show Stinney as a murderer coldly indifferent to what he had done only hours before. These three words are the only reference to a dance in all surviving documents and newspaper accounts. It was not until 2014 that Stinney's younger sister shed light on

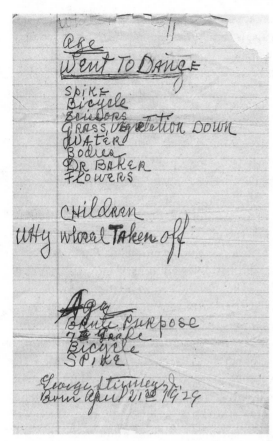

Evidence from
Indictment file
of George Stinney.
Clarendon County,
Court of General
Sessions. Series
L14095, Indictment
#1853. South Caro-
lina Department
of Archives and
History.
- - - - - - - - - - - - -

the cryptic "Went to Dance"; the family, she said, had gone to a neighborhood party that night before they learned that two White girls in the
village were missing.[29]

The list continued in this order:

Spike
Bicycle
Scissors
Grass Vegetation Down
Water
Bodies
Dr. Baker
Flowers
Why wheel taken off

And then, the word "Age" appears again, followed by "Brute Purpose." In the Jim Crow world of 1944, brute force signaled that the rape of a White woman by a black man.

Three more words followed:

7th grade
Bicycle
Spike

The prosecution's reference to George's grade in school was made to show that Stinney had normal intelligence, that he knew right from wrong. The final note on this list read "George Stinney Jr. Born April [sic] 21st 1929." This was a reminder to the jury, for the third time, that Stinney was more than fourteen years old. The message was clear: McLeod wanted a verdict of guilty, a sentence of death, and no recommendation for mercy.[30]

Next, John G. Dinkins, who had injected himself into the trial as a co-prosecutor, rose to address the jury. Like McLeod, he asked the jury not to consider the plea for mercy. Thirty-nine years later, the jury foreman could clearly recall what must have been an emotionally powerful climax to Dinkins oration, as he sought to seal Stinney's fate. Nothing, Dinkins insisted, nothing less than the electric chair would do. "Mr. J. G. Dinkins had just talked to us before we went there [to the jury room]," recalled foreman William Clarkson, "and he said 'What mercy should he have—what mercy did he show those little girls?'" [31]

After Dinkins's rhetorical flourish, Judge Stoll would have charged the jury. No record survives of what he said or how he explained the law to the jurors. The jurors were then ushered into the jury room adjoining the courtroom to begin their deliberations. Clarkson immediately called for a vote; "There wasn't anything to discuss," he later declared, adding that there was no need "to beat around the bush." Thus, without discussion, without deliberation, the twelve men voted unanimously that George Stinney Jr. was guilty. They did not consider the possibility of mercy. When, in 1983, the interviewer asked Clarkson, "Did anyone on the jury give much consideration to granting mercy because he was only fourteen?" Clarkson answered, "No, not that I remember of. No not that I know of. I don't remember anyone saying let's . . . talking [sic] about mercy." In less than ten minutes, the jurors were ready to return to the courtroom and deliver their verdict. The swiftness of their decision was not unprecedented in cases involving Black violence, real or alleged, against Whites.[32]

With no recommendation for mercy, only one thing remaining to complete the ritual of a trial for a capital offense: the judge must pronounce the death sentence in formulaic and at times archaic language and then fix the date for execution. Judge Stoll turned to Stinney and recited the words that told the young man to prepare for his death:

> It being solemnly demanded of the prison at the bar, if he hath anything to say why sentence of death should not be passed upon him, and he having answered nothing further unless as he had before said; Wherefore it is considered by the Court and pronounced as the judgment of the law, that you, the said George Stinney, Jr., be taken thence to the place whence last you came, there to be kept in close and safe custody until you shall be removed in accordance with the law to the State Penitentiary in Columbia, S. C., at which place on Friday, the 16th day of June, A. D. 1944, between the hours of six o'clock A. M., and six o'clock P. M.[33]

According to all surviving accounts, Stinney had sat impassively throughout the course of his short trial. But now, hearing the tolling of Judge Stoll's voice, his composure momentarily collapsed. The *Manning Times* reporter noted that "only when asked to rise and receive sentence did he appear nervous and slightly excited. He bit his nail and twisted his fingers while facing the judge, but soon regained his composure. . . ." Immediately after his sentence had been read, Stinney was removed from the elegant Clarendon County courthouse and returned to the safety of the jail in Sumter County—"the place whence last you came"—to await transfer to the state penitentiary. In ordinary cases, defendants that were sentenced to death were held in their own county's jail until three weeks before execution. They would then be moved to the state penitentiary's death row. But if there were fear for their safety, they were taken earlier to the penitentiary for "Safekeeping." Stinney fell into this category since the danger of a lynching might still exist. Thus, three days after the conclusion of his trial, Stinney found himself in a cell in Columbia, housed in the secure section of the penitentiary know as Tier F. There he would wait out the time that remained to him until he was moved to death row.[34]

Clarendon County—White Clarendon County—had spoken clearly and resoundingly. After the jury's verdict, there were only two possibilities to save him from the electric chair. The first was an appeal to the Supreme Court of South Carolina and from there, if possible, to

George Stinney's fingerprints, taken when he was transferred to Columbia for "safekeeping" while he awaited execution. Department of Corrections, Central Correctional Institution, Records of Prisoners Awaiting Execution. Series S132004. Inmate George Stinney, File #260.

the Supreme Court of the United States on constitutional grounds. One ground for appeal was the threat of mob violence by spectators in the courtroom that interfered with the jury's ability to hear and weigh the evidence. But the solicitor had commended the members of the crowded courtroom for their restraint and composure, and the *Manning Times* reported that there had been no hint of violence as the spectators filed out. The defense attorneys could have initiated an appeal on other grounds, but they were not inclined to do so. As Plowden would put it to his interviewer, "No need to appeal. No grounds for appeal. No $ to appeal. Just wasn't any ground for an appeal. . . ." An appeal would indeed have required money, money for lawyers and for the printing of a brief and a transcript of the trial. But George Stinney's parents were poor and they may not have been aware that an appeal was possible. As Plowden put it "Never any discussion about an appeal. Family never came to talk to him."[35]

There was, however, one organization with the resources and the relevant experience to undertake an appeal on behalf of George Stinney: the National Association for the Advancement of Colored People (NAACP). If they did not act, Stinney had only one other possibility for surviving past June 16, 1944, and that lay with the governor of South Carolina, Olin Johnston, who had the power to commute the death sentence to life in prison or to grant Stinney a pardon.

POSTSCRIPT. James E. Gamble lost his seventh bid for reelection as sheriff to F. L. Overby, the candidate backed by the mayor of Manning. Alcolu voted handily against Gamble, 109 to 59, perhaps a reflection of his failure to appear in the village on the day following the murders, thereby not taking charge of the case.[36]

Henry (Huger) Newman's career as deputy sheriff ended with his abrupt resignation shortly after the conclusion of George Stinney's trial. He never did run for office, as had been rumored he would. He retired to the land and became a farmer.[37]

Of the three officers of the law, Sidney Pratt fared the best. He was appointed as a constable to the State Tax Commission on March 26, 1947.[38]

Chapter 7
The Silence of the NAACP

We have about a half-dozen cases pending in
the Supreme Court of South Carolina and one
being prepared for the United States Supreme
Court. There simply is no due process for
Negroes in the State of South Carolina.

Thurgood Marshall, 1941

During the eight weeks between George Stinney's conviction and execution, the office of Governor Olin D. Johnston received approximately 175 letters and telegrams and petitions with approximately 1,500 signatures. The message in all of them: commute George Stinney's death sentence to life in prison or, at the very least, stay the execution until the crime was more fully investigated. These appeals came from outside the state as well as from within South Carolina, from White as well as Black writers, from single individuals, from left-wing labor unions, and from mainstream organizations like civic groups, ladies' clubs, clergymen, and interracial committees. Only one other case in Johnston's governorship ever received more protest and appeals; that case arose several months before Stinney's and ended in Johnston commuting a death sentence to life imprisonment. Perhaps this had given Stinney's supporters hope.[1]

Among the many protests and pleas for executive clemency for Stinney was one from the South Carolina Conference of the NAACP. The conference centralized and coordinated the activities of local branches of the NAACP throughout the state. It had sat by silently for more than two months, from the moment of George Stinney's arrest on March 25 through his trial and conviction on April 24, and for almost six weeks while he was confined in the state's penitentiary awaiting his moment in the electric chair. It had at last made a tepid move five days before his execution when the four hundred delegates to its annual convention sent a telegram to the governor, declaring the execution of Stinney would be a "blot" on South Carolina. In a separate meeting, the conference's newly established Youth Council sent its own telegram protesting the execution.[2]

Several months after George Stinney's disfigured body had been laid to rest, the national NAACP's monthly publication, *The Crisis*, briefly mentioned the conference's telegram, and a month later it mistakenly reported that the local Sumter branch had also sent the governor a protest telegram. It had not. In fact, it had not discussed the case or voted to protest the jury's decision. The three men who signed the telegram did not even identify themselves as members of the NAACP, although two of them were. Instead, they referred to themselves as members of the "Better Citizens Association of Sumter." It would appear, that, even in Sumter, in what was reputedly the NAACP's premiere branch in the state, the South Carolina NAACP did not seek to associate itself with the Stinney case, despite all its involvement in earlier cases of African Americans tried, convicted, and sentenced by South Carolina's criminal courts.[3]

If there were any one organization that might have made a difference in saving George Stinney's life, it was the NAACP. Unions, especially ones that leaned to the left, were hardly taken seriously in conservative South Carolina. Protesters from outside the state were dismissed as meddlers who had no business interfering in South Carolina affairs. The South Carolina legislature expressed this attitude clearly by passing a resolution condemning outside agitators. On Thursday, March 2, 1944, less than a month before the murders in Alcolu, US congressman L. Mendel Rivers of South Carolina read into the Congressional Record an article from the *Washington Post*, entitled "Race, Equality 'Agitators' Denounced," that cited this resolution which demanded that "henceforth the damned agitators of the North leave the South alone" in its interracial relations, and affirmed the "belief in and allegiance to established white supremacy." But unlike leftist unions and other well-meaning people from outside the state, the NAACP's local branches throughout the nation, as well as its national organization, had amply demonstrated the ability to bring—and sometimes win—suits in the courts on behalf of African Americans who had been tried and sentenced to death. As in those earlier cases, the NAACP could have provided Stinney with a competent attorney for his trial, one who would have presented a defense in his behalf, unlike his two court-appointed attorneys. Following his conviction, it could have brought an appeal on constitutional grounds because of the inadequacy of his defense. Why did it do none of these things?[4]

Since its creation in 1910, the NAACP had fought valiantly against America's systematic debasement of African Americans and the unabashed denial of the principle of equality, often at great personal cost and peril to individual members. During the 1930s, its agenda included employment discrimination, inferior provision for the education of Black children, restrictive covenants that buttressed segregated housing, and differential pay for Whites and Blacks. Their campaign included the call for a federal anti-lynching law, a project that never succeeded because of resistance by Southerners (and President Roosevelt's failure to support such a bill in Congress). The organization sent its attorneys into the courts to challenge all manner of discriminatory practices, including trials and convictions in criminal courts. As the keynote speaker noted during his address at the national organization's annual conference in 1939, this spectrum of activities was "typical of the N.A.A.C.P.," and it most definitely encompassed "unfair trials of Negroes in court. . . ." Here, then, was the testimony to the organization's engagement with the cases of African Americans who received unjust and discriminatory treatment in the nation's judicial systems.[5]

Although the national NAACP entered a criminal proceeding for the first time in 1910, its record of continuous involvement in pursuit of equal justice in the criminal courts dates to 1919. In that year, there was an outbreak of gunfire near the town of Elaine, Arkansas, in which one White man was killed and another wounded. Seventy-five Black men were soon quickly convicted of murder and insurrection. Twelve were sentenced to death and sixty-seven to prison terms ranging from one to twenty-one years. From its headquarters in New York City, the NAACP recognized that defending these men would enhance its standing as the premier organization fighting for equal rights and this would enable it to increase its fundraising. It was ultimately successful in saving the lives of the twelve men condemned to death and winning the release of the other sixty-seven. This struggle took almost seven years, during which the NAACP engaged and paid attorneys, planned legal strategies, and raised the necessary funds for appeals, retrials, briefs, trial transcripts, and court fees. This case established that a trial conducted in a mob atmosphere violated the defendants' right to due process; thus, *Moore v. Dempsey* is recognized as a landmark in civil rights law. For the NAACP, it marked the beginning of its expertise in suing for equal treatment based on the individual's rights under the Constitution.[6]

In the Elaine, Arkansas, case and in many others that followed, the national office of the NAACP in New York intervened, but branches throughout the country also acted to counter the unequal system of justice that Blacks faced—and not only in the South. The voluminous records of the NAACP's legal department are filled with the files of hundreds of cases in which local branches, state organizations (including South Carolina's), and the national office in New York City defended accused individuals during their trials and frequently brought appeals following their convictions, losing some, but winning others. Thus, years before George Stinney's case, the precedents for action were ample and the accumulated experience was extensive. Results of these legal battles were reported in the pages of *The Crisis*, making knowledge of how the courts could be used in the struggle for fair and equal treatment in the institutions of justice widespread throughout the organization.

NAACP leaders in South Carolina were thus well aware of what could be achieved by providing legal representation for accused Blacks and by financing appeals on their behalf once they had been convicted. As far back as 1926, the national office helped finance the appeal of the conviction of a defendant in Fairfield County for killing a White man in self-defense. The man had invaded the defendant's home, intending to carry off two of his teenage daughters. The NAACP managed to get the South Carolina Supreme Court to reduce the defendant's sentence of life in prison for murder to six years for manslaughter. Between 1939 and 1943, the national office and local branches in South Carolina worked together to provide attorneys and funds for seven men in five separate cases. In two of these cases, the national office appealed all the way to the US Supreme Court, petitioning for writs of certiorari that would require a new trial for three convicted men.[7]

In September 1941, James B. Hinton, an insurance executive, Baptist pastor, and an active member of the South Carolina NAACP Conference reported proudly to the national office a remarkable local success: the prosecution and conviction of a White man who had raped a fourteen-year-old Black girl. Hinton would also play a critical role in the case of Sammie Osborne who killed his employer in the summer of 1941. Osborne was a seventeen-year-old farm hand; his employer was a farmer with an unsavory reputation even among part of the White population of Barnwell County. The farmer was abusive, shouting at Osborne, kicking him, and beating him in the head with a when he refused to work in damp fields because of a wounded leg. Osborne ran away after the farmer threatened that he and a crowd would kill Osborne that night. Fearful of returning to his own home where he would be found by his tormenter, the young man stayed overnight at a friend's house. But sometime after midnight, his employer broke in, brandishing a club and a gun. He proceeded to kick and beat Osborne while he lay in bed and to point the gun in his face. Fearing for his life, Sammie Osborne reached for a nearby shotgun and shot his assailant dead.[8]

At his trial, presided over by future senator and presidential candidate Strom Thurmond, Osborne pled self-defense. But according to the prosecution, Osborne had ambushed his employer after luring him to the house where he was staying. The jury concurred with the prosecutor. Osborne was sentenced to death and, despite Osborne's insistence that he alone had killed the farmer, his friend was sentenced to fifteen years in prison.

Hinton acted forcefully and aggressively, as he led the South Carolina NAACP's efforts to save Osborne's life. On September 24, 1941, he sent a special delivery letter to Thurgood Marshall, urging that immediate action was necessary. Osborne was sentenced to die in only five weeks. "The case was a cut and dried one before it even begun [sic]," Hinton wrote, for the prosecution had been assisted by every prominent attorney in the county, including the speaker of the South Carolina House of Representatives. Osborne had been ably defended by two White, court-appointed attorneys, one of whom had pressed the South Carolina NAACP after the trial to appeal the verdict to the South Carolina Supreme Court. He cited excellent reasons for believing an appeal would succeed. The conference leadership agreed to sponsor the appeal, but Hinton pointed out that it could not pursue things on its own. He believed the appeal, which would cost $750 for the attorney's fee and the preparation of the trial transcript, required participation by all three levels of the organization, from the local branch to the South Carolina Conference to the national office in New York. Hinton asked the national office to contribute $250.

Marshall had doubts. The lawyer who would represent Osborne in the appeal process was, after all, the son of the state's incoming governor. Hinton discounted Marshall's concerns: "We do not feel that Mr Harley being the son of the governor of South Carolina will make any difference." And then Hinton added, "We have decided to fight the case anyway, as a mere boy is sentenced to be hanged . . . We cannot permit this boy to go to the chair, at least without a fight."[9]

Over the next three years, the South Carolina leadership demonstrated its determination to save Osborne's life. But the national office seemed to be dragging its feet. Hinton pressed Marshall for funds. The South Carolina NAACP had won a stay of execution for Osborne; it had paid for preparation of the trial transcript and part of the attorney's fees. It was preparing to launch a fund drive, but, as Hinton told Marshall, it still needed money from the national office. In October 1941, Hinton asked Marshall, could the national office see its way to contributing $150 if it could not afford the $250 that was originally requested? "We need [the funds] . . . badly right now," he wrote, "and will appreciate an immediate reply to our letter . . . Please aid us and immediately." Two weeks later, Marshall finally authorized a check for $100. He would send another $50, he told Hinton, if it became available. Meanwhile, the South Carolina conference held a public rally that launched a monthlong fund-raising drive.

In mid-January 1942, conference members met with Osborne's attorney, who suggested a new course of action: accept a commutation of the sentence from death to life imprisonment. The conference turned him down. They would only consider this as a last resort, if and when an appeal failed. The appeal to the State Supreme Court actually succeeded on the grounds that the presiding judge, Strom Thurmond, had not adequately explained the law of self-defense to the jury. A new trial was ordered, but Osborne was again found guilty and once more sentenced to death. This decision was also appealed, this time on the grounds that there had been no evidence introduced during the trial to justify the conviction. This appeal failed. All that was left was an appeal for a reversal by the US Supreme Court, and for this, the conference once again turned to the national office for financial aid and legal advice.

Thurgood Marshall rejected this call for funding. He had reviewed the entire record of the case and decided there was no basis for asking the Supreme Court for a writ of certiorari. When Hinton said the conference would proceed with the appeal anyway, Marshall replied that the national office could only cooperate to the extent of filing papers, but it could not sign them. At its June 1943 term, the Supreme Court declined to issue the writ of certiorari that would reverse the decisions of the trial and the appeals courts. Sammie Osborne died in the electric chair on November 19, 1943. Moments before he entered the execution chamber, he gave the prison chaplain three one-dollar bills on which he had written his name. He told the chaplain to keep one for himself and asked him to give the others to two leaders of the South Carolina Conference who had labored so hard to save his life. He wanted them to have something to remember him by. One of the bills went to James Hinton.[10]

Hinton emerged from the Osborne ordeal with extensive experience and knowledge that could prove useful in future cases. He now knew how the legal department of the national office functioned. He knew that it had to be pushed, that it often took a long time to make critical decisions, and that pressure and persistence were required if local branches hoped to pry funds from it. He also now knew how the appeals process worked at both the state level and before the Federal Supreme Court. He had been repeatedly exposed to judicial procedures, legal forms and writs, and the formulation of legal strategy. And he had raised money from the public, organizing rallies and campaigns that lasted several weeks. When he became the president of the South Carolina Conference in the spring of 1944, James Hinton was prepared for the challenge that arose only four months after Sammie Osborne's execution: the arrest of George Stinney, Jr., on March 25.

When that occurred, the most logical place for the NAACP to initiate Stinney's defense would have been at the level closest to the case—the Clarendon County branch. But in 1944, that branch was, to all intents and purposes, defunct. In 1943, the county's leading activist, Pastor Joseph A. De Laine Sr. had founded the branch in Summerton, a town of almost a thousand some ten miles south of Manning. By December of that year, De Laine had fallen ill and was incapable of functioning. He guarded the branch's meager bank account of $83.20 for the next four years, until he finally turned the funds over to Hinton. In the intervening years, De Laine admitted to Hinton, the other officers of the Clarendon County branch "have not done anything since my health broke on me in 1943. . . . Nothing short of a new organization is needed here. . . . There are a number of the folks about in the county who want to do something but don't have the ability to take the leadership." In a handwritten comment at the top of De Laine's letter, Hinton summarized the state of affairs in Clarendon: "Rev. J. A. De Laine's health failed in December 1943 and the work in Clarendon County stopped during his long illness. This $83.20 was left in the bank for over 4 years."[11]

With the Clarendon branch incapable of functioning in 1944, no alarm could be raised at the local level when Stinney was arrested or while he awaited trial. If anything were to be done, the South Carolina Conference would have to swing into action just as it had at the outset of the Osborne case three years before. As president of the South Carolina Conference, Hinton probably learned almost immediately of Stinney's trouble. Both his hometown papers, the *State* and the *Columbia Record*, had reported what occurred in Alcolu within twenty-four hours of Stinney's arrest. The *Lighthouse and Informer*, an African American newspaper published in Columbia, also carried this news. Then, too, several influential state NAACP leaders who resided in Sumter had full knowledge of the case. The *Sumter Herald* had quickly covered it since Alcolu was only fifteen miles away.[12]

No matter what his source of information, Hinton had a complete month between Stinney's arrest on March 25 and trial on April 24 to engage a competent lawyer on the boy's behalf. But he did not. Nor did he undertake an appeal to the South Carolina Supreme Court following George Stinney's conviction. At no point did Hinton turn to the national office for assistance or advice; the meticulously indexed files in the legal department's extensive archives do not contain a single reference to the Stinney case nor a single communication about it between Columbia and New York. In fact, as we shall see, no one in a position of importance at any level of the NAACP seemed interested in Stinney's fate.

Although Sammie Osborne's age had stirred the Conference to pursue an aggressive course of action, George Stinney's tender age did not have a comparable impact upon the South Carolina NAACP's leadership. The glaring difference between their response to the two cases cries out for explanation. Unfortunately, Hinton and his colleagues apparently did not commit their reasons to paper; no smoking gun has been discovered. There is only one known document in which an African American leader in South Carolina attempted to account for the abandonment of George Stinney in the spring of 1944, a letter written thirty-seven years later by John H. McCray, the editor of the *Lighthouse and Informer* and a prominent activist for Black rights.

In 1981, McCray had written to David I. Bruck, who was then busy researching Stinney's case for an article in the *Washington Post*. In his letter, McCray offered a harsh assessment of the NAACP's failure to act. "Two items come to mind you likely picked up some notes on in your research," wrote McCray. "One is the tendency of Negroes at that time to flee from another of their group on occasions when Whites accused them of crimes, especially crimes for which capital punishment was prescribed." By way of illustration, McCray offered two examples in South Carolina, both of which occurred not long before the Stinney case. In the first example, a Black man named George Thomas was executed in 1942 for rape. "[T]he president of the Negro Ministerial Alliance at Georgetown," McCray said, "opposed efforts of the . . . secretary for the same organization and others who attempted to raise funds in the community with which to furnish the accused with legal assistance." McCray's second example was an acerbic recollection of a meeting convened to consider bringing one of the appeals on behalf of Sammie Osborne: "The Reverend James Hinton, the Reverend J. P. Reeder, the Reverend E. A. Adams [Hinton's predecessor as president of the Conference], and I were present. Adams, who was chairman of the Board of Directors for Victory Savings [an African American bank in Columbia] and also chairman of the Osborne Defense Committee, opposed further legal assistance in the case. 'We have already gotten enough publicity out of the case,' he said, smiling like a fat cat."[13]

McCray's attempt to explain the failure to act on Stinney's behalf is, however, inadequate. NAACP leaders everywhere, in branches all over the nation and in the national office, had an exemplary record of efforts to save Black defendants unfairly accused or convicted of capital offenses, including cases of interracial sexual contact. For example, early in 1941, Thurgood Marshall successfully defended an African American chauffeur accused by his White, upper-class employer of raping and kidnapping her. Later that year, right in South Carolina, the NAACP brought an appeal to the state's supreme court, then a petition for a writ of certiorari to the US Supreme Court, on behalf of two men convicted and sentenced to death for the capital offense of "assault [upon a White girl] with attempt to ravish."[14]

With only McCrays's reflections on the Stinney case, it is impossible to do more than ask: What plausible reasons did the South Carolina NAACP have to ignore George Stinney's plight? To begin with, there was the chronic shortage of funds, so apparent in the Osborne case and in every earlier case in South Carolina. Challenges to court decisions took money: there was the printing of trial transcripts and briefs, lawyers' fees to be paid, travel expenses to obtain affidavits from witnesses, and the cost of hiring expert witnesses. Defense attorneys repeatedly complained they were not being paid and the shortage of funds sometimes put appeals in danger. In one case, a South Carolina attorney had to warn the New York office that he would miss a filing deadline if he did not receive the money to print the documents he needed. The truth was that local branches were perpetually short of funds. In 1940, the Charleston branch was embarrassed to confess that it could only raise $39.11 of the $100 it had promised to contribute toward a case. The South Carolina Conference was no better off; it had no endowment to draw upon even if it wished to defend George Stinney or appeal his conviction. A plea that the public contribute so soon after the Osborne case was unlikely to be greeted with enthusiasm for, despite the rallies and the dedication of the attorneys, Osborne had died in the electric chair. And finally, as James Hinton knew so well, the national office could contribute only erratically to South Carolina projects.[15]

Not that the national office was by its nature tight-fisted. It simply did not have the resources to support the many desperate defendants seeking its assistance. In 1939, the office hoped to raise some funds by asking for contributions in honor of Walter White's twenty-one years as the NAACP's executive secretary. The appeal letter was blunt: "For a number of years the association, because of lack of funds has been forced to turn down pleas for assistance in court cases. In other worthy cases it has had to confine itself to making a small contribution to the expenses instead of prosecuting the fight with full vigor." The lack of funds was often embarrassing. In 1940, Thurgood Marshall found it necessary to write to a White attorney in South Carolina that "[t]he delay in answering your last letter concerning the Benjamin Heywood case has been caused by the usual problem here, namely lack of funds." Hoping to help in some way in the Heywood case, Marshall wrote to a branch in Cleveland, Ohio, pleading for a contribution. "I hate to call on the branches for these cases but we have had so much activity this year our defense fund is exhausted and we cannot raise much money in South Carolina for obvious reasons." The problem was persistent, and it inevitably led to the tragedy that many defendants would not get the assistance from the NAACP that might have saved their lives.[16]

But lack of local funds or help from the national office were not the only reasons the South Carolina Conference did not take up the Stinney case. In the spring of 1944, the conference was preoccupied with several initiatives of great import, and each of them required both concentrated attention and considerable funding. Focused upon those undertakings and gearing up for battle on many fronts, the conference was perhaps reluctant to divert energy and its scarce resources to yet another criminal case in which there was a high risk of defeat. In their judgment, the projects the conference was poised to embark upon would have far wider potential impact than the rescue of one small boy.

The conference was gearing up to do nothing less than directly challenge Jim Crow. The first of their projects was a major struggle to win equal pay for South Carolina's African American teachers. Fully a year before the murders in Alcolu, Hinton had announced plans to fund the suit for equal pay brought in Federal District Court by a Black teacher in Charleston. In February 1944, Judge J. Waties Waring sacrificed his hitherto impeccable reputation and standing among the state's White population by ruling that Charleston's Black teachers must receive the same pay as its White teachers. To a Columbia County Representative in the legislature the looming campaign for equal salaries was the greatest crisis facing South Carolina. He introduced legislation designed to thwart the court's order, warning that the legislature's failure to pass his proposal would lead to lawsuits by the NAACP in *all* of the state's school districts.[17]

The *Columbia Record*, relatively moderate in matters of race, recommended that the state's legislature comply with the court's ruling and appropriate the funds necessary for salary equalization, not just in Charleston but throughout the state. Instead, the legislature searched for ways to defeat the ruling. It focused on raising the bar for teacher certification. Although some White teachers might lose their certification or be certified at a lower level, the clear intention of the plan was to decertify large numbers of Black teachers, or at the least to relegate many to "a lower certification group and lower salary group." The result would be, as a *Columbia Record* editorial noted, "more money to pay their white teachers still larger salaries, increasing the existing racial discrimination." During the state legislature's 1944 spring session, the House of Representatives included a certification measure in its appropriation bill. The bill, complicated and often opaque, failed to pass the state senate. Thus, the legislature's struggle to prevent equalization of teacher pay was deferred.[18]

The legislature's resistance to equal pay was hardly unexpected. In fact, six weeks before George Stinney's arrest, and well before the legislature's efforts to thwart the court order began, Hinton declared that the South Carolina Conference would finance suits against several counties on behalf of equal pay for African American teachers. Here, then, was a significant constraint on funds for any effort that might have been mounted on behalf of George Stinney. As one historian of the salary-equalization movement throughout the South has observed, "Cases had to be pursued one district at a time, which consumed large amounts of time and resources for only limited gains. . . ."[19]

With its second project, the State Conference faced an even more explosive and perhaps more expensive battle: the fight to win the right of Black voters to cast ballots in Democratic Party primaries. In the absence of a viable Republican party in the South, state and local Democratic parties enjoyed unchallenged rule. A victory in a Democratic primary was the same as winning in the general election. White South Carolinians were determined to continue the exclusion of African Americans from the electoral process. For many of these White citizens this exclusion was the bedrock of White supremacy. And it was already being threatened.

The threat came with the April 2, 1944, US Supreme Court ruling that the exclusion of Black voters in Texas was unconstitutional. On hearing this, South Carolina Senator "Cotton Ed" Smith sputtered that he was "too mad to comment." Others however spoke out in threatening terms. At the opening session of the South Carolina legislature, Governor Olin Johnston declared:

> We South Carolinians will use the necessary methods to retain white supremacy in our primaries and to safeguard the houses and happiness of our people . . . The representatives of these agitators, scalawags and unscrupulous politicians that called themselves white men and used the colored race to further their own courses [back during Reconstruction] are in our midst today, and history will repeat itself unless we protect ourselves against this new crop of carpetbaggers and scalawags, who would use the colored race to further own economic and political gains. . . . Now is the time to act. White supremacy will be maintained in our primaries. Let the chips fall where they may![20]

To the state's African American leaders, language such as that last sentence may well have implied the use of force and violence to maintain the white primary.[21]

South Carolina's White political leaders reacted swiftly to this threat of Black voters, formulating plans for legislative action. The state's African American leaders reacted just as fast. A day after the Texas decision, they announced that they were preparing to sue in South Carolina's federal district court for the right of Blacks to vote in the primaries. Technically, it was the Negro Citizens Committee, established in 1942 to challenge the

White primary, that would bring the suit, but when it came to financial resources, there was little difference between this organization and the state NAACP. The battle to overturn the White primary was thus added to the salary equalization struggle and this made funds to hire a defense attorney for George Stinney that April difficult if not impossible to find, even if these organizations wished to do so.[22]

Yet a third great cause commanded the time and resources of Black South Carolinians in 1944. John Henry McCray, the radical editor of the *Lighthouse and Informer*, was leading an effort to create a new political party. McCray proposed that this new organization, the Progressive Democratic Party (PDP), send delegates to the 1944 Democrats' presidential nominating convention in Chicago that July. Here the PDP delegation would challenge the legitimacy of the delegates sent by South Carolina's all-White Democratic party. The new, alternative party hoped to persuade the nation party's credentials committee to allocate eight of South Carolina's eighteen delegates to the PDP. The PDP also intended to field a candidate for the US Senate, and it was ready to aggressively organize voter registration drives among the state's Black population.[23]

Between March, the month when George Stinney was arrested, and June, when he was executed, McCray and his colleagues were absorbed in establishing branches of the PDP in forty-two of the state's forty-six counties. On May 24, representatives of the branches from around the state convened in Columbia. Here they elected eighteen delegates to send to the upcoming national convention of the Democratic party—and they solicited funds to pay these delegates' expenses. Hinton, speaking as president of the state NAACP, wholeheartedly supported McCray's goals and pledged a Conference contribution to the fight. On June 14, two days prior to George Stinney's execution, the new party convened a mass meeting in Columbia to build support for their bold political effort and to publicly urge Blacks to attempt to register to vote.[24]

Three great causes, each requiring resources, time, and intense organizational effort, thus enveloped South Carolina's Black leadership cadre in the spring of 1944. Thanks to the multiplicity and the boldness of their initiatives, it is not surprising that, in the national NAACP's 1944 campaign to enroll a half-million new members, the South Carolina Conference distinguished itself by becoming the first state in the nation to exceed its assigned quota.[25]

In the final analysis, however, perhaps it was not the scarce funds or the multiple major projects that were the key to the decision not to fight for George Stinney's life. It may simply be that Hinton and his colleagues had come to believe that attempts to save the victims of courtroom injustice were futile. The effort to save Sammie Osborne, whose conviction they had fought so long, so hard, and with such great diligence and dedication, had come to nothing. The hopelessness of it all was a raw lesson, a bitter memory that undoubtedly lingered. It was, after all, less than half a year between Osborne's execution on November 19, 1943, and George Stinney's arrest on March 25, 1944.

— — — — — — — — — — — — —

With the Clarendon County Branch incapable of taking action, and the South Carolina Conference unwilling or unable to finance a defense or an appeal, one other possible avenue within the NAACP remained for launching a campaign on behalf of George Stinney's life: bringing the fourteen-year-old on death row to the attention of the NAACP's national office in New York City. The opportunity to do this arose six days before Stinney's execution. Hinton had invited Roy Wilkins, the assistant secretary of the national NAACP, to present the keynote at the conference's annual June 11 meeting. Writing to Wilkins at the end of February 1944, Hinton spoke with pride of the Conference's ambitious challenges to the prevailing racial order. "South Carolina," he noted, "is very much in the limelight now and your coming would aid us greatly." Although Wilkins rarely traveled to the South, he accepted Hinton's invitation. He was, in fact, eager to get to Charleston where he hoped to interview the editorial board of the *News and Courier*, despite that newspaper's tenacious devotion to White supremacy. He planned to make Charleston his first stop and then attend the conference gathering on its first day. His visit would be brief; he would return to New York that same day.[26]

Hinton and Wilkins exchange several more letters in March. Hinton wrote again on June 6, sending his guest speaker travel information. It was ten days before Stinney's execution, but there was no mention of George or his fate.[27]

Following Wilkins's arrival in Sumter, it is reasonable to assume that the two men discussed the Stinney case. Yet in the speech that he delivered, Wilkins apparently did not refer to Stinney or his plight. Although no copy of his address survives in either his papers or those of the NACCP, the *State* covered the event. According to its reporter, Wilkins gave a passionate speech on behalf of equal rights for African Americans. Speaking from the pulpit of Sumter's AME church, he proclaimed that, despite the "white supremacy dogmas" of South Carolina's governor, its two senators, and the editor of Charleston's *News and Courier,* "we will attain our rights. . . . We are leading a revolution against negation of American rights . . . No person in power, including those now in power in South Carolina, ever gave up that power. We will have to take it." But Wilkins then took care to moderate his fiery references to revolution; "there is no need for riot or for hatred. Our revolution must be conducted through the courts."[28]

Wilkins's insistence that the change would come "Through the courts" provided a perfect opportunity for the NAACP's assistant secretary to refer to the Stinney case. The trial, with its all-White jury, its absence of any defense on the part of Stinney's two court-appointed attorneys, and the imposition of the death penalty for a fourteen-year-old boy fit perfectly within any discussion of "white supremacy doctrine" and the "negation of American rights." Yet the newspaper report contained no reference to George Stinney or his trial.

Wilkins returned as scheduled to New York City immediately after his address. Meeting the following day with the NAACP's Board of Directors, he relayed his impressions of his trip to South Carolina. To judge from the letter that he wrote to Hinton on June 13, three days before the electrocution, he made no reference to George Stinney in his meeting with the national Board. He only said, "It was a great pleasure for me to speak for the South Carolina Conference of Branches in Sumter last Sunday. When I reported to the Board of Directors yesterday afternoon on the attendance at the mass meeting and the enthusiasm of the people of South Carolina, they were greatly pleased. . . ."[29]

Wilkins and the board apparently failed to see any potential value in taking up Stinney's cause, although it might have produced a growth in membership, an increase in the NAACP's public presence and its financial strength. The potential for fundraising had certainly figured in earlier decisions to champion cases, beginning with the one in Elaine, Arkansas, in 1919. Thurgood Marshall had, in fact, recognized the possibility of alleviating the legal department's perennial shortage of money afterward as he undertook to save a man who had been brutally tortured into a false confession in a sensational murder trial in Oklahoma. Writing to Walter White, head of the national office, in February 1941, Marshall pointed out, "We could use another good defense fund and this case has more appeal than any up to this time. The beating plus the use of the bones of dead people will raise money. I think we should issue a story this week on the start of the defense fund and when I get back to

New York . . . we can lay plans for a real drive for funds." Marshall also saw the potential for fundraising around the Connecticut case in which a chauffeur was acquitted of raping his White socialite employer. "The NAACP did all right this month," he told White; "We can raise money on these cases. We have been needing a good criminal case and we have it. Let's raise some real money."[30]

Surely the impending spectacle of a five-foot-one-inch tall, ninety-five-pound, fourteen-year-old boy strapped into an electric chair—his face encased in a leather hood, an electrode pressed onto the top of his skull and another wrapped around his small leg—would have elicited wide sympathy and additional financial support, at the very moment when the national NAACP was in the midst of a campaign to enlist 500,000 new members. There was still time in June to bombard the governor with letters and telegrams; in fact, they continued to arrive in Governor Olin Johnston's office even on the day of the execution. There was still time to reach out to major newspapers, White as well as Black, and to political and civic leaders. To be sure, only four days remained between Wilkins's meeting with the NAACP's board and the execution, but the organization had on a previous occasion acted decisively—and successfully—only three days prior to an execution.[31]

On June 14, Hinton sent Wilkins a thank you note for his inspiring keynote address. In it, he also proudly reported that a "Youth State Conference," had been formed the day following Wilkins speech. "Monday afternoon was the high session of our youth, and you would have enjoyed greatly the contributions made, the frank expressions, the problems presented, and the solutions for same." The new organization, he added, anticipated great accomplishments. It intended to raise $500 for the court case to equalize teachers' pay, and it would establish new youth branches throughout the state. But Hinton made no mention of the one concrete achievement of this newly established group: sending a telegram to Governor Johnston protesting the execution that would take place four days later.[32]

With nothing to draw his attention to the Stinney case, Wilkins went about conducting routine business, sending memoranda to office members, writing to clerical staff about vacation pay, and attending to Walter White's memo on finding a business manager for *The Crisis* and the problems of overcrowding in the office. In his weekly newspaper column, *The Watchtower*, Wilkins focused on the regrettable absence anywhere in the country of a good African American restaurant that offered southern cooking. Two weeks later, Wilkins described his recent trip to South Carolina in a *Watchtower* column entitled "Politeness and Rebellion in S.C." No mention was made of the impending execution or even of the two telegrams pleading for Stinney's life send by South Carolina's State Conference and the new Youth Conference.[33]

The Clarendon County Branch's inability to initiate activity on behalf of George Stinney is understandable, given its meager resources. The State Conference's failure to take up Stinney's case is also understandable, given the major attacks on the Jim Crow system, it was engaged in at the time. But the silence of the national office remains difficult to explain. It is true that, after a troubling case in the 1930s, the office had decided only to come to the aid of defendants that were innocent of the charges against them. But, as one historian has noted, the New York based national office was "rarely in a position to evaluate the innocence or guilt of defendants." In the end, the acknowledgement of Stinney's execution came in a brief item in *The Crisis*, three months after his death in the electric chair.[34]

The absence of a campaign by the NAACP's national office to publicize George Stinney's case and his execution meant that the at-large press, including African American newspapers, provided little coverage. The *Chicago Defender*, one of the nation's leading African American newspapers, buried its brief notice of the execution on page 18 of its June 17, 1944, issue. It had not covered the trial or its aftermath. Other papers failed to cover the case at all or, mentioned it only briefly, as the *New York Amsterdam News* did on June 17. The *New York Times* carried a seventy-five-word account, buried deep on page 21, noting that it had taken its report from an Associated Press dispatch. The left-wing press was strangely silent about Stinney's execution. The American Communist Party did not devote any attention to Stinney's plight until June 17, when its *Daily Worker* used six slim paragraphs to report "S. Carolina Executes 14-Year-Old Negro Boy—Gov. Ignores Protests."

— — — — — — — — — —

George Stinney might have benefited more from a noisy campaign to publicize his plight than he did from a telegram to the governor. He might have benefited even more from an appeal carried through the courts. If the conference had pursued an appeal following Stinney's conviction either with or without the assistance of the national office, the case of two young South Carolina men convicted in October 1940 and sentenced to death after jury deliberations that lasted only seven minutes could have served as a model. At least one of the constitutional issues in their case, namely, the quality of the defense provided by their court-appointed lawyers was applicable to George Stinney's case.[35]

Perhaps intervention by the NAACP on behalf of George Stinney would have ultimately failed, as it did in the cases of Benjamin Heywood, Cyrus Pinckney, Alchrist Grant, and Sammie Osborne: they were all executed. But the appeals process bought a condemned man precious time. A stay, or an appeal to the South Carolina Supreme Court, or a new trial if the state supreme court found in favor of Stinney, or an appeal to the Supreme Court of the United States: all would have more than exceeded the period between his conviction at the end of April 1944 and the beginning of 1945, when a new governor would take office, one who perhaps would have been more disposed than the current one to exercise clemency for a child who was sitting in a cell on death row. As capital-punishment attorney David I. Bruck has written, "The execution would have been automatically stayed for at least a year if Plowden had filed a one sentence notice of appeal, and then appealed the case to the state Supreme Court."[36]

The same observation can be made of the NAACP's decision not to act.

POSTSCRIPT. Both Joseph A. De Laine and James M. Hinton were instrumental in the initiation of the first case in the twentieth century that challenged school segregation, namely, *Briggs v. Elliott*, which originated in Summerton in Clarendon County and later became one of the five cases adjudicated in 1954 by the US Supreme Court in *Brown v. Board of Education*. Between 1951 and 1955, De Laine and his wife lost their jobs, their home in Summerton was destroyed by arson, and their subsequent home in nearby Lake City came under attack. They were forced to flee from South Carolina, to which they never could return because of an arrest warrant for assault and battery with intent to kill, issued against De Laine after he defended his Lake City house with gunfire.

James M. Hinton continued after 1944 to lead the movement for equal civil rights in South Carolina, serving as the president of the state's NAACP until 1958. Like De Laine, he faced grave danger. Abducted in 1949, he was beaten and left lying on the ground in the countryside near Augusta. In 1956, his home was attacked by gunfire amid the backlash against *Brown v. Board of Education*.

Chapter 8
The Governor

Please reprieve this child.

> Marguerite Sease to Governor
> Olin Johnston, June 13, 1944

South Carolina is my state, and I don't want it to be known as the state that electrocutes children.

> Eliza S. Gault to Governor
> Olin Johnston, June 14, 1944

Two days after Clarendon County's jury found George Junius Stinney Jr. guilty of murder, Miss Mary C. Preston of Charleston, South Carolina, took her pen in hand and wrote to Governor Olin Johnston. Had any professionals examined his mental condition? she asked. Hers was the first of approximately 175 letters and telegrams that individuals, as well as organizations in South Carolina and a dozen other states, sent to the governor, most of which urged him to exercise his power to halt the sentence of death. Taken together, this correspondence was the second largest the governor would receive in his second term in office. Most were written in early June as the date for execution neared. Many arrived during the last week of Stinney's life. Some even came on the day of his execution. Some, like the eloquent four-page telegram sent by the Catholic Bishop of Charleston, or the three-page letter from the Recorder of the Municipal court of Greenville, rose to heights of sophistication; others, although grammatically faulty, conveyed heartfelt sympathy for the fourteen-year-old boy awaiting his death. Among these, was a brief letter written in an awkward, childish hand on a sheet of lined notebook paper, that appealed not only for Stinney's life but also for the life of the second young man sentenced to die on the same day: "I saw the add on the State About those Boys. Now I don't think it is right to kill any child, I think it would be right to punish them for the Crime done but not to kill them. It sure would be much better for all the people to pray for them. And that is what I am going to do."[1]

On the other hand, some twenty letters came from death-penalty supporters who urged the governor to resist pleas on behalf of Stinney: "Put him in the Electric chair where he belongs," one South Carolinian angrily scrawled across the top of a newspaper advertisement that advocated mercy for Stinney. "Why mercy for this rattlesnake?" the writer asked. "Let the law take its course and terminate the life of this reptile. In that way you can avoid lynchings."

Perhaps the rawest of the letters urging the governor to stand firm came from a writer in Mullins:

> I am writing to say that I am by no means in favor of saving this fellow's life. It may be that if his life is saved, with many negro boys, it will mean that they may rape and kill white girls without any fear of punishment other than life imprisonment, and that with the hope of pardon at some future time. The sight of these little girls as they suffer and die and the hands of this youthful brute is too awful and gastly [sic] to be lost sight of long enough to save the life of him who with fiendish purpose took theirs. . . .[2]

South Carolina's constitution gave the governor the power to commute a death sentence to a term in prison, to postpone an execution, or to grant a pardon to a convicted defendant. Four months before Stinney was to die, Governor Johnston had commuted the sentence of a convicted murderer, police officer Joe Frank Logue. Logue had been convicted of hiring someone to kill another man. Logue's aunt and uncle were convicted as accessories to the murder and, together with the hired killer, these two went to the electric chair. But in February 1944, on the eve of Logue's execution, Governor Johnston spared him by commuting his death penalty to life imprisonment. Johnston listed three reasons for exercising this executive clemency. First, eight members of the jury that convicted Logue asked for this clemency. Secondly, Logue had cooperated fully with the prosecution, testifying against his aunt and uncle. And, finally, a majority of South Carolina's pardon board recommended commutation. Logue was paroled sixteen years later, after spending much of the time outside the state penitentiary, freely moving about without supervision.[3]

Perhaps if the Governor acted with similar compassion toward George Stinney, he, too, could be paroled after spending several years in prison. To be sure, none of the members of Stinney's jury had asked for this consideration and the State Pardon and Parole Board had never met to consider his case. In fact, one of the board members visited Stinney in his cell "for some time" and assured the governor that there was no reason to alter the fourteen-year-old's sentence. Yet the many petitioners who wrote to the governor evidently hoped that Johnston could be moved to act mercifully. Like Logue, Stinney had cooperated with the officers of the law by confessing to the murders of the two girls. Afterward, he led them to the railroad spike (or iron rod) with which he had killed them. He stuck to his confession on at least two occasions, first, while awaiting execution, and then at the execution itself. He wavered only once. Above all, in contrast to Logue who was a mature adult and a seasoned officer of the law, Stinney was only fourteen years old. How could that not carry weight with the governor?[4]

Stinney's age was the point most frequently raised in the letters and telegrams that arrived in Johnston's office. At least one hundred of the correspondents argued that it would be unconscionable to execute a minor. Many shared the sentiments expressed by Rabbi Jacob S. Raisin, the spiritual leader of the oldest Jewish congregation in the state, who argued that Stinney should be saved from the electric chair "not only for humanitarian reasons, since he is a minor, but with the thought of the ignominy which his execution may bring upon the fair name of our State."[5]

Other writers, though they were not lawyers, attempted to tie the argument about age to legal grounds. They asserted that a child of fourteen did not have the capacity to distinguish between right and wrong and therefore could not bear criminal responsibility. In his letter, the Recorder of the Municipal Court of Greenville, underscored the travesty in South Carolina law that proclaimed a person below the age of sixteen was neither to be judged nor punished as an adult, *except in capital cases.* His own experience dealing with many criminals ranging in age from ten to eight persuaded him that "a 14 year old boy cannot conceive, plan and execute a murder with all its legal essential elements of premeditation." This anomaly that allowed a child to be punished for a capital case could only be corrected if the death sentence were commuted to life in prison.[6]

About forty-five of the writers pointed to the clemency granted to another young man who confessed to murder. This case overlapped with Stinney's; the two actually unfolded simultaneously. Early in December 1843, the body of an eight-year-old girl was found on swampland at the US Marine Corp base on Parris Island. She proved to be the daughter of a Marine Corp lieutenant. Sixteen-year-old Ernest Edmund Feltwell, Jr, son of a White Marine gunnery officer, was arrested for the murder in early February. Feltwell at first denied any guilt, but he ultimately confessed. Newspapers reported that, despite his age, Feltwell was only in the seventh grade, a grade that Stinney had reached before turning fourteen.[7]

Because the crime had been committed on US government property, the case was a federal one, and Feltwell's arraignment thus took place in May of 1944 in the US District Court for the Eastern District of South Carolina in Charleston. Judge Julius Waities Waring was on the bench. Although he had once been an advocate of White supremacy, Judge Waring had begun to establish a reputation as a liberal southern judge, particularly in cases involving race. It was Waring who, early in 1944, had ruled for the plaintiffs when the South Carolina NAACP sued to gain salaries for Black teachers equal to those White teachers received In the Feltwell case, the prosecution charged that the boy had killed the child when he attempted to rape her. Feltwell pleaded not guilty to this charge, insisting that he had never intended to kill her. He had murdered her only by accident, he explained, choking her by placing his hand over her mouth in order to stifle her screams.[8]

Judge Waring gave the defense ample time to prepare their case. He had appointed three eminent South Carolina attorneys to represent Feltwell, and they had agreed to take the case without compensation. They took their task seriously; their first step was to request the court send their client to the State Hospital in Columbia for observation, a clear sign they were exploring the possibility of an insanitary defense. When the hospital reported that Feltwell was sane, the lawyers began a thorough investigation, traveling to Parris Island, interviewing many people there, consulting a criminologist with a national reputation, and utilizing a lie detector to measure the truthfulness of Feltwell's confession. They paid for all the expenses entailed out of their own pockets, since the court lacked the funds to cover these costs. In the end, the lawyers advised Feltwell to change his plea to guilty in order to avoid the death penalty.

The advice was wise. If his case went to trial and a jury found Feltwell guilty but did not recommend mercy, Judge Waring would have no choice but to sentence him to death by electrocution. But if he pleaded guilty, the judge could exercise mercy and sentence him to prison. Thus, on June 1, Ernest Edmund Feltwell Jr. rescinded his earlier plea of innocence and pleaded to guilty of murder in the second degree. Judge Waring then sentenced him to twenty years in prison. Waring chose not to place the boy among habitual offenders. Instead Feltwell would be given the opportunity to learn a trade, and he could be released on parole after serving only one-third of his sentence. Many of the letter writers seeking clemency for Stinney pointed out the salient difference in the handling of the Stinney and Feltwell cases—race. And, indeed, the advantages Feltwell enjoyed starkly illuminated the role that race played in the halls of justice in South Carolina in 1944.[9]

Other letter writers stressed the rising racial tensions in the state, tensions that would surely be exacerbated, they argued, if a fourteen-year-old African American boy died in the electric chair. This concern was expressed by a Charleston businessman who, after citing both Stinney's "extreme youth" and the disparity in treatment with the Feltwell case, added: "[C]onsideration of the unusual amount of feeling which has been engendered upon the colored people of our state through the interference and leadership, largely of outsiders, which to my mind necessitates the calmest and clearest thinking and action, as it relates to the two races. I feel were this boy at his age executed it would but add additional fire to the already smoldering timbers due to a feeling that advantage had been taken of the fact that he was colored."[10]

The executive secretary of the South Carolina Conference of Social Work made a similar argument. "At a time when feeling runs so high between the white and Negro races," sparing George Stinney's life might very well "quell the fires of discontent so evident now." Another correspondent worried about "the possibility of race riots in the near future" and thus thought it "doubly advisable to see that the negro does not pay the supreme penalty." He held a jaundiced view of Feltwell's rehabilitation, writing that "the equally guilty white boy will probably live to repeat his crime." The concern about racial tensions also motivated a writer from Greenwood, South Carolina who was "very sure that such incidents [as in the differences between the Feltwell and Stinney cases] can only add to the growing tension, which seems to me to be very grave at this time."[11]

Some petitions for clemency stressed the issue of mental disorder. A postcard from Brooklyn, New York, read, "He needs a good psychiatrist rather than the electric chair." There were over a dozen letters and telegrams that charged that executing a child was something that could occur only under a regime like Hitler's. A telegram that arrived the day before Stinney's execution read: "Beseech you spare young George Stinney child execution is only for Hitler." In a less dramatic fashion, a South Carolina man urged "that this State . . . not do a thing like the countrys [*sic*] we are fighting."[12]

Some pleas for clemency were accompanied by affirmations of White supremacy. For example, a major in the US Army stationed at Fort Jackson in Columbia wrote to say that he was a Southerner who believed in White supremacy, but that he opposed execution because of Stinney's "extreme youth." Yet another, a woman who identified herself as a White Southerner who expected African Americans to know their place, and who thought that Eleanor Roosevelt "stirred up plenty of trouble between black and white," argued that the differential treatment in the Feltwell and Stinney cases "just isn't fair play." To her, "a law is a law not one for white & one for colored." And in a third example, a writer explained that he was a Southerner, that he did not like Blacks, that he wished they were all back in Africa, that Stinney's crime was a horrible one—but that he should not be executed: "After all, he is a child and should be treated as such."[13]

— — — — — — — — — — — — —

White women's voices were the loudest in the call for clemency. Of the eighty-four individual South Carolinians who wrote to the governor, seventy-nine can be identified by gender, race, education, or profession, or by a combination of these factors. A full 62 percent of the letters in which gender can be determined came from South Carolina women. Over 64 percent of those who wrote these letters and telegrams can be identified conclusively as White, either because they identified themselves by their race or because they were listed that way in the census of 1940, or because the content of their letters inferred this was so. Only three South Carolinians were African American. Over 34 percent of the letter writers are known to have attended college and, in some cases, postgraduate programs, a striking statistic in an era before the advent of mass higher education. Equally striking, eleven of the twenty-seven with higher education credentials were women.[14]

Few of the South Carolina women writers worked outside of their homes. Of the twenty-nine women for whom information about employment is available, only ten, or 34.4 percent, were employed outside their households. The available profiles of male writers were far different. Twenty-three of twenty-five of these men, including nine clergymen, were employed outside their homes.[15]

The campaign for clemency was also waged by groups such as unions, churches, and ministers' associations. The largest of these collective efforts was a Charleston petition campaign that garnered almost 1,500 signatures, primarily from the African American community.

Women church groups sent the governor letters that focused on the unequal treatment of Whites and Blacks in the courts of law. Three days before Stinney's scheduled execution, Mrs. D. L. Johnston wrote on behalf of women of the First Presbyterian church of Greenville, South Carolina. She pointed directly to the different fates of Ernest Feltwell and George Stinney, both tried for murdering young girls. "The ladies of a circle of the First Presbyterian church which met at my home this morning" she said, "expressed themselves very strongly of [sic] the matter of the white people dealing equal justice to the negro race in the courts of our state." Two days later, the executive board of the Women's Auxiliary of Charleston's venerable St. Philips, the state's oldest Episcopalian church, telegrammed the governor to register their opposition to Stinney's execution. The Methodist women of Lyman chose to express their concern through their minister, who wrote to Johnston on their behalf. Pastor M. Wallace Fridy confessed that he knew little about Stinney's case, but he was moved to write because the women of the community were so deeply concerned that such a young boy had been sentenced to die. Pastor Fridy urged the governor to review the situation. The Executive Board of the Civic Club of Charleston also protested to Johnston, arguing that the members were "opposed to the execution of minors."[16]

Two South Carolina unions, The Tobacco Workers Organizing Committee of Charleston who cited its 2,000 members and the National Maritime Union of Charleston, with its 7,500 members, each contacted the governor on the same day. Both had decidedly radical connections and significant African American memberships. The National Maritime Union, the older of the two unions, had long struggled against racial discrimination in the shipping industry, citing the statement by Karl Marx that "Labor with a white skin can never be free while labor with a black skin is branded." Even its white members in the South supported racial equality in employment on board ship, the NMU claimed. The Tobacco Workers Organizing Committee had been organized in 1942 with the help of the Communist Party; its mission was to protest low wages, segregation, and other adverse working conditions in the industry's factories. It had a large following among African American women. The two unions appeared to have coordinated their protests, for they used identical language to compare the George Stinney and Ernest Feltwell's cases. There had been, they concurred, "an obvious miscarriage of justice."[17]

The NAACP had been reluctant to embrace the cause of George Stinney and had made little or no effort to reach out to the African American press. But these two unions, each with strong roots among African American workers, channeled word of the impending execution in South Carolina to their counterparts in the larger world. As a result, telegrams protesting Stinney's execution arrive in the governor's office from leaders of the National Maritime Union in New York, the Tobacco Workers Organizing Committee in Richmond, Virginia, two unions in Winston Salem, North Carolina, and the office of the CIO Maritime Committee in Washington, DC. "Merchant seamen from all over the country . . . were shocked. . . ." read one, a sentiment common to these and other labor organizations writing from Virginia to New Jersey to Pennsylvania and New York.[18]

The president of the South Carolina Commission on Interracial Cooperation (CIC), an organization that sought to bring together moderate Whites and African Americans, added his voice to those calling for clemency for Stinney. The CIC had begun in 1919 in Atlanta but spread to several southern states. Although the organization worked to improve housing and education for Blacks and to curtail lynching, by later standards, it would appear moderate in the extreme. It did not seek to dismantle segregation or the Jim Crow institutions that sustained it. The result was that it was assailed as too radical by many White Southerners and not radical enough by many African Americans. Despite these attacks from the right and the left, the CIC labored on. The South Carolina branch had put forward a six-point program to mitigate the realities of Jim Crow just a few weeks before the murders in Alcolu.[19]

Other interracial committees functioned in many cities, including Charleston. Charleston's Inter-Racial Committee produced "A Petition to Governor Johnston in Behalf of George Stinney" signed by approximately 1,500 women and men. It declared that "It is not the practice of state courts in these United States to execute minors" and asked for clemency

"In the name of simple humanity." Charleston's African American ministers led this petition drive. The Charleston African American ministerial association, representing forty thousand Blacks in that city, also made the case for clemency. They assured the Governor that their members "do not question the action of the court that convicted and sentenced George"; they were asking for clemency for a child who they believed had a mental capacity well below that of a normal fourteen-year-old.[20]

Charleston's White ministers had already spoken up for Stinney through their association. Three days prior to the letter from the African American ministers' organization, their Charleston Ministers' Union had conveyed its opposition to the forthcoming execution, basing its "plea for lenience entirely upon the extreme youth of the criminal." Not content to let the matter rest there, the secretary of the Union wrote as an individual several days later, citing another of the reasons many petitioners had offered: "Along with others of the ministry I see that the tension between the two races in South Carolina is increased every day. We believe that any unwise action on the part of the State, as well as on the part of individuals, at this moment, will hasten trouble. I am firmly of the opinion that if this boy is executed a feeling between the two races will be further incited."[21]

The Reverend William R. Pettigrew, minister of the Charleston's Citadel Baptist Church also communicated directly with the governor, writing that almost two hundred members of his church had joined him in a petition for commutation of Stinney's death sentence. Their reasons were many, and they serve as a summary of most of the arguments made by the many others who appealed to the governor:

> We plead for the boy's life on the basis of his extreme youth, the conscience-troubling contrast between the sentence he has received and the sentence given Ernest Feltwell, and because his execution will give the negroes of South Carolina a "martyr" and another battle cry with which to arouse their followers.
>
> As a minister in the midst of a city where race animosities are already running high, I can say to you that the job of dealing with the situation and trying to avert serious trouble is already difficult enough. I sincerely trust that you may see your way clear to spare the boy's life.[22]

The Reverend Pettigrew's hope that the governor would find a "way clear to spare the boy's life" was, however, behind the times. The governor had publicly announced his decision three days before the minister wrote his letter. Olin D. Johnston intended to allow the electrocution of George Stinney to proceed as scheduled.

— — — — — — — — — — — —

Like many politicians who routinely respond to communications from their constituents, answering politely even the inane or pathetic ones, Governor Johnston dutifully answered his mail. His responses evolved tellingly over the course of the first week of June. Early in the month they were simple, to the point, and focused on the brutality of the murders. For example, his June 2 letter to Miss Susan Pringle Frost of Charleston read: "I have your letter in regards to George Spinney [*sic*], Jr. The Courts have settled this matter and I see no reason why clemency should be extended. As you know from the case, the little girls were only 7 and 11 years of age and they were brutally murdered. Very truly yours. . . ."[23]

Three days later, the governor began to shift the burden of Stinney's fate to those who had convicted him. They were the ones to act in this matter; they were the ones to blame. This more defensive shift can be seen in his June 5 letter to Miss Elize Moorer of Charleston: "I have your letter concerning the case of George Stinney. As you know, this case was passed on by 12 jurors and a judge, and, although the boy is as you say young, the victims were 11 and 8 [*sic*] years of age, respectively, and I would suggest that you contact the judge, the jury, and the solicitors in regards to this matter. Sincerely yours. . . ."

And then, in a June 9 postscript to Miss Moorer containing a devastating assertion, the governor pulled out all stops by invoking the most incendiary of all issues: "P. S. I have just talked with the officer who made the arrest in this case. It may be interesting for you to know that Stinney killed the smaller girl to rape the larger one. Then he killed the larger girl and raped her dead body. Twenty minutes later he returned and attempted to rape her again but her body was too cold. All this he admitted himself."[24]

The governor did not stop there. He added a startling assertion: "[T]he colored people of Alcolu would have lynched this boy themselves had it not been for the protection of the officers." From this point on, this baseless claim became a standard part of Johnston's litany of reasons against mercy for Stinney. It would not matter if the members of the Black community in Alcolu denied its validity. Perhaps, as the *Daily World*, an African American newspaper in Atlanta, reported, the governor had come to believe this allegation because Blacks had assisted in the search for the murderer of the two girls. "Some of those in the posse describe the white men as 'talking about a rope party,' after the boy was taken into custody. But "Negroes did not share in this feeling, they said."[25]

By June 9, all the elements justifying the governor's refusal to halt the execution or grant commutation of the sentence were in place. In his response that day to the Port Agent of the National Maritime Union in Charleston lengthy telegram, Johnston wrote:

> I have your communication concerning George Stinney, Jr. As you know, I had nothing to do with this matter. It was entirely in the hands of the judge, jury, and the solicitor.
> I understand that, although this boy was about 14 years of age, he brutally murdered two little girls, ages 11 and 8 [sic]. I would suggest that you contact the solicitor, the judge, and jury in regards to this matter.
> I have just talked with the officer who made the arrest in this case. It may be interesting for you to know that Stinney killed the smaller girl to rape the larger one. Then he killed the larger girl and raped her dead body. Twenty minutes later he returned and attempted to rape her again but her body was too cold. All of this he admitted himself.
> One other thing, the colored people of Alcolu would have lynched this boy themselves had it not been for the protection of the officers. Sincerely yours. . . .[26]

On the following day, June 10, South Carolinians who had urged Governor Johnston to stand firm learned that their position had prevailed. In his public statement Olin Johnston had declared "the brutality of the crime was more important than the age of Stinney." Despite the finality of the governor's decision, pleas to spare George Stinney's life continued to arrive, some of them postmarked June 16, arriving after Stinney had been electrocuted at 7:30 that morning.[27]

— — — — — — — — — — — —

The timing could not have been worse for the effort to save George Stinney's life, for his death sentence collided with Olin DeWitt Talmadge Johnston's frustrated ambition to win a seat in the US Senate. That ambition was deeply engrained. Born into poverty, or at best very modest circumstances, in 1896, Johnston had risen by dint of diligence and hard work. He began work in a textile mill at the age of eleven and had no more than ten months of schooling between the ages of eleven and seventeen. Yet by the age of fourteen he would declare his aspiration to become South Carolina's governor. At eighteen, he completed a high school diploma from the Textile Industrial Institute in Spartanburg, but when he applied to college, neither Clemson nor Furman would recognize the Institute's diploma. Wofford College agreed to take him as a special student, requiring him to take approved high school courses along with his freshman college courses. After military service in World War I, Johnston returned to earn his BA and, three years later, he graduated from the University of South Carolina law school. To pay for his education, Johnston had sometimes worked at two jobs a day.[28]

Olin Johnston did not wait to earn his law degree to enter politics. He began his rise to prominence with a seat in the state house of representatives and, by 1930, he made his first run for the governorship. He focused this ultimately losing campaign on the economic issues facing lower-class White workers. In 1934, he ran once again and won, despite the appeal to White supremacy by his opponent. In his first term in office, Johnston again emphasized economic issues affecting mill hands, trying, as historian Bryan Simon noted "to keep the volatile language of white supremacy in the background."[29]

In 1938, Johnston made a bid for a seat in the US Senate. His opponent was the thirty-six-year incumbent, the redoubtable Ellison DuRant Smith, popularly known as "Cotton Ed." Cotton Ed was a fierce opponent of Franklin Roosevelt's New Deal and an equally fierce proponent of White supremacy. He ran on a three-pronged platform: "States rights— white supremacy—tariff revenue." One of his favorite anecdotes centered on an incident at the Democratic national convention two years earlier. Smith had stormed out of the convention hall when an African American clergyman rose to deliver the invocation. As Smith told it during the 1938 campaign:

> I had no sooner taken my seat when a newspaper man came down the aisle and squatted down by me and said, "Senator, did you know a nigger is going to come up yonder in a minute and offer the invocation?" I told him, I said, "Now don't be joking me, I'm upset enough the way it is." But, then, Bless God, out on that platform walked a slew-footed, blue-gummed, kinky-headed Senegambian!
>
> And he started praying and I started walking. And as I pushed through those great doors, and walked across the vast rotunda, it

seemed to me that Old John Calhoun leaned down from his mansion in the sky and whispered, "You did right, Ed."[30]

Although Johnston shared this commitment to White supremacy, he did not invoke the issue of race until a week before the Democratic primary. His standard speech stressed support for Roosevelt and the New Deal. "I am squaring off," he declared, "for the humanitarian Roosevelt policies." But in that last week, in a radio address, Johnston sought to bolster his flagging support by a resort to racist rhetoric. He wildly accused Smith of pandering to Black voters. But he was no match for Smith who asserted that a "program to destroy white supremacy" was afoot, as evidenced by the introduction of an anti-lynching law in Congress. It did not help Johnston that President Roosevelt traveled to South Carolina to support his candidacy since this raised the specter of outside interference. Johnston lost the primary and was forced to settle for another term as governor.[31]

Johnston tried for the Senate a second time in 1941. That year a special election was called to replace Senator James F. Byrnes who had been appointed to the US Supreme Court. Johnston faced two opponents. None of them played the race card, although on several occasions, Johnston did decry federal spending for education if it were to require school integration. Overall, the campaign was considered a tepid one, a contest devoid of fireworks. But Johnston did not emerge the winner.[32]

Despite these two defeats, in the summer of 1943 Olin Johnston was readying to run for Cotton Ed's seat once again. And this time he was prepared to take the offensive on race issues. He delivered speeches and wrote letters making clear his conviction that Blacks were inferior to Whites, that White supremacy laws and institutions were necessary, and that the recent race riots in Detroit began because "the races mixed too freely" there. Olin Johnston had, in effect, adopted Cotton Ed's modus operandi of exploiting race for political advantage.[33]

On the day that Ed Smith hinted that he would stand once again for reelection, Johnston proclaimed that South Carolina possessed the ability to deal with the inherent differences between the races. The state's Whites, he said, dealt fairly with African Americans, providing them with educational and employment opportunities. But he would never allow racial mixing in schools, churches, and homes. In a speech before three thousand members of the South Carolina Home Defense Forces, he issued a warning to "outside agitators," concluding with this inflammatory flourish: "If any outside agitators come into our state and agitate for social equality among races, I shall deem it my duty to call upon you men to help expel them from our state."[34]

The *Columbia Record* concluded that the two candidates seemed to agree on the race question. By July 1943, the newspaper was denouncing both men, declaring Smith unfit to serve because of his advocacy of isolation at war's end, and Johnston for resorting to Cotton Ed's long-established race-baiting. But Johnston's decision to stir the racial cauldron won popular support. Letters poured into his office congratulating him, extolling his new direction, and assuring him that this was indeed the right strategy for his campaign in the 1944 primary. Once embarked on this new path, Johnston forcefully and consistently utilized every possible opportunity during the spring of 1944 to advocate White supremacy. His letters to constituents continued to emphasize his commitment to upholding Jim Crow laws in South Carolina. In April, he convened a special session of the state legislature in order to subvert the US Supreme Court's ruling that Democratic primaries were unconstitutional because only Whites were permitted to vote in them. South Carolina legislators speedily endorsed his proposal to declare the Democratic Party a private club, permitted to select its own members. This legislative ploy, engineered by Olin Johnston, was widely praised. One supporter wrote that "South Carolina will demand your candidacy for the United States Senate, requiring you to continue serving as its first Statesman. . . ." And within three weeks of George Stinney's execution, Johnston attacked Thomas Dewey, the Republican nominee for the presidency, for having met with a delegation of African Americans. This prompted New York's *Herald Tribune* to declare that Johnston had the dubious distinction of "having thrown out the first mud ball in the 1944 Presidential campaign." The newspaper predicted there would be "more of the same, no doubt, and much dirtier."[35]

The Democratic primary campaign was set to officially begin only two days before George Stinney's execution. One thing was clear to the governor: he could not risk upending his newly established White supremacy credentials by staying the execution or commuting the sentence of a Black murderer and rapist of a White child.

The relationship between Johnston's political aspirations and Stinney's fate did not escape the notice of two of the women writing on George Stinney's behalf. On June 11, Mary E. Carr wrote to the governor's wife, imploring her to intervene with her husband to save Stinney's life. "People are saying," she wrote, "that the Governor will not change this sentence because of political reason and the fact that he has made "'white supremacy' a big plank in his platform for the Senate." Yet many, like herself, "are hoping that he will do the noble thing in this instance even at the risk of sacrificing an ambition of his own. If he is the big man I have been led to believe, he will certainly take a stand. Then, and then only, can he look his Lord, himself and his own children in the face. Otherwise, he will go down through life as Pilate of old, consoling himself with the thought that he washed his hands of it." Mrs. F. W. Holmes was even more direct in her concern that political ambition rather than justice or mercy was uppermost in the governor's calculations. On June 15, she wrote to Johnson, asking him bluntly "Can it be that you think your election may be furthered by your refusal to extend clemency [sic] to the boy?"[36]

The answer to Holmes's question was yes. Olin Johnston decided that he must wash his hands of a man's fate just as Pilate had once done. If he wanted to defeat Cotton Ed—and he did—he could not act with mercy. George Junius Stinney Jr. had to die in the electric chair.

POSTSCRIPT. Olin DeWitt Talmadge Johnston decisively defeated Ellison DuRant Smith's bid for a seventh term. As for Cotton Ed, he died suddenly in November 1944, a month and a half shy of completing his final term in office. Johnston served in the Senate for the next twenty years until his death in 1965, consistently opposing all civil rights legislation.

Ernest Edmund Feltwell Jr. did not serve his full sentence. He was released sometime before 1957, when he married and established a family.

Chapter 9
"This Case Will Not Die"

On November 3, 2013, the front page of a local South Carolina newspaper, the *Sumter Item,* carried the news: "Lawyers seek retrial of executed teen." Sixty-nine years after George Junius Stinney Jr. met his death in the electric chair, his story was back in the news. In truth, George Stinney had never been entirely forgotten by the press, or by authors, or documentary film makers. In 1985, the distinguished criminal lawyer David I. Bruck had cited Stinney's execution in his *Washington Post* article that called for the end to the death penalty for juveniles. Three years later, David Stout published the novel *Carolina Skeletons*, based on Stinney's trial and execution. In 1991, a television drama based on Stout's book aired. This was soon followed in 1993 by *Billy*, a novel that its author, African American author Albert French, declared had been based on the Stinney case. Then in 1996 Stephen King's blockbuster novel, *The Green Mile*, appeared in bookstores everywhere. By December 1999, it had become a blockbuster film. In that same year, the controversial social critic Christopher Hitchens penned an article in *Vanity Fair* that began with a shocking declaration: "The United States of America executes its own children." The first case Hitchens cited was George Stinney's.[1]

It was not until 2006, sixty-two years after a judge and jury sentenced the fourteen-year-old boy to the electric chair, that an African American in Clarendon County decided to examine the case in earnest. George Frierson was a school board member in Clarendon County who a local newspaper identified vaguely as "an activist." He started collecting newspaper articles, death certificates and other documents relating to the murders of Betty June Binnicker and Mary Emma Thomas and to Stinney's arrest, conviction, and execution. People in Manning remembered seeing Frierson around town carrying a large orange binder full of the evidence he believed pointed to a miscarriage of justice. Years later he would confess to an interviewer, "At times, it has been a bit lonely, my work on this case. At times I have been worried about my safety. But I'm convinced that this young man is innocent, and I can't just sit back and let history record him as guilty."[2]

Fortunately, Frierson was not the only South Carolinian interested in the Stinney case. In 2009, a local lawyer named Steve McKenzie had also begun to do a little research on the execution. But the demands of McKenzie's law practice forced him to put aside all thought of Stinney and his fate. Then, in 2013, after a conversation about courtroom injustice, McKenzie was prompted to share his research with Matt Burgess, a twenty-four-year-old junior member of the firm. According to an account published years later in a March 2018 series on the case, McKenzie handed Burgess the rather flimsy file that had been gathering dust for the past four years. It was an invitation to act that Burgess could not resist. The idealistic Burgess soon began to scour the web for more information on the Stinney case. He apparently found several articles from the 1980s, probably including the Bruck piece, all written as the nation's legal system was grappling with the constitutionality of juvenile execution. He was soon fully convinced there had been a miscarriage of justice that sent Stinney to his death.[3]

Burgess decided to contact members of the Stinney family, including any siblings who might still be alive. He wanted to propose that the case should be reopened. George's surviving sisters and brother were hesitant. Although George's youngest sister Amie, now a great grandmother, had always maintained George's innocence, she had little interest in Burgess's proposal. She said that she had made her peace in the matter a long time ago: "There is a God who sits high and looks low," she had earlier told a reporter, adding "I know that anyone who had anything to do with this will have to come before a just God." But Burgess persisted. In the end, he persuaded the Stinney siblings to let him draft a request in December 2013 for a new trial.[4]

Throughout the months that followed, South Carolina newspapers retold the story of the grisly murders, the arrest of George Stinney, the threats to lynch him, and the brief trial that ended in a conviction after ten minutes. Rather quickly, the new suit filed by Burgess and McKenzie on behalf of the Stinney family survivors captured the attention of national figures. In late December, civil rights leaders from across the country journeyed to Clarendon County to join over one hundred others in a candlelight vigil outside the courthouse where the statue of the Confederate soldier still stood.[5]

Weeks passed before a hearing date was set. In their later series, South Carolina's *Post and Courier* recalled that, from the start, Burgess was afraid a judge might question the legal standing of an appeal to reconsider Stinney's guilt or innocence—and quickly dismiss the case. Worried, he had asked his old law school professor Miller Shealy for advice. Shealy proposed using a six-hundred-year-old English common law device, a writ of *coram nobis*. Known in legal circles as a "Hail Mary Pass," this writ allowed a court to change an original judgment if a fundamental error were unearthed. After suggesting this tactic, Shealy offered to join the Stinney legal team.[6]

Burgess's fears were, in part, justified. When the hearing at last began on January 21, 2014, the presiding judge, Carmen Mullen, made it clear that the issue was not Stinney's guilt or innocence; the question before her, as she saw it, was whether Stinney had received a fair trial. Whether a fair trial had occurred was, of course, the question posed by *coram nobis,* and Mullen suggested that she would be open to its use. "No one here," she declared, "can justify a 14-year-old child being charged, tried and executed in 83 days."[7]

The atmosphere in the court room as the lawyers began to present their case must have been tense. The *Sumter Item* reported that "the ghost of Jim Crow justice" hovered over the proceedings. The irony could not have been lost on the crowded courtroom that the 3rd circuit solicitor who would argue the case for the state of South Carolina was Ernst "Chip" Finney III, the eldest son of the state's first African American supreme court justice.

In his opening address to the court, Finney characterized the original verdict as unfortunate. "Back in 1944," he conceded, "we should have known better, but we didn't. The fact of the matter is it happened, and it occurred because of a legal system that was in place." Sealy, however, saw the verdict differently. It was, he insisted, a miscarriage of justice even by the "old South Carolina standards" of the Jim Crow era. "It was appalling," he told the judge.[8]

McKenzie, Shealy, Burgess and a third colleague from the firm, Ray Chandler represented the Stinneys, all acting pro bono. Despite the judge's warning that Stinney's guilt or innocence was not the issue, they did make an attempt for a new trial based on the merits of the case. They put forward six witnesses at the hearing before Judge Mullen. The

Stinney siblings, Katherine, Amie, and Charles, all of whom had been quite young in 1944 and were now quite old, could not produce a seamless account of what happened on those fateful days in March. Katherine Stinney Robinson, who had been nine or ten years old at the time and was now seventy-nine, was vague about whether she had seen the victims stop to talk to her brother and younger sister. She did recall that when George was taken into custody, she had not been at home; she was at a beauty parlor with her brother Charles. Amie Rufner, the youngest of the Stinney siblings at seventy-seven, had been only eight in 1944. In both an affidavit and in live testimony, she swore that she and George were grazing the family cow when the victims crossed their path but that both of them—and the cow—had returned home together for the rest of the afternoon. George only left the house later, she recalled, when he accompanied his father on the search for the missing girls. She could not say what happened when uniformed men came to the family home because she had hidden in the chicken coop until George was taken away in handcuffs. On cross-examination, Finney had no trouble undercutting the reliability of Amie's testimony. When he questioned her about the contents of a 2009 notarized statement that had made no mention of her brother accompanying her father, Ruffner replied that she could not recall ever signing such a document.[9]

But if Katharine and Amie's memories were faulty, or if some of their recollections were contradictory, there were two things that the Stinney sisters were certain of: neither law enforcement nor Stinney's attorneys ever interviewed them about the day's events and neither woman had been called as a witness in the 1944 trial.

Bishop Charles Stinney, too ill and frail to appear in the courtroom, sent a sworn affidavit and a video deposition that was played at the hearing. He recalled law enforcement searching the family home (presumably for bloodied clothing) and that his sister Katharine was not at home at the time. Otherwise, his testimony did not provide a coherent narrative of events.

Perhaps Stinney's lawyers' most compelling witness of events was Wilford "Johnny" Hunter, who was in jail at the same time as George. In his sworn affidavit, Hunter provided an impression of Stinney as small and frail and recounted a conversation the two had while incarcerated. According to Hunter, when he asked Stinney why he was in jail, George replied that he was accused of killing two White girls and "they were going to electrocute him . . . and that he didn't kill the girls and that they made him say those things."

McKenzie's team also called two expert witnesses in an effort to challenge the likelihood that Stinney had committed the murders. The forensic pathologist, Dr. Peter J. Stephens, dismissed the autopsy report filed by Dr. Bozard as inadequate even by 1944 standards. Stephens challenged the police assertion that George had used a railroad spike to kill Betty June and Mary Emma; because of the badly executed autopsies, it was simply impossible to determine what the murder weapon was. The forensic psychiatrist, Dr. Amanda Salas, who had written about the case in her thesis in 2010, offered expert testimony on the reliability of Stinney's confession. Dr. Salas argued that, without an adult present during the alleged confession, a fourteen-year-old would be highly suggestible to pressure from the law enforcement agents to give a false confession. This was, she suggested, even more likely in the case of an African American boy, arrested by White men in the segregated world of South Carolina in 1944.[10]

By the second day of the hearing, McKenzie and his team recognized that Mullen was unlikely to grant a retrial or to declare the conviction wrong on the merits of the case. They might argue that George Stinney could not have committed the murders, citing Amie's testimony that he was at home with her until evening. They might have argued that a small and frail ninety-five-pound boy did not possess the strength to remove the front bicycle wheel. Or, they might have argued that no bloody clothes belonging to Stinney had been recovered or at least presented as evidence at the trial. But the truth was that all the evidence that could prove Stinney's innocence or guilt—the murder weapon, any bloody clothes, George's confession—had disappeared. No transcript was ever made of the trial and there was no record of any appeal since George's attorneys had never filed one. The Stinney family had not been firsthand witnesses to the trial because they had been forbidden to attend. In fact, no one who had been in the courtroom that day was known to be alive. All that remained was a small collection of documents relating to the defendant's arrest, indictment and trial, including the handwritten notes of Deputy H. S. Newman, a handwritten order issued after the coroner's inquest was completed, the arrest warrant for Stinney, his indictment for the murder of Betty June, and a typewritten medical report signed by Dr. Bozard.[11]

Bowing to reality, Stinney's counsel withdrew its request for a new trial and asked to proceed instead on the writ of coram nobis. The argument thus shifted to the *process* by which George Stinney had been tried, convicted, and executed. This allowed them to use their witness's testimony more effectively. Why hadn't the Stinney children been interviewed? Why were they not called to testify at the trial? They also raised questions about the defense provided to Stinney in 1944. Why was there no lawyer present when George's alleged confession was obtained? Why had George's court appointed defense team failed to point out the autopsy's possible inconsistencies? Why had they failed to cross-examine any of the prosecution's witnesses? Why had they failed to ask for a change of venue, especially after a threat of lynching had been made? Why had they failed to appeal the conviction? McKenzie's team also raised key questions about due process in the trial itself. Why did George Stinney face an all-White jury in a county with a large African American population? Why was a trial for the murder of two people begun and concluded in one afternoon? With all these questions swirling about, Miller Shealy felt justified in declaring that "the dirty hands of the state" was now the issue in 2014.[12]

The hearing lasted only two days, but it would take almost a year before Judge Mullen issued her ruling. During that time, the case remained alive in the press. It was the subject of a *New York Times* editorial and even *People Magazine* carried an article about Stinney and his execution. By summer, the Stinney family was expressing their doubts that Mullen would rule in their favor. As McKenzie told a reporter from *The Item* on August 24, the family believed "South Carolina will just sweep this under the rug again."[13]

They were wrong. On December 17, 2014, Mullen's clerk forwarded the judge's decision to the Clarendon County Clerk of Court, with a brief cover letter asking that the filing be expedited. "This court," wrote Judge Carmen Mullen, "finds fundamental, Constitutional violations of due process exist in the 1944 prosecution of George Stinney Jr and hereby vacates the judgment." In her twenty-eight-page decision, Mullen reviewed a litany of violations in the case that followed closely the arguments presented by McKenzie, Shealy, and Chandler; among them, admitting a coerced confession as evidence, an action contrary to Fourteenth Amendment guarantees; failure to provide effective assistance of counsel at all critical stages in a criminal prosecution; failure by counsel to request a change of venue despite pretrial publicity and juror prejudice; failure of the defense counsel to cross examine witnesses or file an appeal; and improper jury composition. On the final page of her ruling, Mullen reminded the public that "a violation of the Defendant's procedural due process rights tainted his prosecution." For that reason, she continued, the court hereby was granting relief in the form of a writ of *coram nobis*, "not on the grounds that the judgment against him was wrong on the merits, but that the courts have failed in a capital case to discharge their proper functions with due regard to the constitutional safeguards in the administration of justice."[14]

In the end, it was less a vindication of George Junius Stinney Jr. than a condemnation of a judicial system and the men who supported it in the land of Jim Crow.

Ave Atque Vale

Eli Faber left behind a postscript to his
manuscript. Its title "Ave Atque Vale" is
borrowed from Catullus. The dictionary
translation is "Farewell and goodbye," or
in modern parlance, "I salute you . . . and
goodbye."

This postscript ponders how the tragic
story of George Junius Stinney Jr. came to be.

There were far too many uncertainties in the prosecution of George Junius Stinney Jr. for him to have been found guilty beyond a reasonable doubt of the murder of Betty June Binnicker. How, then, was it possible, even in the midst of a Jim Crow regime, and even in an era that predated the legal revolution of the 1960s reserving the rights of accused children and adolescents, for a tragedy such as his to have occurred in the middle of the twentieth century in the United States of America?

There can be no question that White racism and the accompanying features of the doctrine of White supremacy, particularly beliefs about Black males' predatory sexuality, were at the core of the matter. But two other factors contributed as well. First, the political ambitions and calculating careerism of several of the leading figures in this story played their part, from the arresting officers to the defense attorneys appointed by the court, and to the governor of the state. Second, the failure of African American leaders to intervene on behalf of Stinney contributed to his terrible death. An appeal on constitutional grounds to the Supreme Court of the State of South Carolina and from there, if necessary, to the United States Supreme Court, as the NAACP had successfully accomplished in previous cases, might have saved his life.

Because of the rapidity with which the officers of the law embraced the idea that it was Stinney who was responsible for the murders of the two girls, they looked no further for other possible perpetrators. They obtained a confession under highly dubious circumstances and decided they had solved the case. Subsequently during Stinney's trial, his court-appointed defense attorneys did not cross-examine these law officers, instead doing nothing to undermine their credibility.

If in fact it was not George Stinney who committed the murders, then the injustice he suffered extended to Betty June Binnicker and Mary Emma Thames, whose murderer simply walked away, disappearing silently down the railroad tracks of Alcolu.

One hopes and prays that all three are at peace in their eternal resting place.

POSTSCRIPT. "Ave Atque Vale" is often used, the dictionary tells us, in a eulogy for a hero. Those of us who knew Eli Faber, an historian who labored right up until his death to complete his book on "the boy in the electric chair," believe it is an appropriate eulogy for him.

Abbreviations

Census 1940: United States Census for 1940: South Carolina
DIBC: David I. Bruck Collection, University of South Carolina, South Caroliniana Library, Manuscript Division
Reports: Reports and Resolutions of the General Assembly of the State of South Carolina
Stinney Papers: L 14095, Box 9, Clarendon County, Court of General Sessions, Indictments, Roll 1853, South Carolina Department of Archives and History
2014 Hearing: Author's notes of the 2014 hearing to review George Stinney's case

Notes

Chapter 1

1. *New York Times,* June 17, 1944, 1, 8.

2. Mack Thompson, convicted of assault with intent to rape, was sentenced to death, but Governor Robert A. Cooper commuted the sentence to life imprisonment. Cooper explained that he commuted Thompson's sentence to life in prison because of his mental condition: "a low grade moron, and therefore not fully responsible for his criminal act"; *Statement of Pardons, Paroles and Commutations Granted by Robert A. Cooper Governor of South Carolina 1920* (Columbia: Gonzales and Bryan, 1921), 27. I am grateful to Barry Latzer for the latter reference. In the second instance, Clarence Lowman was sentenced to death for murder in 1925; he was not executed but was lynched in 1926. The the prison records failed to record what happened to him. For both cases, see *The State,* June 10, 1944, 9.

3. Various other accounts place the age of Mary Emma Thames, the younger of the two children, at eight: *Columbia Record,* March 27, 1944, 3; Robert Lewis Alderman, *Sad Days in the Little Village,* March 4, 2004. However, the census of 1940 recorded that she was three at the time, as her parents would have reported, making her seven in 1944; Census 1940, E.D. 14-22, 5A. Further confirmation is provided by her gravestone, which records the dates of her life as March 14, 1937–March 24, 1944; https://www.findagrave.com/memorial/43346907/mary -emma-thames. Accessed July 2, 2019.

4. DIBC, Gamble interview, 1–2. According to Gamble's account, the county sheriff who took George to the penitentiary had not only provided the Bible but also given the boy a candy bar. Documentation for the remainder of the information provided in this paragraph is in several of the subsequent chapters here.

5. "Annual Report of the Board of Directors and Superintendents of the South Carolina Correctional Institutions for the Year Beginning July 1, 1943 and Ending June 30, 1944," 32, in *Reports and Resolutions of the General Assembly of the State of South Carolina,* 1945. *The State,* June 10, 1944, 9. For Stinney's stature: South Carolina Department of Archives and History, Department of Corrections, Record of Executed Prisoners, 1939–1962, File 260.

6. Documentation for the information in this paragraph is in several of the subsequent chapters below.

7. *Columbia Record,* June 13, 1944, 1.

8. *News and Courier,* June 16, 1944, 1; *Greenville News,* June 16, 1944, 16; *Manning Times,* June 21, 1944, 1.

9. *Manning Times,* June 21, 1944, 1; *Sumter Herald,* June 22, 1944, 1. For Gamble's full recollection, see Gamble interview, 3.

10. *Sumter Herald,* June 22, 1944, 1.

11. Ibid.; and *Sumter Daily Item,* June 16, 1944, 1.

12. Gamble Interview, 3.

13. As documented by vintage film footage in "Our Brother's Keeper: CCI," 1993, video, State Library, Columbia. (CCI is the abbreviation for Central Correctional Institution.) DIBC, Interview with Roston Stukes, March 23, 1983, 2: "And when they took him out of there, they carried him back and put him on a table. And it locks your bones. . . . He was just in a sitting position when they took him out." Stukes was an eyewitness at the execution. For an earlier South Carolina eyewitness account of the corpse's rigidity in a sitting position, see Earl D. Paulk, *Execution of Six Men as Witnessed by the Author,* Fifth ed. (n.p.: n.p., 1952), 25.; "George Stinney, Youngest Executed," radio interview June 30, 2004, retrieved December 11, 2011, at http://soundportraits.org/on-air/youngest _executed/. Court Hearing 2014: testimony of Aime Ruffner.

14. *The State,* June 17, 1994, B7.

15. All of these individuals were White. The two men, Robert Lewis Alderman and George Jones, who the author had the privilege to interview several times, were especially important as deeply knowledgeable informants about life in the lumber-mill village where the murders occurred. The story told by the dying woman was relayed to the author by the pastor who conducted her funeral when he heard it from her relatives. Whether it was accurate or was an imagined occurrence is beside the point that powerful memories lived on, underscoring the fact that the Stinney case remained a major event in the lives of those who lived in the village where the murders occurred.

Chapter 2

1. Alcolu was chartered by the state legislature on December 22, 1891, for thirty years, but the charter was never renewed. Hence, the census and the South Carolina state tax commission did not classify it as an incorporated entity; South Carolina State Planning Board, *Towns of South Carolina,* Pamphlet No. 8 (n.p.: Columbia, 1942), 13. In 1940, the village had 191 households; the surrounding areas of Plowden Mill Township had 198 households. Most of the residents there were engaged in farming while Alcolu's economic life centered on its sole industry: milling. All demographic data are from Census 1940. Another ten households, all belonging to a carnival, resided within the village in tents on the day of the census. Not actually part of the village or its economic life, they are excluded from all information here about the residents of Alcolu and Plowden Mill Township. All data for Alcolu and Plowden Mill Township are in South Carolina's Enumeration District 14–22. The names of individuals who are cited are followed in parentheses by the page number in E.D. 14–22; e.g., John M. Hudson (3B).

2. The year 1935, for example, was a particularly bad one for fires in Alcolu. Late in January, the church where the White population worshiped burned to

the ground, and eight other buildings also caught fire but were saved from destruction. The church was subsequently rebuilt in an exact replica but with additional classrooms. In late May or early June, a fire in the lumber mill threatened to destroy the entire complex, but the mill's sprinkling system successfully doused it. Both fires were reported by the *Manning Times,* June 5, 8, and 19, 1935, 1. The line through the village belonged to the Atlantic Coast Line.

3. Richard Alderman, "A Little Village, a Special Time, a Wonderful People . . . Remembered. . . ." Alderman read this aloud at the Alcolu reunions in August 2006 and August 2008.

4. Mary Ellen Taylor Bilton, interview.

5. Robert Lewis Alderman, interview; John Dollard in *Caste and Class in a Southern Town* (New Haven: Yale University Press, 1937), 8, described "Southerntown," the Deep-South community he studied in the mid-1930s as "a 'good town for Negroes,'" while "Sturdevant, ten miles away, is known as a 'bad town'; race contacts there are shot through with a tenser feeling, and there have been more incidents." Charles Stinney, interview.

6. *Northwestern Lumberman,* July 19, 1890, 42; Robert Lewis Alderman, *A Little History of the Village of Alcolu, South Carolina and the Story of its Founders Mr. and Mrs. David Wells Alderman,* 2nd ed. (n.p.: n.d., 2004), 13–14; Walter Edgar, ed., *The South Carolina Encyclopedia* (Columbia: University of South Carolina Press, 2006), 963–64; *South Carolina in 1884. A View of the Industrial Life of the State. A Brilliant Showing, 1880–84* (Charleston: The News and Courier, [1884]), [1].

7. For the development of the lumber industry in the South during the late-nineteenth century, see Edward L. Ayres, *The Promise of the New South: Life After Reconstruction* (New York and Oxford: Oxford University Press, 1992), 123–31. Gunnar Myrdal, *An American Dilemma: The Negro Problem and Modern Democracy* (New York and London: Harper & Brothers Publishers, 1944), 1090–96, presents a description and analysis of the industry as it existed in the South contemporaneously with the Stinney case. For the New South Movement in general, in addition to Ayers, see C. Vann Woodward, *Origins of the New South, 1877–1913:* N.p.: Louisiana State University Press, 1951. For a thorough exploration of the role played by southerners and southern capital in the development of the cotton mill industry, see Broadus Mitchell, *The Rise of Cotton Mills in the South* [Baltimore, 1921].

8. *South Carolina in 1884,* in the sections devoted to Clarendon County and Marion County (no pagination). Information about the county seal was provided by the archivist of the Clarendon County Archives and History Center, June 17, 2014. The original seal contained the words "Lumber and Agriculture" in its upper-left quadrant. The current seal has the words "Forestry and Agriculture," a change made at a date not known to the archivist. Clarendon's swamps were where Revolutionary War hero Francis Marion hid out and harried the British in guerilla-like fashion, earning his nickname "the Swamp Fox." One of his victories occurred in Tearcoat Swamp, only a few miles from the future Alcolu. On the engagement at Tearcoat Swamp, see Mark Mayo Boatner, III,

Encyclopedia of the American Revolution (New York: David McKay Company, 1966), 1092, and for Marion, 675–79. For the location of Tearcoat Swamp and its proximity to the Pocotaligo and Black rivers, see the map in Hugh F. Rankin, *Francis Marion: The Swamp Fox* (New York: Thomas Y. Crowell Company, 1973), 62–63.

9. Six years later, a national lumber industry publication reported that a group of investors had purchased sixteen thousand acres of swampland along the Santee River in Clarendon County, a site located "in the very heart of this richly timbered region," where they would harvest the cypress trees that grew there in order to manufacture shingles. A generation later, one of the lumber industry's leading trade publications could still single out the cypress stands along the Black River as "one of the richest cypress sections in South Carolina," adding that "experts who have seen this timber make the unqualified statement that it cannot be excelled." And as late as 1937, a pamphlet published by the county's newspaper extolling Clarendon's strengths would assert that the county had "thousands of acres of virgin fertile woodland. . . . Over 60 percent of our total area is in woodland. It is admitted that timber grows faster in this area than anywhere else in our country." See *South Carolina in 1884*, in the section devoted to Clarendon County (no pagination). For the timber industry's reliance on African American labor, see the editorial in the *Columbia Record*, July 5, 1943, 4; see also Myrdal, *American Dilemma*, 1090ff; and William P. Jones, *Black Ulysses: African American Lumber Workers in the Jim Crow South* (Urbana: University of Illinois Press, 2005), passim.

10. [Jesse Samuels Plowden], *History of Descendants of Plowden I in America* (n.p.; n.p., 1937), 4–5, 17. In the late 1700s or early 1800s, Edward Plowden built a grist and flour mill in a fork between two branches of the Black River, where he owned several thousand acres. He subsequently relocated and constructed another mill nearby. Eventually, another member of the family, apparently a nephew, Hampton Plowden, constructed yet another mill, and it is this one, bearing the name Plowden's Mill, that gave its name to "the upper township in the fork of Black River." In every case, Plowden mills were associated with the Black River. For the location of Plowden Mills in 1856, see the map in Sylvia H. Clark, *Shadows of the Past: An Illustrated History of Clarendon County, SC* (Virginia Beach, VA: The Donning Company Publishers, 2005), 9; a form of legal recognition dated to 1888, the year that Alderman obtained a US Post Office designation for it. Alderman, *Little History*, 19–20.

11. Tom Johnson, *Fragments of Fallen Flags: Railroads of Clarendon County, S. C. 1886–1940* (n.p.: n.p., 2003), [3–30], for a highly detailed description of the railroad and its track route, as well as its general history. See also Thomas Fetters, *Logging Railroads of South Carolina* (Forest Park, IL: Heimburger House Publishing Company, 1990), 97–103.

12. A rendering of the village dated February 24, 1902, shows that its industrial section contained a saw mill, a planing mill, a shingle mill, boilers for power, storage areas, a "log way," several Alcolu Railroad sidings, shops to service the railroad, and an area where lumber was stacked. The residential section, along

two thoroughfares that later became Highway 521 and Hotel Street, was separated from the mill complex by the depot and the tracks of the Atlantic Coast Line railroad. Four structures related to the mill stood on the other side of the tracks adjacent to the residential area: two warehouses; the company store; and the company office. Approximately thirty houses are indicated in the residential section. Clarendon County Archives, Jeffrey Black Collection, Plat of Alcolu, with the notation, "A. C. L. R. Co. of S. C. Local Report of Freight Received Feb. 24th 1902." The chapel's existence is known from Gresham, *Clarendon County Directory, 1900*, 10. (The first asterisked item in this chapter provides the full citation to this source.)

13. Johnson, *Fragments of Fallen Flags, 10*. According to a key informant, the company still owned 100,000 acres when it went out of existence in 1947; George Jones, interview. Johnson, 3, 25, 27. Alderman, *Little History*, 53–54.

14. Howard Hanlon, *The Bull Hunchers: A Saga of of the Three and a Half Centuries of Harvesting the Forest Crops of the Tidewater Low Country* (Parsons, WVA: McClain Printing Company, 1970), 258; Myrdal, *American Dilemma*, 1091; *Year Book of the Department of Agriculture Commerce and Industries of the State of South Carolina 1928*, in *Reports*, 1929: 1, 89–90; Hanlon, *Bull Hunchers*, 266; *Manning Times*, March 4, 1931, 1; Fetters, *Logging Railroads*, 103.

15. This composite portrait of Alcolu in the 1940s is based upon the interviews conducted with past as well as present residents of the village. Two households, Richard L. Durant's and Paul A. Fann's, resided under one roof. Hence the final number of house totals is 190, not 191; the latter was the number of households. The five larger homes belonged to Paul R. Alderman (valued at $20,000); Paul R. Alderman Jr. (valued at $7,000); Malvina E. Alderman (valued at $15,000); Lewis M. Jones, manager of the company store (valued at $10,000); and Homer K. Brinson (valued at $500), whose occupation is not known. Census 1940 (3B; 3B4A: 4A; and 10B).

The account of how African American children received Christmas gifts was provided by Katherine Stinney Robinson; Robinson interview, and Hearing 1914. Francis Batson, "Tell Us a Story, Please," 6–7, dates construction of the store and auditorium to 1914.

16. Hardy Green, *The Company Town: The Industrial Edens and Satanic Mills that Shaped the American Economy* (New York: Basic Books, 2010), 57. https// en.wikipedia.org/wiki/Tabitha_Babbitt, accessed on September 5, 2019. George Jones interviews. Jones insisted on several occasions that a great deal of myth and misinformation surround the history of babbitt in Alcolu, particularly the nearly universal belief that the company paid its employees their wages in babbitt. Jones's corrective is reliable in view of the fact that his father, Louis M. Jones Sr. and his elder brother, Louis M. Jones Jr. served as company-store manager and assistant manager, respectively; he thus had first-hand knowledge of the function of babbitt in the village. Babbitt was issued not only in company towns but also by the owners of regular stores. For images of this alternative currency issued by individual stores elsewhere in Clarendon County, see Clark, *Shadows of the Past*, 85. In addition to the monopolistic nature that company currency

bestowed upon the company store, yet another abusive practice existed, as Congressman John Luecke of Michigan informed Congress in the late 1930s: company scrip was discounted for cash at company stores, with discounts against the scrip ranging from 5 to 25 percent; Stetson Kennedy, *Southern Exposure* (Doubleday & Co.: Garden City, NY, 1946), 49–50.

17. This and subsequent paragraphs describing the population of Alcolu are based on a close reading of Census 1940; Paul Norgren, "Negro Labor and Its Problems: A Research Memorandum Prepared Under the Direction of Paul H. Norgren" (New York: n.p., 1940) noted (in chapter 2: 28) that the annual labor turnover in the sawmill industry throughout the United States far exceeded the levels in all other industries. In 1934, the turnover figure for all industries was 49.2 percent, while in the sawmill industry it reached 87.8 percent. In the South, Norgren reported (chapter 2: 9–9a), sawmill labor was interchangeable with agricultural labor, with Black farmers flowing in and out of the lumber industry.

18. Green, *Company Town*, 4–5. In addition to the economic exploitation of workers in many mill towns, including child labor and industrial accidents that maimed and killed workers, a host of such social problems as deadly violence, juvenile delinquency, alcoholism, prostitution, cockfighting, gambling, and pool halls reportedly accompanied life in many of them; Bryant Simon, *A Fabric of Defeat: The Politics of South Carolina Millhands, 1910–1948* (University of North Carolina Press: Chapel Hill and London, 1998), 19, 49. For details describing the social problems in an Alabama cotton-mill town, see the memoir by a journalist who spent part of his youth there: Rick Bragg, *The Prince of Frogtown* (New York: Alfred A. Knopf, 2008), 24, 29, 40, 49–52, 54–55, 61, 71, 98, 128–29, 177. Green, op. cit., also describes the social issues that characterized life in many company towns, at 58, 120–21, 142, 166–67. A far more positive view of life in a mill town is to be found in Jacquelyn Dowd Hall et al., *Like a Family: The Making of a Southern Cotton Mill World* (Chapel Hill and London: University of North Carolina Press, 1987).

19. For operating the mill's saw, Thames earned $845 in 1939, which gave him an income less than the average of all of the company's White employees, which stood at $948. Mary Emma Thames's father, in other words, appears to have been utterly average in his standing among Whites in the Alcolu community, both in terms of his education and his earning capacity.

20. According to Binnicker's eldest daughter, Vermelle Tucker, the family arrived during 1940; DIBC, Interview with Vermelle Tucker, March 23, 1983, 1. She identified his job as "a logging foreman"; DIBC, Tucker, interview, 1. Herbert Brown, on the other hand, described him as a night watchman; Herbert Brown, interview.

21. In the 1940 census, 24 Black male heads of households ranged in education from none through third grade; 67 had completed fourth grade; 19 had gone on through grades five through seven; and 1 had completed one year of high school (Census 1940, South Carolina, E. D. 43-3 (6B). In 2006, George Jr.'s brother, Charles Stinney identified his father as a farmer; Charles Stinney interview. Aime Ruffner, the younger of his two sisters, described him in January

2014 more precisely as a sharecropper; 2014 Hearing. The 1940 census record described him as working for the entire year as a laborer in a sawmill.

22. Myrdal, *American Dilemma*, 208, 283.

23. *Northwestern Lumberman*, April 5, 1890, 2.

24. Katherine Robinson interview. Alderman, *Little History*, 82, describes the company's cranes as "one industrial ton locomotive crane" and "one Ohio 25 ton industrial locomotive crane."

25. *Twenty-fifth Annual report of the Railroad Commissioners for the State of South Carolina, 1903* (The State Company, State Printers, Columbia [1904]), 838.

26. A two-track society organized along lines of both class and caste is the thesis throughout Dollard's *Caste and Class in a Southern Town*.

27. Location of the Stinney home: Katherine Robinson interview and Amie Ruffner testimony: 2014 Hearing.

28. Herbert Brown interview. Alderman, *Little History of the Village of Alcolu*, 82, reports on the basis of inventories taken at the time the Alderman company dissolved itself in 1947, that there were fifty White homes with three to seven rooms and 120 African American homes with two to seven rooms. Robinson interview.

29. The "shanties" were recalled in 1983 by Roston Stukes: DIBC, interview with Roston Stukes, March 23, 1983, 3.

30. In 1940, the Manning high school for White children went through the 11th grade; the Training institute ended in the tenth grade. South Carolina did not create a twelfth grade for White students until 1947. See, Clark, *Shadows of the Past*, 173, 175.

31. *Briggs v. Elliott*, 342 U.S. 350 (1952), consolidated with *Brown v. Board of Education of Topeka*, 347 U.S., 483 (1954).

32. Robert Lewis Alderman interview, explaining why William L. Hamilton, the principal of the African American school in Alcolu, was called "Professor."

33. Although salaries improved in the 1940s, the differential between White and Black incomes was maintained. In 1944, the average White male employee in Alcolu earned $1,765, the average Black male employee, $979; in 1945, the average White male earned $2,000, the average Black male, $1,199; and in 1946, the average White male received $2,200, the average Black male $1,315. These averages are derived from the annual reports the company made to the State of South Carolina Department of Labor," as per n. 44, supra.

34. The information about sports in this paragraph is based upon a composite of interviews conducted with present and former residents of Alcolu. For Jimmy Carter's remembrances, see Jimmy Carter, *An Hour Before Daylight: Memories of a Rural Boyhood* (New York: Simona & Schuster, 2001), 229–30. See also James R. McGovern, *Anatomy of a Lynching: The Killing of Claude Neal* (Louisiana State University Press: Baton Rouge, 1982), 46, where the author describes how Claude Neal and Lola Cannidy, the former brutally lynched and mutilated for allegedly raping and murdering the latter in Jackson County, Florida, in 1934, "had played together as children. . . . It was not uncommon in the South for Black and White children to play together. . . . Association between boys and

girls of the two races terminated when they reached puberty. . . ." Johnson, *Growing Up in the Black Belt*, 319–20, reported that between the ages of ten and fifteen, African American children tended to cease all contact with Whites; playing with White children "begins to become taboo for Negro children at about the age of 10."

35. In 1944, the average White female working for the company earned $750 while the average Black female earned $875. See the annual reports the company made to the South Carolina Department of Labor. On medical treatment: checkbook stubs discovered in 2014 in an abandoned storage structure provided the names of employees treated by physicians at the company expense. African American patients treated in 1944 included Paul Smith and B. O. Thames, Mack Hannah; Roy Cantry; and Moss Wright (check stubs 8610, 8611, 8648, and 8649). For the description of "Southerntown," see Dollard, *Caste and Class*, 2–3; Roy Wilkins, "Politeness and Rebellion in S.C.," *New York Amsterdam News*, July 1, 1944, 11A. For Wilkins's trip to South Carolina during the week preceding the execution, see the discussion in chapter 7.

36. Robert Lewis Alderman interview; Alderman, *Little History*, 74, 78–79; Francis M. Batson, "Tell Us A Story, Please," 66.

37. DIBC, interview with Lee Burke, March 23, 1983.

38. Robert Lewis Alderman interview, in which he cited as his source William L. Hamilton, principal of the African American School in Alcolu.

39. The information in this paragraph is a composite of interviews with present and former residents of Alcolu.

40. George Jones, interview; DIBC, Stukes, interview, 2–3.

41. Mary Ellen [Taylor] Bilton's experience offers a good example of the help a resident of Alcolu could rely upon if injured in an accident. She was struck by a car outside her family's house on Highway 521 in 1936 at the age of five and taken to Baptist Hospital in Columbia, where the company carried an insurance policy. The surgery to save her leg could not be performed there, and she was moved to another hospital in Columbia where it could be done. The insurance policy covered all the costs. During her recuperation in Alcolu, to which she returned in a semi-body cast, she was required to travel to Columbia every two weeks to be seen by her doctor; an African American employee who worked in the company office drove her there in a car owned by the Aldermans. Mary Ellen [Taylor] Bilton, interview; for help when a child lost a parent, Jewel Brown, interview; for the provision of churches and schools, see Clifton Hodge, interview; in addition, information on physicians, and their office hours, George Jones, interview. Reunion comments, Mary Ellen Bilton, interview; and Tyler Wyman, statement to author. For details of what occurred in the Clarendon County jailhouse after Stinney was arrested, see chapter 3.

42. For the freedom of play that children had contemporaneous with life in Alcolu, see Howard Chudacoff, *Children at Play: An American History* (New York and London: New York University Press, 2007), 126–53; the chapter's title, "The Golden Age of Unstructured Play, 1900–1950," conveys the theme. For the latitude children had to roam about unsupervised in the early 1940s in an Ohio

town, see Kenneth L. Woodward's reflections upon the opposite experiences of children in the early twenty-first century: "Several times before the age of eight, my best pal and I packed a bag with sandwiches, a cache of our favorite toy soldiers and stuffed animals we slept with, and set out 'to run away from home.' We weren't trying to escape; we just wanted to explore what lay beyond the neighborhood, convinced that wherever we went the world would wear a friendly face. Our parents never knew because we always returned in time for dinner. When I tell these stories to my grandchildren they are incredulous. That's because the America they inhabit is a far more dangerous and fearful place." Woodward also observes that, in the America of 2016, "even in upscale neighborhoods, fearful parents keep kids on a short tether because drugs and danger can be found in every community. It is rare to see kids roaming unattended or squads of bicycling preteens freewheeling down suburban streets." Kenneth L. Woodward, *Getting Religion: Faith, Culture, and Politics from the Age of Eisenhower to the Era of Obama* (Convergent: New York, 2016), 18–19, 406.

43. Census 1940: Paul O. Batson, minister (10B), salary in 1939, $2,700; Francis S. Roberts, saw filer (5B), salary $2,821; and Thomas H. Jenkins, bookkeeper (3B), salary $2,300.

44. Francis Batson telephone interview. For his written account of his run-in with Stinney, see "Tell Us A Story Please," 56.

45. Robert Lewis Alderman, interview; Alderman, *Little History,* 81–83.

Chapter 3

1. I am indebted to Ms. Gail Kotler for tracking down local weather conditions on March 24, 1944, in the newspaper archives at the South Carolina State Library, Columbia. In 1983, Betty June Binnicker's older sister recalled the day was a warm and sunny one; DIBC, interview with Vermelle Tucker, March 23, 1983 [1].

2. DIBC, interview with Vermelle Tucker, March 3, 1983 [1, 5]. Her age is derived from the 1940 census, when the family still resided in Orangeburg County; Census 1940, E.D. 38–32, 5; Joanne Poe interview. Passiflora incarnata is known not only as maypop but also as purple passion flower, among other names. It is the state flower of Tennessee. According to another account, they sought honeysuckers—the latter a variant of honeysuckle. Joanne Poe, interview; Joanne Poe and Mary Ellen Bilton, interviews; and Robert Lewis Alderman, interview, citing Amelia Burke Alderman. Whether these invitations actually occurred or are the products of retrospective imagination is a matter for speculation, an exercise in social psychology.

3. Hearing 2014: testimony of Katherine Stinney Robinson and Aime Ruffner. Ages in 1944
derived from Census 1940, E.D. 43–3, 6B.

4. Hearing, 2014.

5. Ibid, including Charles Stinney's videotaped deposition explaining why he and his mother had been absent from their home and confirming that they had attended a party that evening.

6. Alderman, *Sad Days in the Little Village,* 1; Hearing 2014: testimony of
Aime Ruffner and Charles Stinney for the participation by George Stinney Sr.
and George Stinney Jr. in the search; DIBC, Tucker, interview, [1–2], Joanne Poe,
interview; Lions and Masons: Mary Ellen Bilton, interview; *Manning Times,*
March 29, 1944, 1; *Sumter Herald,* March 30, 1944, 1. For the participation of
African Americans in the search: *The State,* March 26, 1944, 1; and DIBC, interview with Lee Burke, March 23, 1983, 3, in which Burke recollected that "Some
of them was out there, the colored people, the old colored people and the young
ones was out there helping look for [the girls]." (The bracketed words are in the
interview transcript.) Notification of Newman and his arrival at Alcolu: Huger
Newman statement in Stinney Papers; Richard Alderman, "A Little Village, a
Special Time a Wonderful People. . . Remembered. . .", [2]. Alderman's reminis-
cence was part of the remarks he delivered at the reunions of present and former
Alcolu residents in August 2006 and August 2008.

7. The log pond, measuring 118 feet by 407 feet, was 7 feet deep; Robert Lewis
Alderman, *A Little History of the Village of Alcolu, South Carolina,* 2nd ed. (n.p.:
n.p., 2004), 81.

8. Francis M. Batson, *Tell Us a Story Please,* 56. Batson did not mention the
brush that had been piled on top of the corpses, but this detail—important because of the deliberateness of the murderer that it implied—figured in other
descriptions of the murder scene, as did the water in the ditch, which he also
omitted in his account. For another description that includes those details, see
DIBC, Burke interview, 1. According to the account of Stinney's trial provided
by the *Manning Times,* April 26, 1944, 1, it was Scott Lowder who discovered the
bodies.

9. DIBC, Burke interview, 1; Stinney Papers: Huger Newman's account; For
the source of this Alderman quotation, see the asterisked item at the beginning
of this chapter. Alderman also repeated this sentiment to the author during several interviews. Another informant, on the other hand, thought that life quickly
picked up and returned to normal in the aftermath of the murders. George
Jones, interview.

10. For discussion of the problems Gamble encountered during his run for
office, see chapter 6, infra, at n. 36; [1]DIBC, interview with S. J. Pratt, March 26,
1983.

11. The entire account of what transpired in the Manning jail and later at
the scene of the crimes presented below is based upon this interview, passim. It
should be noted that Deputy Sheriff Huger Newman's account in Stinney Papers,
which has the virtue of having been written shortly after the events of March
24–25, 1944, was much sparser and it gave no credit to Pratt's role. Newman
wrote that, after he viewed the bodies and the bicycle at the location of the murders, "from information I received I arrested a boy by the name of George Stiney
[*sic*], he then made a confession and told me where a piece of iron about 15
inches long were, he said he put it in a ditch about 6 feet from the bicycle wheel
which was lying in the ditch the piece of iron were found in water where he said
it were at."

In 2003, twenty years after Pratt revealed what he knew about George Stinney Jr. Robert Louis Alderman interviewed John Doe during the course of research for the book he was writing about Alcolu's history. Alderman asserts he had no interest in or intention to discuss or to ask questions about the Stinney case. However, shortly after their conversation began, John Doe, without warning, suddenly raised Stinney's name and began to speak insistently and with great emotion about the case. As Doe recounted the events of March 24–25, 1944, Alderman sensed he had a compelling desire to discuss the case, and therefore let him continue with his recollections. During the course of his discourse, Doe stated forcefully and with great conviction that George Stinney Jr. was "the meanest boy I have ever known." These words closely approximate those that Pratt attributed to Doe when he arrived in the village to join Deputy Sheriff Newman's investigation, thereby effectively establishing Doe's identity. Robert Louis Alderman interviews, 2006, 2008, and 2013.

Alderman could not have been influenced by Pratt's 1983 interview; he did not know of it until the author informed him of it in December 2013, ten years after Alderman's conversation with John Doe. Revealing Doe's identity even now could cause harmful and damaging consequences to relatives who are still alive. The possibility of such consequences argues for maintaining the same discretion about his identity that Constable Pratt invoked during his interview in 1983. John Doe is deceased.

12. Ibid.

13. For the contradictory accounts about the murder weapon, see the discussion in chapter 6.

14. Saul M. Kassin, Steven A. Drizin, Thomas Grisso, Gisli H. Gudjonsson, Richard A. Leo, and Allison D. Redlich, "Police -Induced Confessions: Risk Factors and Recommendations," *Law and Human Behavior*, 39, no. 1 (2010): 3–38.

15. DIBC, Stukes, interview, March 23, 1983, 1.

16. DIBC, Pratt, interview, 2. Deputy Sheriff Newman's handwritten account in Stinney Papers is unfortunately incomplete. It does not include the alleged confession to rape or any other form of sexual assault. At the bottom of the yellow legal-sized paper on which Newman wrote his account, the word "over" appears, but nothing is written on the reverse, and there is no second page.

17. For elaboration and documentation of the myth and the horrors it justified, see the discussion in chapter 4.; South Carolina State Archives, Olin Johnston Papers, S544003, Pardons, Paroles and Commutations, 1943–1945, Mrs. Winnie Ferguson of Greenville, South Carolina, to Governor Olin D. Johnson.

18. DIBC, Stukes, interview, 1; DIBC, Burke, interview, 3.

19. DIBC, Stukes, interview.

20. For Pinewood as the destination: Charles Stinney, interview.

21. Stinney Papers, report by A. C. Bozard, M. D. and C. R. F. Baker, M. D., March 25, 1944. Bozard signed the document; Baker did not.

22. Ibid.

23. Mary Ellen Taylor Bilton, interview; DIBC, Burke, interview, 1.

24. John Hammond Moore, *Carnival of Blood: Dueling, Lynching, and Murder*

in South Carolina, 1880–1920 (University of South Carolina Press: Columbia, 2006), 210, and n. 13 on 211. Moore includes the instance of Bruce Tinsdale in 1941 among his listing of all known lynching victims in South Carolina between 1880 and 1947 but notes that this may have instead a case of "whitecapping," in which "a few individuals sought to teach the victim 'a lesson,' but he resisted so strenuously that he was killed." The circumstances of Tinsdale's murder do suggest that, rather than a lynching, this was instead an attack that resulted in homicide. The day following Stinney's execution, Charleston's *News and Courier* wrote in an editorial that the last lynching in South Carolina occurred in 1930; June 17, 1944, 4.

Chapter 4

1. Hearing 2014, Charles Stinney, videotaped testimony; and Charles Stinney, telephone interview with author. Amie Stinney's age derived from Census 1940, E.D. 43–3, 6B.

2. Determining the exact number of lynchings is fraught with difficulties, making a perfectly complete listing impossible; see the discussion in John Hammond Moore, *Carnival of Blood: Dueling, Lynching, and Murder in South Carolina* (Columbia: University of South Carolina Press, 20060, 54–55. A more recent calculation by the NAACP places the total between 1882 and 1968 at 4,743, of whom 72.7 percent were Black; cited by Charles M. Blow, "The Flag is Drenched with Our Blood," *New York Times*, September 28, 2017; Gunnar Myrdal, *An American Dilemma: The Negro Problem and Modern Democracy* (New York and London: Harper & Brothers Publishers, 1944), 560–61.

3. So terrible was death by burning that, prior to a Texas lynching in 1905, the intended victim pleaded to be shot or hanged rather than burned, but "nothing less than burning would satisfy his captors. . . ." *New York Times*, September 8, 1905, 6:1. Photography (including picture postcards) provides an incomparably vivid source of documentation for lynching. Many such images—primarily of African Americans but also of Whites, most in the South but also other parts of the country, and some with evidence of torture—have been reproduced in James Allen, Hilton Als, Congressman John Lewis and Leon Litwack, *Without Sanctuary: Lynching Photography in America* (n.p.: Twin Palms Publishers, 2000).

4. Terence Finnegan, *A Deed So Accursed: Lynching in Mississippi and South Carolina, 1881–1940* (Charlottesville and London: University of Virginia Press, 2013), 167–73; "Annual Message of Thomas G. McLeod Governor to the General Assembly of South Carolina, Regular Sessions Beginning January 11, 1927," in *Legislative Reports*, 1927, II, 17–19; Moore, *Carnival of Blood*, 209–11. Moore actually lists fifty-two, but on the basis of the information he provides, it would appear that three were not true lynchings, including the murder of Bruce Tinsdale in 1941, which is why he is not cited in the discussion here as the last lynching before 1944. The NAACP, on the other hand, did list Tinsdale as the victim of a lynching. Ibid, 75, 78–80.

5. The entire story of Claude Neal's lynching is recounted in James R. McGovern, *Anatomy of a Lynching: The Killing of Claude Neal* (Baton Rouge and

London: Louisiana State University Press, 1982). The account by an eyewitness, confirmed by others, is on page 80.

6. Jason Morgan Ward, *Hanging Bridge: Racial Violence and America's Civil Rights Century* (New York: Oxford University Press, 2016), 4.

7. Cited by Moore, *Carnival of Blood*, 63; Ray Stannard Baker, "What is Lynching?: A Study of Mob Justice, South and North. 1-Lynching in the South," *McClure's Magazine* 24 (January 1905), 306–7.

8. One Southerner wrote during the 1880s that, in order to assure that African Americans knew their place in southern society, "at times lynchings are planned and carried through not under the fierce compulsion of mob hysteria but by men who have calmly besieged themselves to the performance of a painful duty which according to their rights is necessary for the good of society." Cited by Vann R. Newkirk, *Lynching in North Carolina: A History, 1865–1941* (Jefferson, NC, and London: McFarland & Company, Inc., 2009), 9–10. In the case of the three members of the Lowman family in Aiken, South Carolina, in 1926, the White lawyer who defended them during their trial wrote to the NAACP's national office that, when they were about to be acquitted for murder, "the lynching scoundrels saw . . . that a verdict of NOT GUILTY was inevitable . . . and so when Court adjourned for the night, the trial to be resumed the next morning they got up their crowd and pulled this outrageous lynching . . ." Further, he wrote in a second letter, "It was pre-arranged, deliberately planned, and perfectly executed. Those who were on the inside, knew the jail, the proper keys to use, and where the prisoners were kept were in the mob and perhaps led it. My own opinion is that certain officials there delivered those poor prisoners over to the mob, there can be no doubt about that. . . . I have within the last day or so learned that the lynching had been planned for some several weeks. . . ." L. G. Southard to Walter White, October 8, October 13, 1926, NAACP Papers, case of Jim Davis, Part 8, Series A, reel 7, frames 840,841. For example, prior the the lynching by burning alive of Henry Lowry in 1921, a Memphis newspaper ran the following headline on its front page: "LYNCHING PARTY ON WAY TO ARK. TO PASS THROUGH MEMPHIS"; Negro Who Killed Two on Christmas Day Taken from Officers at Sardis, Mississippi." The paper then actually provided the route the lynchers would be taking with their victim to Arkansas. The headline in a subsequent issue of the paper read, "MAY LYNCH 3 NEGROES THIS EVENING. LOWRY NEARS TREE ON WHICH IT IS PLANNED TO HANG HIM: TAKEN THROUGH MEMPHIS TODAY. RUMORED OTHERS WILL DIE." Cited by Frank Shay, *Judge Lynch: His First Hundred Years* (New York: Ives Washburn, Inc. 1938), 172–74. Tuskeegee Institute News Clippings Fill, Reel 222, frame 562. Joel R. Williamson, "C.Vann Woodward and the Origins of a New Wisdom," in John Herbert Roper, ed., *C. Vann Woodward: A Southern Historian and His Critics* (Athens and London: University of Georgia, 1997), 218. See also Amy Luise Wood, *Lynching and Spectacle: Witnessing Racial Violence in America, 1890–1940* (Chapel Hill: University of North Carolina Press 2009).

9. Clarence H. Poe, "Lynching: A Southern View," *Atlantic Monthly* 93 (January 1904): 155, 161; Baker, "What is a Lynching?" 299, 311; Jessie Daniel Ames,

The Changing Character of Lynching: Review of Lynching, 1931–1941 (Atlanta: Commission on Interracial Cooperation, Inc. 1942), 13–14; Myrdal, *American Dilemma,* 597.

10. For examples, see Terrence Finnegan, *A Deed So Accursed: Lynching in Mississippi and South Carolina, 1881–1940* (University of Virginia Press, 2013); Tuskeegee Institute News Clippings File, Reel 222, frame 556; McGovern, *Anatomy of a Lynching,* 67; *The State,* July 7, 1938, 1.

11. Ben Robertson, *Red Hills and Cotton: An Upcountry Memory* (New York: Knopf, 1942), 7, 10, 12–13, 62, 82–84. For discussion of tensions along class lines within the White population see Dollard, *Caste and Class,* 76–77, 93–95; James C. Cobb, *The Most Southern Place on Earth: The Mississippi Delta and the Roots of Regional Identity* (Oxford University Press, Reprint Edition, 1994), 175–77; Myrdal, *American Dilemma,* 582. Among poor Whites, Myrdal included farm laborers, sharecroppers, the permanently unemployed, most textile workers, and unskilled laborers; Rick Bragg, *Ava's Man* (New York: Vintage Books, 2001), 90. Bragg knew firsthand the contempt of more fortunate Whites during his boyhood, as he recounted in two other memoirs: *All Over But the Shoutin'* (New York: Vintage Books, 1998), 55, 97–99, 104, 106–7, 119–20; and *The Prince of Frogtown* (New York: Alfred. A. Knopf, 2008), 128–29. Particularly harrowing is his description of how his first-grade teacher would not allow him to sit or read with children above his economic and social class.

12. Tom Watson of Georgia was in the forefront of the populist effort during the 1890s to create a political movement in the South uniting poor Whites and Blacks: "Watson appealed to the negroes to make common cause with the poor and lower middle class Whites," in "Why Was Frank Lynched?," *Forum* 56 (December 1916): 681. The effort by White populists to combine political forces with Blacks can best be followed in C. Vann Woodward, *Tom Watson: Agrarian Rebel* (New York: Rinehart & Co., 1938; republished by Beehive Press, 1973, and by Golden Springs Publishing, 2016).

13. Walter White, *Rope and Faggot: A Biography of Judge Lynch* (South Bend, IN: University of Notre Dame Press, 2002), 19, provides the following data for lynchings: 1890–1900, 1665; 1900–1910, 921; 1910–1920, 840, 1920–1927, 304; Arthur F. Raper, *The Tragedy of Lynching* (Chapel Hill: University of North Carolina Press, 1933), 47.

14. W. Cabell Bruce, "Lynch Law in the South," *North American Review* 155 (September 1892): 379–81; Thomas Nelson Page, *The Negro: The Southerner's Problem* (New York: Charles Scribner's Sons, 1904), 21–22, 27, 47–48, 80, 94–97; Clarence H. Poe, "Lynching: A Southern View," *Atlantic Monthly* 93 (January 1904): 159–161, 164–65; ROMA CATHOLIC, "When Lynching is Right," *New York Times,* August 30, 1903, 8; Henderson M. Sommerville, "Some Co-operating Causes of Negro Lynching," *North American Review* 177 (October 1903): 509–10.

15. "He Defends Lynch Law," *New York Times,* August 12, 1903, 9.

16. Ida B. Wells, *A Red Record: Tabulated Statistics and Alleged Causes of Lynchings in the United States, 1892–1893–1894* (Chicago: Donohue and Henneberry

[1894]), 20; Page, *Negro: Southerner's Problem*, 93; Raper, *Tragedy of Lynching*, 1; Shay, *Judge Lynch*, 8.

  17. Baker, "What is a Lynching," 312–213; Poe, "Lynching: A Southern View," 156.

  18. Poe, "Lynching: A Southern View, 156–57; J. Cardinal Gibbons, "Lynch Law: Its Causes and Remedy," *North American Review* 181 (October 1905): 507; Sommerville, "Some Co-operating Causes," 507–8; Page, "Lynching and Race Relations," 247–48.

  19. Percentages calculated on the basis of the numbers listed in Ames, *Changing Character of Lynching*, 11.

  20. Unitedmethodistwomen.org/news/lynching-is-an-indefensible-crime -jessie-daniel-ames, accessed July 13, 2019; Ames, *Changing Character of Lynching*, 1–2.

  21. Baker, "What is a Lynching?" 309. Newkirk, *Lynching in North Carolina*, 95–96, 126, describes North Carolina's efforts during the 1920s to curtail lynching because of fear that northern industrialists were "concerned about mob violence." In 1941, businessmen in one of North Carolina's counties sought, without success, to convince the NAACP to reclassify a lynching as a murder, as they were concerned that "a lynching would undermine their efforts to attract industry"; see also "Facts about Worth County Killing (May 28, 1920) in Tuskeegee Institute News Clipping File, Series II, Miscellaneous Files, 1899–1966, Reel 222, frame 549a–549b.

  22. Ames, *Changing Character of Lynching*, 12; Myrdal, *American Dilemma*, 566.

  23. DIBC, Stukes, interview, 1.

  24. DIBC, Interview with Lee Burke, March 23, 1983, 1–2.

  25. DIBC, Interview with Lee Burke, March 23, 2; 1.

  26. DIBC, Stukes, interview, 1, 3.

Chapter 5

  1. For the text selected by Pastor Batson; Herbert Brown, interview; DIBC, interview with Vermelle Tucker, March 23, 1983, 3.

  2. *Daily World* in Tuskegee University's Newspaper Lynching Collection, Reel 233, frame 7199. [The archivist mislabeled this with a date of July 23, 1944]; DIBC, interview with Lee Burke, March 23, 1983, 3.

  3. *Manning Times*, March 29, 1944, 1; https://www.findagrave.com/memorial /43346907/mary-emma-thames, accessed July 2, 2019.

  4. *Columbia Record*, March 30, 1944, Section Two, 88.

  5. *Summer Herald, March 30, 1944; Manning Times*, March 29, 1944,1; For the separate findings by the coroner's jury for the two murders, and the arrest warrant issued by Coronor C. M. Thigpen directing Sheriff James E. Gamble to apprehend Stinney, see Stinney Papers, March 29, 1944.

  6. McLeod became Solicitor of the Third Circuit in 1917 and was continuously reelected until he retired in 1954. For his reputation as an honest prosecutor, See

Shepard K. Nash, Mortimer M. Weinberg and William M. Reynolds, "Franklin Alexander McLeod," *South Carolina Law Quarterly* 10 (1957–58): 598–99. For the powers of the two courts, see 1942 {S.C.} Code of Law, 762.

7. *The State,* March 29, 1944, 4

8. For the documentation, see chapter 1, n. 2, supra.

9. *The State,* March 29, 1944, 4. For an example in actual practice, see a June 1910 statement on a loose sheet of paper on the letterhead of the Clerk of Court of Clarendon County inserted after page 240 in South Carolina State Archives, Criminal Journal, Clarendon County, 1905–16, 1924. "You shall well and truly try wether [*sic*] the Mental condition of the Prisoner at the Bar is such and whether he be now insane that he can understand the meaning of Punishment and a true verdict give accordingly to the evidence so help you God."

10. In the 1939 case, Judge Henry Johnson wrote to the governor on December 18 of that year that Frank Dash, Jr., convicted and sentenced to death for murder, had the mental ability of a six or eight-year-old child. However, the judge continued, "mere *mental weakness* will not exempt one from responsibility for his criminal acts . . . the test of sanity in this State is the ability to distinguish between right and wrong. . . ." South Carolina State Archives, Department of corrections, Execution Files, Folder 225; For Newman's education, Census 1940, E.D. 14–16, 19B; For Alcolu, Census 1940, E.D. 14–22, passim. Twenty-five (33.3 percent) had gone through the sixth grade or less; ten had completed the seventh grade (13.3 percent); and forty (53.3 percent) had gone past the seventh grade, ranging from one year of high school to, in one case (Pastor Batson), five in college; *Columbia Record,* June 6, 1944, 2; *The State,* June 11, 1944, 1 and June 15, 1944, 5; DIBC, Pratt interview, 2, DIBC Lee Burke interview, 3, and DIBC interview with Charles A. Plowden, March 18, 1983, 1,3.

11. *Manning Times,* April 5, 1944, 1.

12. Of the county's 31,500 people in 1940, roughly only a sixth of its inhabitants resided in its five incorporated towns and two unincorporated towns, which ranged in size from 210 in Foreston to 2,381 in Manning, the county seat. The remaining five-sixths of the county's population resided either in the countryside or in minute hamlets. See, South Carolina Research, Planning and Development Board, *General Statistics on South Carolina,* Pamphlet No. 12 (Columbia: n.p., 1948), 1, 4. 8–9, 10–11, 13; for the exclusion from urban ranking, see South Carolina Research, Planning and Development Board, *General Statistics, Pamphlet No. 12* (Columbia: n.p. 1948), 36; for the impact of the Santee-Cooper Waterways, see *Manning Times,* January 22, 1941 and Walter Edgar, ed., *The South Carolina Encyclopedia* (Columbia: University of South Carolina Press, 2006 and Sylvia H. Clark, *Shadows of the Past: An Illustrated History of Clarendon County, SC* (Donning Company Publishers: n.p. 2005), 122–25. For the economic conditions of tenant farmers and sharecroppers, see, for example, the vivid descriptions in Theodore Rosengarten, *All God's Dangers: The Life of Nate Shaw* (New York: Alfred A. Knopf, 1974).

13. The list of the grand jurors for 1944 spring term of the Court of General Sessions is in *Manning Times,* January 19, 1944, 1. Limitations and outright

mistakes in this newspaper list include incorrect addresses for several individuals, initials for first and middle names that were shared by other individuals with the same family names, and in one instance two individuals who shared the same complete name, George W. Burke. Both the newspaper and the census listed one juror, William J. Millsap of Gable as W. J. Millsay. The census also listed him as an African American although the 1920 census listed him as White as does the 1930 census. The eight jurors who could not be traced in the census are Danny Beard, W. H. Holliday, Jr, Thomas J. Jackson, Oscar P. Johnson, H. M. Pritchard, B. E. Richburg, D. J. Touchberry, and John T. Walker. The three identifiable jurors who were not farmers were James A. Creighton, the grocery store proprietor, in E.D. 14-5, 2B; H. Burgess Sprott, the drug store manager, in E.D. 14-11, 12B; and Hugh M. McCutcheon, the electrician, in E.D. 14-20, 7B.

14. The four farm owners were Robert L. Bagnal, E.D. 14-17, 16B; J. Raymond Broadway, E.D. 14-5, 6A; William J. Millsap, who had completed two years of college; and Eugene C. Walker, E.D. 14-22, 16B. John Elliot Childers of St. Paul Township, the superintendent of a farm, had completed the eighth grade, E.D. 14-26, 21A. P.C. Cochran, E.D. 14-14, 11B; Charles T. Ridgeway, E.D. 14-25, 7A; John W. Ridgeway, E.D. 14-30, 3A; and one of the two George Burkes, the older of whom managed a farm in Plowdon Mill Township and had completed two years of high school while the younger, a farm laborer, had finished seventh grade.

15. Stinney Papers.

16. Stinney Papers.

17. *Manning Times*, March 29, 1944, 1; and April 5, 1944, 1.

18. Ibid., April 26, 1944, 4.; Julian Weinberg interview.

19. South Carolina State Archives, Criminal Journal, Volume H, Clarendon County, 1905–16, 1924, 443–44; For Wideman's own description of his career, see *Manning Times*, August 16, 1944, 4. In this statement he identified the position of Magistrate as equivalent to that of Justice of the Peace. For a summary of his life, ibid, May 18, 1949, under "Deaths." In his 1940 attempt, Wideman received 653 votes, while his opponent trounced him with 1067, see *Manning Times*, August 28, 1940, 1.

20. At thirty-two years of age, Plowden was a graduate of The Citadel, South Carolina's revered military college, followed by the University of South Carolina's law school, although there is evidence that he did not relish a career as a lawyer. In addition to his membership at the bar, Plowden was a banker, having established the Bank of Summerton. He built a noteworthy career: he became chairman of the House Ways and Means Committee in 1950; a director of National Bank of South Carolina; the first director of the State Research, Planning and Development Board in 1951; and served again as Clarendon's representative in the House between 1972 and 1974. Two years later, South Carolina's governor appointed him to the state tax commission, on which he served until several months prior to his death in 1984. Most lastingly of all, he was credited with rewriting South Carolina's tax code. *Manning Times*, May 19, 1984, 1, 17; *The State*, May 5, 1984, C1. Plowden's opponent in 1942, and again in the Stinney case,

John G. Dinkins, served as mayor of Manning beginning in 1926 and as chairman of the county Democratic Party since 1924. See *Manning Times,* January 22, 1941, 1; May 12, 1966, 1. For the entirely of his long career in public life, see *Biographical Directory of the South Carolina Senate, 1776–1985,* 2 Vols. (Columbia: University of South Carolina Press, 1986, I, 395–96. In the race for the state senate in 1942, Dinkins defeated Plowden by a vote of 2,093 to 1,102, *Manning Times,* August 26, 1942.

21. DIBC, Burke, interview, 4.

22. DIBC, interview with Lt. James E. Gamble, May 6, 1983, 1.

23. Dr. Michael Biden, telephone communication, April 23, 2012; Dr. Robert H. Goldberg, J.D., M.D., Eduardo Martinez, telephone communication, May 9, 2012, and email communication, May 11, 2012; Dr. Mark L. Tall, Chief Medical Examiner of Rockland County, Pomona NY, and Clinical Associate Professor of Pathology, Mount Sinai School of Medicine, NYC, written communication, April 30, 2012; Dr. Cyril Wecht, telephone communication, April 2012; and Dr. Victor W. Weedn, M.D., J.D., email communication, April 23, 2012. For quote, Dr. Victor W. Weedn, email communication, April 23, 2012.

24. *Manning Times,* May 3, 1905, 5; Criminal Journal, Clarendon County, 1905–1916, 1924, 248049, 310.

25. See chapter 2, supra, for these reports about Stinney's behavior.

26. DIBC, Charles N. Plowden interview, 4.

27. South Carolina State Archives, Olin Johnston Papers, S544003, Pardons, Paroles, and Commutations, 1943–1945, Mary C. Preston to Governor Johnston, April 26, 1944; Julia Simpson to Governor Johnston, June 10, 1944; William Capore Jr. to Governor Johnston, June 10, 1944; Emily Moorer to Governor Johnston, June 10, 1944.

28. Dr. Robert Goldberg to the author, email letter, May 11, 2012.

29. *The State,* June 17, 1994, B7: "Stinney's sister, Catherine [*sic*] Robinson, said the fact that there was no blood on her brother's clothing proves he was innocent. She says while her brother was in jail he wrote his parents, telling them the same thing. . . ."

30. Lorraine Bailey in a radio broadcast entitled "George Stinney, Youngest Executed," June 30, 2004, https://storycorps.org/stories/george-stinney-youngest-executed/, accessed July 21, 2006; DIBC, interview with Lt. James F. Gamble, May 6, 1983, 1.

31. DIBC, Burke Interview, 3; DIBC, Stukes Interview 3; DIBC, Pratt Interview.

Chapter 6

1. For Stoll's service on the bench, see South Carolina Archives, Criminal Journal, Volume H, Clarendon County, 1905–16, 1924, 181–82, 189, 191, 197, 223, 224, 230, 260, 284, 326, 353, 355, 368, 410–11, 466–67; and Volume L, 1917–1918, 1925–35, 433, 440, 487, 514, 554. For his life, see *The State,* October 31, 1958, 6b and *Columbia Record,* October 30, 1958, 5D.

2. *Manning Times,* April 26, 1944, 1.

3. According to the *Sumter Daily Item*, April 25, 1944, 1, the trial commenced at 2:30; according to the *Manning Times*, April 26, 1944, 1, it began at 12:30. Both papers indicate that the proceedings spanned a single afternoon; for Stinney's location in the Sumter jail, see DIBC, Gamble interview, 1. There had been rumors shortly after the arrest that he had been taken to the state penitentiary in Columbia, where he would have been held in the classification "Safekeeping" to await his trial. See *News and Courier*, March 26, 1944, 1, *Sumter Daily Item*, April 25, 1944, 1, and *The State*, March 26, 1944. Ben G. Alderman may have helped cultivate this story, telling Lee Burke that "Pratt is carrying him to Columbia." DIBC, interview with Lee Burke, March 23, 1983, 2. On Stinney's isolation see Hearing 2014, Dr. Amanda Salas, psychologist, and expert witness, who testified that she met with and interviewed one Johnny Hunter, who claimed to have shared a cell in the Sumter jail with Stinney and to have had extensive conversations with him. Unfortunately, Hunter was not called as a witness and was thus not cross-examined, so there was no test of his veracity.

4. Clarendon County Archives, "Clarendon County, SC Courthouse- 1909" (2004); Sylvia H Clark, *Shadows of the Past: An Illustrated History of Clarendon County, SC* (Virginia Beach, VA: Donning Company Publishers, 2005), 95. The original blueprints are in the Clarendon County Archives in Manning.

5. The front window of the courtroom is preserved under indoor wooden shutters, its lime-green and gold panes glow in the sunlight that streams through them when a court attendant draws back the shutters; Gene Waddell and Rhodi Windsor Liscombe, *Robert Mills's Courthouses and Jails* (Easley, SC: Southern Historical Press, n.d.), 4, 43, 49.

6. William Burke, Jr interview, for the persistence of the prisoner's dock.; *Manning Times*, April 26, 1944, 1, for Stinney's clothing; DIBC, Lee Burke, interview, March 23, 1983, 3; *Manning Times*, April 26, 1944, 1.

7. *Sumter Daily Item*, April 25, 1944, 1; DIBC, S. J. Pratt, interview, March 26, 1983, 1; DIBC, W. N. Clarkson, interview, May 7, 1983; DIBC, Roston Stukes, interview, March 23, 1983, 2, who commented "Courtroom was segregated. Pretty fair bunch of black people at trial. . . . They just had a certain place where they'd sit." See also, *The State*, June 15, 1944, 5.

8. In old English criminal practice, BY GOD AND MY COUNTRY is the established formula of reply by a prisoner arraigned at the bar when asked, "Culprit, how wilt thou be tried?" The Law Dictionary Featuring Black's Law Dictionary Free Online Legal Directory, 2nd ed, https://thelawdictionary.org/by-god-and-my-country/, accessed July 19, 2019. See also, W. N. Clarkson interview, May 7, 1983, 1: "They asked him, 'How will you be tried?' "By God and my country" just like anybody else would have said. I guess his lawyer had told him what to say."

9. The entire list of thirty-six is in *Manning Times*, April 12, 1944, 1. The problems described in Chapter 4 that adversely affect identification of the grand jury's members apply to the voir dire panel. Twenty-three were farmers who owned their farms. In education, these men ranged from seventh grade through one year of college. Another seven were also farmers but did not own their farms. One, Charlton Coker was described in the census as a farm laborer who

had gone only as far as the sixth grade while the other six ranged in education from seventh grade through four years of high school. The remaining four members of the voir dire panel held nonrural occupations, including William N. Clarkson, the proprietor of a retail general store, who figures prominently in this chapter as he was foreman of the jury. For the dismissal of Alcolu residents, see Lee Burke, interview, March 23, 1983. In Burke's words, "they didn't let any of us from Alcolu be on it [the jury]. DIBC, Clarkson, interview, 1, 2.

10. The entire account of the trial proceedings that follows is based primarily upon the article in the *Manning Times*, April 26, 1944, 1, 4, which is the fullest contemporary reporting that exists. Supplementary material drawn from DIBC is cited as necessary.

11. The two alleged confessions were also reported by the *Sumter Herald*, April 27, 1944, 1.

12. In 1983, her name was Vermelle Tucker; DIBC, Vermelle Tucker interview, March 23, 1983, 1.

13. For Lowder's employment and age, see Census, 1940, E.D. 14–22, 3A; the *Columbia Record*, March 25, 1944, 1, attributed the discovery of the bodies to Donald Padgett and Francis Batson. For sixteen-year-old Francis Batson's account of discovering the two corpses, see the discussion in chapter 3.

14. DIBC, S. J. Pratt, interview, 2.

15. Pratt could not remember meeting with Governor Olin Johnston in the privacy of the governor's office or telling him at that time the details of how Stinney allegedly killed the two girls and sexually molested Betty June Binnicker, see DIBC, S. J. Pratt, interview, 4.

16. See *Columbia Record*, June 9, 1944, 2.

17. DIBC, Clarkson interview, 1. When Ruby Bates, one of the two alleged White rape victims in the notorious 1931 Scottsboro case began to retract her story accusing nine back youths of having raped her, for which eight had been condemned to death, she wrote: "I want to make a statement to you Mary Sanders is a goddam lie about those negros jassing me those police man made me tell a lie . . . I was jaze but those White boys jazzed me . . ." Cited in Dan T. Carter, *Scottsboro: A Tragedy of the American South* (London, Oxford, and New York: Oxford University Press, 1969), 186–87. See also James Baldwin, "If Black English Isn't a Language, What Is?," an essay on the OpEd page of the *New York Times*, September 25, 2010, in which Baldwin wrote "*Jazz* . . . is a very specific sexual term, as in *jazz me baby*, but White people purified it into the Jazz Age." DIBC, Clarkson, interview, 3.

18. DIBC, Burke, interview, 3.

19. While interviewing a group of Clarendon County leaders convened by Matt Evans, the county treasurer, the author asked how one would have best begun a career in local politics in the 1940s. One of the participants, herself an important local public servant, responded immediately, "go see the sheriff." In a separate interview, Sheriff Gamble's son listed the many duties of a county sheriff and this clarified why the position had such political importance. As the county's primary law officer, the sheriff was familiar with every corner and hiding

place in the county—and probably most of its secrets. He could do favors for moonshiners illegally distilling alcohol; he could let off juveniles guilty of minor offenses; and as tax collector, he could go easy on those who could not pay their assessments on time; for the reelection race, see *Manning Times*, July 12, 1944, 8; and August 16, 1944, 4.

20. *Columbia Record*, June 16, 1944, 1, 8; *Manning Times*, May 17, 1944, 1.

21. For Pratt's position as Chief Constable before he was replaced by Governor Johnston, see *The State*, June 27m 1942, 1. Thirty-nine years later, Pratt's interviewer jotted down that Pratt "went to Clarendon County at beginning of Governor Johnston's second term." DIBC, Pratt, interview, 1.

22. *News and Courier*, March 26 and March 30, 1944, both on 1; *The State*, March 26, 1944, 1; *Sumter Herald*, March 30, 1944, 1. According to Governor Olin Johnson, Pratt and Newman informed him when the met with him in his office that Stinney was perched on a coal chute when he saw the two girls enter the woods. He then followed them "with the intention of making love to the larger girl." This coal chute version has had long currency among some present and former Alcolu residents who describe the chute as standing adjacent to the railroad tracks. *The State*, June 10, 1944. [This is the only account in which Newman is described as having been present in the private meeting with Johnston.] For persistence of the coal chute story, see David Young interview.

23. For Newman's entire statement, see chapter 5; *News and Courier*, March 30, 1944; *The State*, March 26, 1944.

24. Pratt, interview, 2; Gamble, interview, 1.

25. Carter, *Scottsboro*, 214–15.

26. In January 2014, Katherine Stinney Robinson and her younger sister, Aime Ruffin, provided this information under oath during the hearing to reopen their brother's case with the hope of nullifying the verdict rendered in 1944. Hearing 2014: Testimony of Robinson and Ruffin; DIBC, Stukes interview, 1, 3.

27. DIBC, Charles Plowden, interview, March 18, 1983, 1, 3, 4. Unlike the other interviews in the Bruck collection of papers, this one was not transcribed. It is in handwritten form as notes taken by Bruck during the discussion with Plowden. The author consulted with Bruck by telephone and in a written communication in order to clarify what Plowden stated at several points; DIBC, Clarkson, interview, 3. The interviewer noted that Clarkson did not think the defense called any witnesses, thus providing verification of this significant feature of the trial.

28. DIBC, Plowden, interview, 2, 4.

29. Stinney Papers; Hearing 2014, testimony of Amie Ruffin.

30. Significantly, the prosecutor's list did not include any mention of bloodstained clothing or shoes, strongly suggesting that none of these things had been introduced into evidence.

31. DIBC, Clarkson, interview, 3.

32. DIBC, Clarkson, interview, 2; between November 2 and November 18, 1919, five separate juries convicted twelve African Americans accused of murder and insurrection in the Elaine, Arkansas riot cases, reaching their decisions after deliberating for eight minutes, seven minutes, nine minutes, six minutes,

and four minutes, respectively. Richard C. Cortner, *A Mob Intent on Death: The NAACP and the Arkansas Riot Cases* (Middletown, CT: Wesleyan University Press, 1988), 16–18. In one of the Scottsboro, Alabama, trials in 1933 the jury convicted two Black men for the capital offense of "assaulting with intent to ravish" after a seven minute deliberation; case of Alchrist Grant (alias Pompey) and Cyrus Pinckney, NAACP Papers, Part 8, Series B, Reel 24, frame 458.

33. Stinney Papers.

34. *Manning Times,* April 26, 1944, 1.

35. For the crowd's reportedly sober behavior, see *Manning Times,* April 26, 1944, 4; *Sumter Daily Item,* April 25, 1944, 1; DIBC, Pratt, interview, 4–5; DIBC, Gamble, interview, 1; DIBC, Plowden, interview, 2–3.

36. *Manning Times,* August 16, 1944, p. 4.

37. Ibid., April 13, 1967, p. 4.

38. South Carolina State Archives, State and District Officers of South Carolina–1943 [*sic*]–Secretary of State.

Chapter 7

1. South Carolina State Archives, Olin Johnston Papers, S544003, Pardons, Paroles, and Commutations, 1943–1945, for this body of source material. Cited hereafter as Johnston Pardons.

2. Both telegrams are preserved in Johnston Pardons. The parent organization's telegram was mentioned in *The State,* June 12, 1944, 2 and in the *News and Courier,* June 13, 1944, 1.

3. *The Crisis,* August 1944, 266; September 1944, 296–97. Like the other two telegrams, the one from Sumter is preserved in Johnston Pardons. It was signed by James T. McCain, Dr. Edwaard E. Jones, and Dr. B. T. Williams. For the Sumter NAACP meetings on March 26, April 23, and May 29, 1944, where Stinney's ordeal might have been discussed, see National Association for the Advancement of Colored People, Sumter Branch, Caroliniana Library, University of South Carolina, Manuscript Collection, 25–30. At the monthly meeting on June 25, 1944, nine days after the execution, the branch was once again silent.

4. *Congressional Record, Proceedings & Debates of the 78th Congress,* Appendix Volume 90- Part 8, January 10, 1944 to March 24, 1944, pp. 1036–37. The *Washington Post* went on to note that John Long had introduced the resolution and "received congratulations from many members after it had been adopted."

5. Judge William H. Hastie, "A Look at the NAACP," in *The Crisis,* September 1939, 263–264.

6. For a full account of this case, see Richard C. Cortner, *A Mob Intent on Death: The NAACP and the Arkansas Riot Cases* (Middletown, CT: Wesleyan University Press, 1988).

7. Case of Jim Davis: NAACP Papers, Part 8, Series A, reel 7, frames 818–90. These cases are discussed later in this chapter.

8. The Sammie Osborne case is in NAACP Papers (microfilm version), Part B, reel 10, frames 872–935.

9. NAACP Papers, Osborne case, frame 888.

10. The text of the petition to the US Supreme Court for a writ of certiorari is available in John E. Stansfield, *Osborne v. State of SC Supreme Court Transcript of Record with Supporting Pleadings* (Gale MOML Print Editions, n.p., n.d.). For the account of the three dollars Osborne gave to the chaplain, see *The State*, November 20, 1943.

11. Rev. J. A. De Laine to James Hinton, February 5, 1948; J. A. DeLaine to Roy Wilkins and the Board of Directors of the NAACP, November 28, 1961, both in Joseph A. De Laine Papers, University Libraries, University of South Carolina, South Carolina Library, Digital Collections. The 1948 letter is in http://digital .tel.sc.edu/cdm/ref/collection/jad/id/594; the 1961 letter is in http://digital.tel .sc.edu/cdm/compoundobject/collection/jad/id/320/rec/3, both accessed September 21, 2013.

12. *The State*, March 26, 1944, 1; *Columbia Record*, March 25, 1944, 1. John McCray, editor of the *Lighthouse and Informer* ceased publication in 1954. The newspaper's copies were disposed of as scrap paper; http://library.sc.edu/socar /mnscrpts/mccray.html, 1, accessed on September 24, 2013. Only a few issues are known to have survived in the collections of the South Caroliniana Library, University of South Carolina, but none of these were published during the spring of 1944. It is thus not possible to know whether Hinton learned about the case from its pages. For McCray's life and activities as an editor and civil rights champion, see Wim Roefs, "Leading the Civil Rights Vanguard in South Carolina: John McCray and the *Lighthouse and Informer, 1939–1954*," in Charles M. Payne and Adam Green, eds. *Time Longer than Rope: A Century of African American Activism, 1850–1950* (New York and London: New York University Press, 2003), e62–491. *Sumter Herald*, March 30, 1944, 1.

13. David I. Bruck, "Executing Teen-Age Killers Again: The 14-Year-Old Who, in Many Ways Was Too Small for the Chair," *Washington Post*, September 15, 1985. A copy is available in DIBC. DIBC, File 4, John MCray to David I. Bruck, May 19, 1981.

14. For a succinct account of the Connecticut case, see Daniel J. Sharfstein, "Saving the Race," http://www.legalaffairs.org/printerfriendly.msp?id=758, accessed on January 7, 2014. The South Carolina convictions were in the case of Alchrist Grant and Cyrus Pinckney, NAACP Papers, Part 8, Reel 24, frames 443ff.

15. Case of Benamin Haywood: Dr. W. H. Miller to Thurgood Marshall, May 10, 1940, NAACP Papers, Part 8 Series B, reel 6, frame 398. For other examples of these varied difficulties, see ibid. case of Jim Davis, Part 8, Series Aa, reel 7, frames 820–29, 875–76; case of Arthur Patterson and John Baker, Part 8, series B, reel 1, frames 473–475, 478–79; and the case of Alchrist Grant and Cyrus Pinckney, supra, frames 443, 504, 506, 517. These were all South Carolina cases.

16. *The Crisis*, June, 1939, 185; NAACP Papers, Haywood case; Thurgood Marshall to Chester K. Gillespie, June 7, 1940, frame 405.

17. *Columbia Record*, March 3, 1943, 1,2; February 14, 1; March 2, 1, and March 18, 1944, 1, 12. For Judge Waring's role in the case and his subsequent liberal rulings in salary equalization cases, see Richard Gergel, *Unexampled Courage: the Blinding of Sgt. Isaac Woodard and the Awakening of President Harry S. Truman*

and Judge J. Waties Waring (New York: Farrar, Straus and Giroux, 2019), 102–10. For an early appreciation of Waring among the African American community, see Carl T. Rowan, *South of Freedom* (New York: Alfred A. Knopf, 1952), 87–100. Rowan made clear not only the respect Waring commanded among the Black community but also the personal price he and his wife had to pay, causing them eventually to leave South Carolina.

18. *Columbia Record*, March 4, 1; March 8, 1; March 9, 1; March 14,1, 10; March 15, 1; March 16, 1, 8B; March 17, 1, 12; and March 21, 1944, 4.

19. John A. Kirk, "The NAACP Campaign for Teachers' Salary Equalization: African American Women Educators and the Early Civil Rights Struggle," *Journal of African American History*, 94, no. 4 (Fall 2009): 533.

20. *Columbia Record*, April 4, 1944, 10, for Smith's comment; April 15, 1944, 1, 14, for Johnston's. The Texas case was *Smith vs. Allwright*. See John Henry McCray Papers, Caroliniana Library, University of South Carolina, Manuscript Collections, dated Ca. Sept 1961, in which McCray recalled Governor Johnston saying of his scheme to negate the Supreme Court's decision through state legislative action, "Should this not be enough, then we have other resorts."

21. McCray wrote that Black leaders saw this as threatening violence.

22. *Columbia Record*, April 3, 1 for the Negro Citizens Committee and April 13, 1944, 2.

23. *Columbia Record*, May 10, 1; May 18, 1; May 24, 1; May 27, 1944, 1. For the history of the PDP, See Roefs, "Leading the civil rights Vanguard," 473–76.

24. McCray Papers, Call no. 1353, Roll 7, minutes of the meeting of May 24, 1944; MacCray to "Dear Fellow Citizens," June 12, 1944; McCray to Wm. L. Dawson, June 22, 1944; and McCray to a Mr. Bruce, June 22, 1944. For Hinton's statement and his pledge of funds, see McCray Papers, minutes of the meeting of May 24, 1944.

25. *Pittsburgh Courier*, June 24, 1944, 5. In Charleston, the *News and Courier*, June 13, 1944, 1, reported that the South Carolina NAACP had established a goal of 100,000 members.

26. Hinton to Wilkins, Febraury 26, 1944, NAACP Papers, Group II, Box A 570, folder captioned "SPEAKERS Roy Wilkins- South Carolina 1944055. Cited hereafter as NAACP Wilkins. Wilkins to Herman Anderson, July 8, 1944. "Although I travel considerably, I do not get into the South very much. I was in Georgia in the winter of 1941 and I was down South again last month in South Carolina. NAACP Papers, Group 11, F 15, folder captioned, "Wilkins, Roy Correspondence 1944–49.

27. Wilkins to Hinton, NAACP Wilkins, March 7, March 20, 1944; Hinton to Wilkins, ibid. June 6, 1944.

28. *The State*, June 12, 1944, 2. For additional coverage of the speech, see the *News and Courier*, June 13, 1944, 1 and the *Sumter Daily Item*, June 12, 1944, 2.

29. Wilkins to Hinton, NAACP Wilkins, June 13, 1944.

30. Cortner, *Mob Intent on Death*, 52. For the Arkansas case, see Thurgood Marshall to Walter White, February 2, 1941, http://americanradioworks.public

radio.org/features/marshall/lyons.html, accessed February 13, 2014. See also, Tushnet, *Making Civil Rights Law,* op.cit.

31. The National Office's publicity expertise had been on display ten years earlier, following the lynching of Claude Neal, when Walter White "telegrammed information to wire services, leading radio commentators, the editors of New York newspapers, the seventy NAACP branches, and the New York correspondent of the London *Herald,*" James R. McGovern, *Anatomy of a Lynching: The Killing of Claude Neal* (Baton Rouge: Louisiana State University, 1982), 118. The National Office also demonstrated its publicity knowhow when it attempted to build support for anti-lynching legislation pending in Congress during the 1930s. See Vann R. Newkirk, *Lynching in North Carolina: A History, 1865–1941* (Jefferson, NC: McFarland & Company, Inc., 2009), 121.

32. Hinton to Wilkins, NAACP Wilkins, June 14, 1944.

33. Wilkins to Miss Baker, June 13, 1944; Wilkins to the clerical staff, June 14, 1944; and Walter White to Wilkins, June 14, 1944, NAACP Papers, II, A, 612, folder captioned "Staff-Roy Wilkins General 1944." For the Watchtower essays, see *New York Amsterdam News,* June 17, 1944, 11 A; July 1, 1944, 11A.

34. *The Crisis,* September 1944, 296–297. For the quote see Tushnet, *Making Civil Rights Law,* 28–29.

35. Case of Alchrist Grant and Cyrus Pinckney, NAACP Papers, Part 8, Series B, reel 24, frames 433ff. The other major constitutional issue in this case was the exclusion of African Americans from service on grand juries and petit juries. The US Supreme Court had declared this unconstitutional in *Ex Parte Virginia* (1880, 100 US 339); and *Strauder vs. West Virginia* (1880, 100 US 303). However, an appeal on behalf of Stinney that included this argument would have had to demonstrate that Clarendon County barred Blacks not only from jury membership but also from inclusion in the pools from which members of juries were selected. In the absence of pertinent original sources, it is not possible to determine whether either applied.

36. David I. Bruck, "Executing Teen-Age Killers Again," *Washington Post,* September 15, 1985, D1.

Chapter 8

1. Miss Mary C. Preston (Charleston), April 26, 1944, Olin Johnston Papers, South Carolina Archives S5544003: Pardons, Paroles and Commutation, 2 boxes. Citations to the letters, telegrams and petitions to and from Johnston provide the name of the writer, the place from which she or he wrote, and the date of the communication. The largest, comprised of seven file folders, was in the case of Joe Frank Logue, discussed below. The correspondence in the Stinney case is in one folder by far the second largest. In bulk, it is about one-half of the Logue files. For the telegram, Bishop Emmet M. Walsh (Charleston), June 12; the letters, James M. Richardson (Greenville), June 12 and Mrs. J. Warren Cassidy (Patrick), undated.

2. M. Rosenfield (Florence), June 14; W. R. Barnes (Mullins), June 9, 1944.

3. The *Columbia Record*, February 26, 1944, 4, took note in an editorial that Logue was a policeman in Spartanburg when he committed his crime: "He was supposed to enforce the law, not break it;" South Carolina State Archives, Records of Prisoners Awaiting Execution, 1939–1962, Files 248, 249, 250. After a stay of his death sentence on an appeal that ultimately failed, Logue was scheduled for electrocution on February 25, 1944. Governor Johnston commuted his sentence to life imprisonment on February 24, 1944. Unlike the state's execution file, the author of a work about the case dates the commutation to February 25 and calls Logue by his full first name, Joe Frank. See, T. Felder Dorn, *The Guns of Meeting Street: A Southern Tragedy* (Columbia: University of South Carolina Press, 2001), passim, for a full account of the episode, including the details mentioned here. For Johnston's explanation for the commutation to life imprisonment: Johnston Papers, Pardons, Paroles and Commutations, Frank Logue, Folder l.

4. *The State*, June 11, 1944, 1. The State Pardon and Parole Board member recounted that, when he met with Stinney in his cell, "At first he denied killing the girls. . . ."

5. The South Carolina NAACP, for example, made this argument in its telegram to the governor on June 13: "By this execution South Carolina will lose prestige among states which have more enlightened methods of dealing with juvenile delinquents;" Jacob. S. Raisin, Rabbi of K. K. Beth Elohim (Charleston), June 10, 1944.

6. For example, the Interracial Committee of Winston Salem, North Carolina, wrote to the governor on June 15, citing "the universally recognized irresponsibility of children for their acts; James M. Richardson (Greenville), June 12, 1944.

7. For examples, see the communications sent to the governor by Elise Moore (Charleston), June 1; William L. Capon Jr. Acting Rector of St. Michael's Church (Charleston), June 10; Marguerite Sease (Greenville), June 13; J. M. Perry (Greenville), June 14; 500 War Workers of Morey Machinery (Astoria, NY), June 15; Maxwell I. Reiskind, chairman, Legislative Committee on behalf of the Executive Committee of the American Labor Party of Richmond County (NY), June 16, 1944. For excellent coverage of the Feltwell case, see Charleston's *News and Courier*, February 10, May 23, and June 1, 1944.

8. Waring's career can be followed in Tinsley E. Yarbrough, *A Passion for Justice: J. Waities Waring and Civil Rights* (New York and Oxford: Oxford University Press, 1987). For an appreciation of Waring by a prominent African American journalist, see Carl Rowan, *South of Freedom* (Baton Rouge and London: Louisiana State University Press, 1952), 83–100.

9. A plea to second-degree murder with the possibility of a sentence to life imprisonment was a strategy that George Stinney's attorneys cannot be faulted for failing to pursue. South Carolina, along with nine other states in the mid-twentieth century, did not provide for degrees of murder in its statues: Frank Brenner, "The Impulsive Murder and the Degree Device," 22 *Fordham Law Review* 3 (December 1953). The author is indebted to Barry Latzer for this

reference. The case can be followed in the *Columbia Record*, May 23, June 1, 1944; *Beaufort Gazette*, February 10, May 25, 1944; and for the fullest account, Charleston's *News and Courier*, February 10, May 23, June 1, 1944.

10. W. C. Wilbur (Charleston), June 12, 1944. The letterhead on Wilbur's stationery identified him as a real estate and insurance broker.

11. Adele Johnston Minahan (Columbia), June 14, 1944; Marguerite (Mrs. Ivens Christopher) Sease (Greenville), June 13, 1944; Mrs. Elizabeth F. MacLeod (Greenwood), June 12, 1944. For additional expressions regarding the impact of the impending Stinney execution on racial tensions, see also Miss Elizabeth W. Hard (Greenville), June 10; Mrs. Emily Moorer, June 10; and Elise Moore (Charleston), June 1, 1944.

12. Vivian Schlessel (Brooklyn, NY) undated; Home Owners Federation, Mrs. N.D. Davis, secretary (Cleveland, Ohio), June 15; Harry R. Arnold (Spartanburg), undated.

13. Major James D. Gardner Jr. (Fort Jackson, Columbia), June 13; Mrs. C. M. Hunt (no location given), June 12, Angus H. McGregor (Miami, Florida), June 13. McGregor identified himself as a former member of the American Prison Association and the National Council of Juvenile Agencies. The letterhead of his stationery states that he is an inventor, operating in a firm with associates.

14. To arrive at identifications, the 1940 census, self-descriptions in letters and telegrams, and inferences in some cases have been utilized. Some are known to have been White because they identified themselves as such: Major James O. Gardner, Jr; "a white lady"; Helen (Mrs. J. W.) Hammersmith; the remainder have been located in Census 1940. Two identified themselves as Black: Edward Pinckney (Aiken), June 16 and the Reverend Z. M. Matthews (Hartsville), June 12. The third, Reverend Andrew William Hill, Trinity First Baptist Church (Florence), June 12, is known to have been African American from Census 1940, ED 21–17, sheet 18B.

15. Kathryn Moye, a social worker and the secretary o the Charleston Inter-racial Committee; Ruth Gotjen, a stenographer; Virginia Nevelle, proprietor of a rooming house; Mrs. J. C. Adams, a packer in a cracker factory; Mrs. J. A. Raley, manager of a bakery; Mrs. C. L. Amich, waitress; Susan Pringle Frost, who owned a realty business; Miss Fay DeShields, a teacher; Miss Elizabeth W. McClean, a teacher; and Marjorie Patterson, a clerk. The men were C. Browning Smith, retired army officer; J. M. Perry, attorney; Huger Sinkler, attorney; Alison Lee, newspaper manager; George Murphy, farmer; Harold R. Arnold, radio engineer; W. L. Williams, professor of mathematics, University of South Carolina; William C. Wilbur, real estate and insurance; Frank Williams, ensign, US Navy; James O. Gardner, major, US Army; James M. Richardson, attorney and Recorder of the Greenville Municipal Court; and C. B. Barksdale, executive in an insurance company.

16. M. Wallace Fridy, Pastor, Lyman Methodist Church, June 9; Mrs. D. L. Johnson, June 13; Executive Board of the Women's Auxiliary of St. Philips Episcopal Church of Charleston, June 15. For St. Philips, see Walter Edgar, ed. *The South Carolina Encyclopedia* (Columbia: University of South Carolina Press,

2006), 829. Eliza Huger Kammerer, chairman [sic] of the Legislative Committee of the Civic Club, June 13. That this was an organization of women is apparent from its constitution.

17. *The NMU Fights Jim Crow* (n.p.: National Maritime Union, 1943), 2, 3, 10, 12. Ten percent of its members were African American, this publication claimed. In actuality, racism was a very difficult problem within the NMU, in part because of discrimination by shippers and shipowners. See Gerald Horne, *Red Seas: Ferdinand Smith and Black Sailors in the United States and Jamaica* (New York and London: New York University Press, 2005), 57–80. For the women's membership in the TWOC, see Jessie Kindig, *Moranda Smith* (1915–1950), https://www.black past.org/african-american-history/smith-moranda-1915-1950/, accessed February 15, 2019.

18. Frank Green, Tobacco Workers Organizing Committee, Charleston, June 9; E.E. Williams, Port Agent, NMU, Charleston, June 9, 1944. Josh Lawrence, Political Action Director, Port of New York, NMU, June 15; Ferdinand Smith, National Secretary, NMU, New York, June 15; Joseph Sweat, Director, NMU, New York, June 15; Gladys Lee, Chairman, Political Action Committee, NMU office, staff, June 16. A. J. Marcus, Chairman of Tobacco Workers Organizing Committee, CIO, Richmond, Virginia, June 15; William Deberry, International Rep TWOC, CIO, June 14, referring to "organized labor and interested citizens of Winston Salem; Frank Hargrove, Chairman, Tobacco Workers Organizing Committee, CIO, Winston Salem, June 14. Arthur E. Phillips, Secretary CIO Maritime Committee, Washington, DC. Phillips added that his organization represented 200,000 maritime workers involved in the war effort. Robbie Mae Riddick, President, Amalgamated Local 26, Suffolk, Virginia, June 14, claiming a potential membership of three thousand Black and White workers; Stanley Lefccourt, Shop Chairman, workers of the Paterson Fur Dressing Company, Paterson, New Jersey; John Vincovitch, Manager, International Fur and Leather Workers Union, Easton, Pennsylvania, June 15; "Management and Employees of Kenmore Fabrics, New York," June 15; "office staff of the United Electrical Radio & Machine Workers of America," UOPWA local 1227, June 15; "a group of young office girls, local 16, UOPWA, June 16; Charles Sherman, Chairman, Legislative Committee of Morey Machinery Vern, Washington CIO local 1227, June 15; Irwin A. Guttko, UERMWA 448, CIO, Union City, New Jersey, June 16; Stanley Lefcourt, Shop Chairman, workers of the Paterson Fur Dressing Company, Paterson, New Jersey, June 16; Maxwell I. Reiskind, Chairman, Legislative Committee, on behalf of the executive committee of the American Labor Party of Richmond County, West Newbrighton, New York, June 16, 1944.

19. M. A. Wright, President, South Carolina Interracial Commission, June 15, 1944. For the CIC movement in general, see Gunnar Myrdal, *An American Dilemma,*, 842–50; Morton Sosna, *In Search of the Silent South* (New York: Columbia University Press, 1977), 20–41; and from a critical perspective, Glenda Elizabeth Gilmore, *Defying Dixie: The Radical Roots of Civil Rights, 1919–1950* (New York and London: W. W. Norton & Company, 2008), 19, where Gilmore writes that the CIC "meant to make Jim Crow work more smoothly." For the CIC

particularly in South Carolina, see Carol Sears Botsch, "South Carolina Council on Human Relations," www.polisci.usca.edu/aasc/scchr.htm, accessed on February 19, 2019.

20. Rev. S. Anderson; Rev. R. E. Brogdon, Pastor of Emmanuel A.M.E. Church; Rev. F. Doctor; Rev. R. I. Lemon; Rev. J. W. Murphy; Rev. C. Rexford Raymond; Rev. Aaron Washington; and Rev. B. J. Whipper. Interdenominational Ministers Union of Charleston, June 8. The letter was signed by Rev. J. W. Curry, President, Rev. J. E. Beard, Chairman, Rev. R. I. Lemon, and Rev. C. S. Ledbetter, Secretary.

21. Charleston Ministers' Union, Rev. F. W. Brandt, President, Rev. R. Wright Spears, Secretary, June 5. For the quote, R. Wright Spears, Minister, Trinity Methodist Church (Charleston), June 10, 1944.

22. W. R. Pettigrew (Charleston), June 13, 1944.

23. Johnston to Miss Susan Pringle Frost (Charleston), June 2. Frost, a prominent figure in Charleston, had been an active suffragist and was a leader in efforts to preserve the city's historic homes (Edgar, *Encyclopedia*, 345–46). All of Johnston's letters to those who wrote to him or sent him telegrams are in the same location as their communications to him.

24. Johnston to Eliza Moore (Charleston), June 5, 9, 1944.

25. *Daily World*, n.d., Tuskegee Institute Clipping Files, Reel 223, frame 7199.

26. Johnston to Mr. E. E. Williams, Port Agent, National Maritime Union, Charleston, June 9, 1944.

27. *The State*, June 10, 1944.

28. Katherine Davis Cann, *Common Ties: A History of Textile Industrial Institute, Spartanburg Junior College & Spartanburg Methodist College* (Spartanburg, SC, Hub City Writers Project, 2007); John E. Huss, *Senator for the South: A Biography of Olin D. Johnston* (Garden City, NY: Doubleday and Company, 1961). Although an uncritical, hagiographic biography, this work spells out the broad outlines of Johnston's life and career.

29. Bryant Simon, *A Fabric of Defeat: The Politics of South Carolina Mill Hands, 1910–1948* (Chapel Hill and London: University of North Carolina Press, 1998), 57, 138.

30. Olin Dewitt Talmadge Johnston Papers, South Carolina Political Collections, University of South Carolina, Box 141, Folder: Johnston, Olin D., Campaigns 1938. Hereafter, Johnston Papers; Simon, *Fabric of Defeat*, 204–5.

31. For example, Johnston Papers, Box 120, Folder: 1938, June, July, radio speech at Florence, June 24, 1938; Huss, *Senator for the South*, 93–97.

32. This assessment of the 1941 campaign is based upon the coverage in *The State*, beginning on June 29 and ending on September 19, 1941. For comments within the newspaper about the campaign's placidity, see August 3, 7 (a "Quiet" campaign—"no major issues to provoke pros and cons"), August 15 (a "campaign that has been mild and free of 'mud slinging'"), August 30, September 3, 7.

33. Olin Johnston Papers, South Carolina State Archives, S544007, General Subjects File, 1943–1945, 3 boxes, Folder: Negro Question, passim.

34. *Columbia Record*, July 17, 1943. A separate column on the same page reported Senator Smith's announcement in Washington, DC.

35. *Columbia Record,* Juny 17, 1943; The *Herald Tribune* published its editorial on July 7, 1944, but it is cited here from its reprint in *New York Amsterdam News,* July 15, 1944.

36. Mary Carr, June 11, 1944. Miss F. W. Holmes, June 15, 1944.

Chapter 9

1. *Sumter Item,* November 3, 2013; David I. Bruck, "Executing Teen Killers Again," *Washington Post,* Sept 15, 1985; David Stout, *Carolina Skeletons* (1988, Mysterious Press, 1988.); "Carolina Skeletons," Tracy Keenan Wynn, teleplay, 1991; Albert French, *Billy* (Viking 1993, Penguin Books, reprint edition, 1995); Stephen King, *The Green Mile* (New American Library 1996) "The Green Mile," Castle Rock Entertainment, 1999); Christopher Hitchens, "Old Enough to Die," Vanity Fair, June 1999. Recent books and productions include: Frances Pollock, "Stinney," an opera; "83 Days," teleplay by Ray Brown, 83 Days Film Company (2018); Karyn Parsons, *How High the Moon* (Hachette Books, 2019); Kendall Bell, *Triple Tragedy in Alcolu: the Execution of 14-year-old George Stinney Jr accused of the murders of Betty June Binnicker and Mary Emma Thames* (Bella Rosa Books, 2020).

2. *The Item,* September 6, 2009, September 17, 2013.

3. *Post and Courier,* March 26, 2018. This newspaper ran a five part series on the Stinney case from March 25 to March 29, 2018, written by Deanna Pan and Jennifer Hawes.

4. For Amie Stinney's comment, see *The Item,* September 6, 2009 and *The State,* September 17, 2013.

5. *Clarendon Citizen,* December 4, December 16, 2013.

6. See, e.g., *The State,* January 21, 2014; *The Item,* January 22, 2014; For the choice of the "hail Mary pass" see *Post and Courier,* March 27, 2018.

7. *Post and Courier,* January 21, 2014; *The Item,* January 23, 2014.

8. *New York Times,* January 23, 2014; *Washington Times,* January 21, 2014.

9. The witnesses testimonies here and below are drawn directly from Judge Mullen's summation in her decision: *State of Carolina vs. George Stinney, Jr.,* December 16, 2014. For Finney cross-examination, see *Post and Courier,* January 21, 2014.

10. *The Item,* January 23, 2014; *New York Times,* January 23, 2014.

11. The list of the items that remained from trial records appear in Mullen decision, *State of Carolina vs. George Stinney, Jr;* see also, *The Item,* January 22, 2014.

12. *The State,* January 21, 2014.

13. *New York Times,* June 16, 2014; *People Magazine,* March 10, 2014; *The Item,* August 24, 2014.

14. *State of Carolina vs. George Stinney, Jr.,* December 16, 2014. For a discussion of how this case fits into the legal history of South Carolina death penalty cases for juveniles, see Sheri Lynn Johnson, John H. Blume, Hannah L. Freedman, "The Pre-Furman Juvenile Death Penalty in South Carolina: Young Black Life Was Cheap," *South Carolina Law Review* 331 (2017).

Bibliography

Primary Sources

MANUSCRIPT COLLECTIONS

Association of Southern Women for the Prevention of Lynching Papers, Microfilm

Beineke Library, Yale University, New Haven, CT
Walter White Papers

Clarendon County Archives and History Center, Manning, SC
Tax Book 1898
Jeffrey Black Collection, "Plat of Alcolu" (1902)
Clarenden Courthouse 1909 Blueprint
D. W. Alderman & Sons Company papers (uncatalogued)
Clarendon County Directory 1900

Oral History Archives at Columbia University
1957: The Reminiscenses of J. Waites Waring

Commission of/on Interracial Cooperation Papers, 1919–1944, Microfilm

Library of Congress, Washington, DC, NAACP Papers (Accessed in microfilm edition at the Schomburg Center for Research in Black Culture)
Cases of John Baker and Arthur Patterson, Part 8, Series B, Reel 1, 462–586
Case of Eugene Brunson, Part 8, Series A, Reel 15, 926–64
Case of Jim Davis, Part 8, Series A, Reel 7, 820–90
Cases of Alchrist Grant and Cyrus Pinckney, Part 8, Series B, Reel 24, 433–517
Case of Benjamin Haywood, Part 8, Series B, Reel 6, 316–54
Case of Sammie Osborne, Part 8, Series B, Reel 10, 872–935
Roy Wilkins Papers

South Caroliniana Library, University of South Carolina, Columbia, SC
David I. Bruck Research Files
Joseph A. DeLaine Papers
John Henry McCray Papers
National Association for the Advancement of Colored People, Sumter Branch, Manuscript Collection

South Carolina Political Collections, Hollings Special Collections Library, University of South Carolina, Columbia, SC
Governor Olin D. Johnston Papers (Olin Dewitt Talmadge Johnston Papers)
Modjeska Monteith Simkins Papers, 1909–1992

South Carolina State Archives, Columbia, SC
Campaign File, 1942–1944 (S544016)
Criminal Journal, Clarendon County, 1905–1918, 1924–1935
General Correspondence, 1942–1945
General Subjects File, 1943–1945 (S544007; 3 boxes)
Governor Olin D. Johnston Papers
Pardons, Paroles, and Commutations, 1943–1945 (S544003; 2 boxes) Pardons and Paroles, General Correspondence, 1943–1944 (S544014)
Records of Prisoners Awaiting Execution, 1939–1962, Files 248, 249, 250
Record of Executed Prisoners, 1939–1962
Year Book of the Department of Agriculture, Commerce and Industries of the State of South Carolina, 1928

Southern Regional Council Papers Microfilm, Digital Collections

Tuskegee Institute News Clippings File
Lynching File, Microfilm Reels, 221–233
Series II: Miscellaneous Files, 1899–1966

U.S. Congressional Record
Proceedings & Debates of the 78th Congress, Appendix Volume 90- Part 8, January 10, 1944, to March 24, 1944

Legal Cases
State of Carolina v. George Stinney, Jr. (December 16, 2014)
Briggs v. Elliott, 342 U.S. 350 (1952), consolidated with *Brown v. Board of Education of Topeka*, 347 U.S., 483 (1954)

Published Primary Sources

Ames, Jessie Daniel. *The Changing Character of Lynching: Review of Lynching, 1931–1941*. Atlanta, GA: Commission on Interracial Cooperation, Inc., 1942.
"Annual Report of the Board of Directors and Superintendents of the South Carolina Correctional Institutions for the Year Beginning July 1, 1943 and Ending June 30, 1944." In *Reports and Resolutions of the General Assembly of the State of South Carolina*, 32. np, 1945.
Baker, Ray Stannard. "What is Lynching? A Study of Mob Justice, South and North." *McClure's Magazine* 24 (January 1905): 306–7.
Batson, Francis. *Tell Us A Story, Please.* Np:, Np., Nd.
Bruce, W. Cabell. "Lynch Law in the South." *North American Review* 155 (September 1892): 379–81.
Commissioners for the State of South Carolina, 1903. Columbia: South Carolina State Company Printers, 1904.

Congressional Record, Proceedings & Debates of the 78th Congress, Appendix Volume 90- Part 8, January 10, 1944 to March 24, 1944.

Gibbons, J. Cardinal. "Lynch Law: Its Causes and Remedy." *North American Review* 181 (October 1905): 502–9.

Gresham, G. T. comp. *Clarendon County Directory 1900.* Greenville: Key & Thomas, 1900.

Hastie, Judge William H. "A Look at the NAACP." *The Crisis* (September 1939): 263–64.

Journal of the Senate of the General Assembly of the State of South Carolina, Being the Regular Session Beginning Tuesday, January 9, 1912. Columbia. SC: Gonzales and Bryan, 1912.

Marshall, Thurgood. "The Legal Attack to Secure Civil Rights." *NAACP Bulletin* (September 1944): np.

———. "Equal Justice Under Law." *The Crisis* (July 1939): 199–201.

McLeod, Thomas G. "Annual Message of Thomas G. McLeod Governor to the General Assembly of South Carolina, Regular Sessions Beginning January 11, 1927." *Legislative Reports* II (1927): 17–19.

National Emergency Council. *Report on Economic Conditions of the South.* Washington: US Government, 1938.

Page, Thomas Walker. "Lynching and Race Relations in the South." *North American Review* 206 (August 1917): 241–50.

Poe, Clarence H. "Lynching: A Southern View." *Atlantic Monthly* 93 (January 1904): 155–65.

Rand, McNally & Co. *Indexed County and Railroad Pocket Map of Shippers' Guide of North Carolina.* New York: Rand, McNally, 1887.

———. *Indexed County and Railroad Pocket Map and Shippers' Guide of South Carolina.* New York: Rand, McNally, 1892.

Smith, Ferdinand C. *The NMU Fights Jim Crow.* New York: National Maritime Union, 1943.

South Carolina Charleston Club. *Constitution of Civic Club of Charleston, South Carolina.* St. Louis: J. Furlong Printing House, 1909.

Railroad Commissioner of the State of South Carolina. *Twenty-fifth Annual Report the Railroad Commissioner of the State of South Carolina.* Columbia: South Carolina State Company Printers, 1915.

Sommerville, Henderson M. "Some Co-operating Causes of Negro Lynching." *North American Review* 177 (October 1903): 509–10.

South Carolina State Planning Board. *Towns of South Carolina. Pamphlet,* No. 8. Columbia: South Carolina State Company Printers, December 1942.

South Carolina State Planning Board. *Towns of South Carolina. Pamphlet No. 8 (Revised).* Columbia: South Carolina State Company Printers, December 1943.

South Carolina Research, Planning and Development Board. *General Statistics on South Carolina. Pamphlet,* No. 12. Columbia: South Carolina State Company Printers, June 1948.

South Carolina in 1884: A View of the Industrial Life of the State. Charleston: The News and Courier, 1884.

Stansfield, John E. *Osborne v. State of S.C., U.S. Supreme Court Transcript of Record with Supporting Pleadings.* N.p.: N.p., N.d.

Statement of Pardons, Paroles and Commutations Granted by Robert A. Cooper Governor of South Carolina 1920. Columbia: Gonzales and Bryan, 1921.

Watson, Tom. "Why Was Frank Lynched?" *Forum* 56 (December (1937): np.

PERIODICALS

American Lumberman
Atlantic Monthly
NAACP Bulletin
Northwestern Lumberman
Southern Lumberman
The Crisis
The Journal of the Southern Regional Council
The Southern Frontier

NEWSPAPERS

Atlanta Daily World
Baltimore Afro-American
Beaufort Gazette
Cleveland Call and Post
Chicago Defender
Clarendon Citizen
Columbia Record
Georgetown Times
Greenville Daily News
Los Angeles Sentinel
Manning Times
News and Courier (Charleston)
New York Amsterdam News
New York Times
Norfolk Journal and Guide
People Magazine
Philadelphia Tribune
Pittsburgh Courier
The People's Voice (New York)
Post and Courier
The State (Columbia)
Sumter Daily Item
Sumter Herald

MAPS

Alcolu Map: 1939/1941
Post Office Map: North and South Carolina 1900.
South Carolina Post Routes 1879.

U.S. Geological Survey: Camden South Carolina 1:100000-scale metric Topographic Map,1986.

U.S. Geological Survey: Sumter South Carolina, 1:1000000-scale Topographic Map, 1990.

Secondary Sources

Aba-Mecha, Barbara W. "South Carolina Conference of NAACP: Origins and Major Accomplishments, 1939–1954." *Proceedings of the South Carolina Historical Association, 1981* (1981): 1–21.

Alderman, Robert Lewis. *A Little History of the Village of Alcolu, South Carolina and the Story of its Founders Mr and Mrs David Wells Alderman.* N.p.: N.p., 2004.

Alexander, Raymond Pace. "The Upgrading of the Negro's Status by Supreme Court Decisions." *Journal of Negro History* 30 (1945): 117–49.

Allen, James et al. *Without Sanctuary: Lynching Photography in America.* Sante Fe: Twin Palms, 2000.

American Lumbermen. *American Lumberman: The Personal History and Public and Business Achievements of One Hundred Eminent Lumbermen of the United States.* Chicago, IL: American Lumberman, 1905–1906.

Arnesen, Eric. *Brotherhoods of Color: Black Railroad Workers and the Struggle for Equality.* Cambridge, MA: Harvard University Press, 2001.

Ayres, Edward L. *The Promise of the New South: Life After Reconstruction.* Oxford: Oxford University Press, 1992.

Bailey, N. Louise. *Biographic Directory of the South Carolina Senate, 1776–1985,* 2 Vols. Columbia: University of South Carolina Press, 1986.

Bass, Jack, and Marilyn W. Thompson. *Strom: The Complicated Personal and Political Life of Strom Thurmond.* New York: PublicAffairs, 2005.

Bell, Kendall. *Triple Tragedy in Alcolu: The Execution of 14-year-old George Stinney Jr accused of the murders of Betty June Binnicker and Mary Emma Thames.* Np: Bella Rosa, 2020.

Berglund, Abraham, George T. Starnes, and Frank T. De Vyver. *Labor in the Industrial South: A Survey of Wages and Living Conditions in Three Major Industries of the New Industrial South* Charlottesville: University of Virginia Institute for Research in the Social Sciences, 1930.

Biographical Directory of the South Carolina Senate, 1776–1985, 2 Vols. Columbia: University of South Carolina Press, 1986.

Boatner, Mark Mayo, III. *Encyclopedia of the American Revolution.* New York: David McKay, 1966.

Bond, Horace Mann, and Julia W. Bond. *The Star Creek Papers: Washington Parish and the Lynching of Jerome Wilson.* Athens: University of Georgia Press, 1997.

Botsch, Carol Sears. *South Carolina Council on Human Relations.* Np, Nd.

Boyle, Kevin. *Arc of Justice: A Saga of Race, Civil Rights, and Murder in the Jazz Age.* New York: Henry Holt, 2004.

Bragg, Rick. *All Over But the Shoutin'*. New York: Vintage, 1998.

———. *Ava's Man*. New York: Vintage, 2001.

———. *The Prince of Frogtown* New York: Knopf, 2008.

Brenner, Frank. "The Impulsive Murder and the Degree Device." *Fordham Law Review* 3 (December 1953): 22.

Brown, Nelson Courtland. *Logging Transportation: The Principles and Methods of Log Transportation in the US and Canada*. New York: John Wiley, 1936.

Bruck, David I. "Executing Teen-Age Killers Again." *Washington Post*, September 15, 1985: np.

Bryant, Ralph Clement. *Logging: The Principles and General Methods of Operation in the US*. New York: John Wiley, 1914.

Cann, Katherine Davis. *Common Ties: A History of Textile Industrial Institute, Spartanburg Junior College & Spartanburg Methodist College*. Spartanburg: Hub City Writers Project: 2007.

Carlton, David L. *Mill and Town in South Carolina, 1880–1920*. Baton Rouge: Louisiana State University Press, 1982.

Carter, Dan T. *Scottsboro: A Tragedy of the American South*. Oxford: Oxford University Press, 1969.

Carter, Jimmy. *An Hour Before Daylight: Memories of a Rural Boyhood*. New York: Simon & Schuster, 2001.

Cash, W.J. *The Mind of the South*. New York: Knopf, 1941.

Chudacoff, Howard P. *Children at Play: An American History*. New York: New York University Press, 2007.

Clark, Sylvia H. *Shadows of the Past: An Illustrated History of Clarendon County, South Carolina*. Virginia Beach: Donning, 2005.

Cobb, James C. *The Most Southern Place on Earth: The Mississippi Delta and the Roots of Regional Identity*. Oxford: Oxford University Press, 1992.

———. *The Selling of the South: The Southern Crusade for Industrial Development, 1936–1980*. Lexington: University Press of Kentucky, 1982.

Collier, John M. *The First Fifty Years of the Southern Pine Association, 1915–1965*. New Orleans: Southern Pine Association, 1965.

Cortner, Richard C. *A Mob Intent on Death: The NAACP and the Arkansas Riot Cases*. Middletown: Wesleyan University Press, 1988.

Cutler, James Elbert. *Lynch-Law: An Investigation into the History of Lynching in the United States*. Montclair: Patterson Smith, 1969.

Dinnerstein, Leonard. *The Leo Frank Case*. New York: Columbia University Press, 1968.

Dollard, John. *Caste and Class in a Southern Town*. New Haven, CT: Yale University Press, 1937.

Dorn, T. Felder. *The Guns of Meeting Street: A Southern Tragedy*. Columbia: University of South Carolina Press, 2001.

Drobney, Jeffrey A. *Lumbermen and Log Sawyers: Life, Labor, and Culture in the North Florida Timber Industry, 1830–1930*. Macon: Mercer University Press, 1997.

DuBose, Sonny. *The Road to Brown: The Leadership of a Soldier of the Cross, Reverend J. A. DeLaine: Recollections of Courage.* Chicago, IL: Williams, 2002.

Edgar, Walter, ed. *The South Carolina Encyclopedia.* Columbia: University of South Carolina Press, 2006.

Egerton, John. *Speak Now Against the Day: The Generation Before the Civil Rights Movement in the South.* New York: Knopf, 1994.

Fetters, Thomas. *Logging Railroads of South Carolina.* Forest Park: Heimburger House, 1990.

Fickle, James E. *The New South and the "New Competition": Trade Association Development in the Southern Pine Industry.* Champaign: University of Illinois Press, 1980.

Finnegan, Terence. *A Deed So Accursed: Lynching in Mississippi and South Carolina, 1881–1940.* Charlottesville: University of Virginia Press, 2013.

Flamming, Douglas. *Creating the Modern South: Millhands and Managers in Dalton, Georgia, 1884–1984.* Chapel Hill: University of North Carolina Press, 1992.

Foner, Philip S., and Roland L. Lewis, eds. *Black Workers: A Documentary History from Colonial Times to the Present.* Philadelphia: Temple University Press, 1989.

French, Albert. *Billy.* New York: Viking, 1993.

Gergel, Richard. *Unexampled Courage: The Blinding of Sgt. Isaac Woodard and the Awakening of President Harry S. Truman and Judge J. Waties Waring.* New York: Sarah Crichton, Farrar, Straus and Giroux, 2019.

Gilmore, Glenda Elizabeth. *Defying Dixie: The Radical Roots of Civil Rights, 1919–1950.* New York: W. W. Norton, 2008.

Green, Hardy. *The Company Town: The Industrial Edens and Satanic Mills That Shaped the American Economy.* New York: Basic Books, 2010.

Green, James. "The Brotherhood of Timber Workers, 1910–1913: A Radical Response to Industrial Capitalism in the Southern USA." *Past and Present* 60 (August 1973): 161–200.

Greenberg, Jack. *Crusaders in the Courts.* Cambridge: Cambridge University Press, 1994.

Hall, Jacquelyn Dowd. *Revolt Against Chivalry: Jesse Daniel Ames and the Women's Campaign Against Lynching.* New York: Columbia University Press, 1979.

Hall, Jacquelyn Dowd et al. *Like a Family: The Making of a Southern Cotton Mill World.* Chapel Hill: University of North Carolina Press, 1987.

Hanlon, Howard. *The Bull Hunchers: A Saga of the Three and a Half Centuries of Harvesting the Forest Crops of the Tidewater Low Country.* Parsons: McClain, 1970.

Hemenway, Robert E. *Zora Neale Hurston. A Literary Biography.* Champaign: University of Illinois Press, 1977.

Hitchens, Christopher. "Old Enough to Die." *Vanity Fair,* June 1999: np.

Herring, Harriet. *Passing of the Mill Village: Revolution in a Southern Institution.* Chapel Hill: University of North Carolina Press, 1949.

Horne, Gerald. *Red Seas: Ferdinand Smith and Black Sailors in the United States and Jamaica.* New York: New York University Press, 2005.

Hornsby, Benjamin F. *Stepping Stone to the Supreme Court: Clarendon County, South Carolina.* Columbia: South Carolina Department of Archives and History, 1992.

Howard, John C. *The Negro in the Lumber Industry: The Racial Policies of American Industry, Report No. 19.* Philadelphia: University of Pennsylvania Press, 1970.

Huss, John E. *Senator for the South: A Biography of Olin D. Johnston.* Garden City, NY: Doubleday, 1961.

Jensen, Vernon H. *Lumber and Labor.* New York: Farrar & Rinehart, 1945.

Johnson, James Weldon. *Along This Way: The Autobiography of James Weldon Johnson.* New York: Viking, 1933.

Johnson, Sheri Lynn, John H. Blume, and Hannah L. Freedman. "The Pre-Furman Juvenile Death Penalty in South Carolina: Young Black Life Was Cheap." *South Carolina Law Review* 68 (2017): 331.

Johnson, Tom. "Fragments of Fallen Flags: Railroads of Clarendon County, S.C. 1886–1940." N.p.: 2003.

Johnson, Charles S. *Growing Up in the Black Belt: Negro Youth in the Rural South.* Washington: American Council on Education, 1941.

Jones, William P. *The Tribe of Black Ulysses: African American Lumber Workers in the Jim Crow South.* Urbana: University of Illinois Press, 2005.

Kassin, Saul M. et al. "Police-Induced Confessions: Risk Factors and Recommendations." *Law and Human Behavior* 39, no. 1 (2010): 3–38.

Katznelson, Ira. *Fear Itself: The New Deal and Origins of Our Time.* New York: Liveright, 2013.

Kennedy, Stetson. *Southern Exposure.* Garden City, NY: Doubleday, 1946.

Key, V. O., Jr. *Southern Politics in State and Nation: A New Edition.* Knoxville: University of Tennessee Press, 1984.

King, Stephen. *The Green Mile.* New York: New American Library, 1996.

Kirby, Jack Temple. *Rural Worlds Lost: The American South, 1920.* Baton Rouge: Louisiana State University Press, 1987.

Kirk, John A. "The NAACP Campaign for Teachers' Salary Equalization: African American Women Educators and the Early Civil Rights Struggle." *Journal of African American History* 94, no. 4 (Fall 2009): 533.

Kluger, Richard. *Simple Justice: The History of Brown v Board of Education and Black America's Struggle for Equality.* New York: Knopf, 1977.

Korstad, Robert Rogers. *Civil Rights Unionism: Tobacco Workers and the Struggle for Democracy in the Mid-Twentieth Century South.* Chapel Hill: University of North Carolina Press, 2003.

Lembcke, Jerry and William M. Tattam. *One Union in Wood: A Political History of the International Woodworkers of America.* Pender Harbour: Harbour, 1984.

Litwack, Leon. *Trouble in Mind: Black Southerners in the Age of Jim Crow.* New York: Vintage, 1998.

Lochbaum, Julia Magruder. "The Word Made Flesh: The Desegregation Leadership of the Rev. J. A. Delaine." PhD diss., University of South Carolina, 1993.

Lowther, Eugene J., and Roland V. Murray. "Labor Requirements in Southern Pine Lumber Production." *Monthly Labor Review* (December 1946): N.p.

Maunder, Elwood R., et al. *James Greeley McGowin-South Alabama lumberman: The Recollections of his Family: Interviews with N. Floyd McGowin, Earl M. McGowin, and Nicholas S. McGowin.* Durham: Forest History Society, 1977.

McGovern, James R. *Anatomy of a Lynching: The Killing of Claude Neal.* Baton Rouge: Louisiana State University Press, 1982.

Mitchell, Broadus. *The Rise of Cotton Mills in the South.* New York: Da Capo, 1969.

—— and George Sinclair Mitchell. *The Industrial Revolution in the South.* New York: AMS, 1969.

Moore, John Hammond. *Carnival of Blood: Dueling, Lynching, and Murder in South Carolina, 1880–1920.* Columbia: University of South Carolina Press, 2006.

Moore, Toby. "Dismantling the South's Cotton Mill Village System." In *The Second Wave: Southern Industrialization from the 1940s to the 1970s,* edited by Philip Scranton, np. Athens: University of Georgia Press, 2001.

Myrdal, Gunnar. *An American Dilemma: The Negro Problem and Modern Democracy.* New York: Harper & Brothers, 1944.

Nash, Shepard K., Mortimer M. Weinberg, and William M. Reynolds. "Franklin Alexander McLeod." *South Carolina Law Quarterly* 10 (1957–58): 598–99.

National Emergency Council. *Report on Economic Conditions of the South.* Washington: US Government, 1938.

Newby, Idus A. *Black Carolinians: A History of Blacks in SC from 1895 to 1968.* Columbia: South Carolinian Tricentennial Commission, 1973.

——. *Jim Crow's Defense: Anti-Negro Thought in America, 1900–1930.* Baton Rouge: Louisiana State University Press, 1965.

Newkirk, Vann R. *Lynching in North Carolina: A History, 1865–1941.* Jefferson: McFarland, 2009.

Norgren, Paul. "Negro Labor and Its Problems: A Research Memorandum Prepared Under the Direction of Paul H. Norgren." N.p.: New York, 1940. Listed also as "Carnegie-Myrdal study. The Negro in America. Research Memorandum for use in the preparation of Dr. Gunnar Myrdal's "An American Dilemma." New York, 1940.

Odum, Howard W. *Race and Rumors of Race: The American South in the Early 1940s.* Chapel Hill: University of North Carolina Press, 2011.

——. *Rainbow 'Round my Shoulder: The Blues Trail of Black Ulysses.* Indianapolis: Bobbs-Merrill, 1928.

Oney, Steve. *And the Dead Shall Rise: The Murder of Mary Phagan and the Lynching of Leo Frank.* New York: Pantheon Books, 2003.

Orvin, Virginia Kirkland Galluchat. *History of Clarendon County, 1700–1961.* Manning: Publisher not identified, 1961.

Page, Thomas Nelson. *The Negro: The Southerner's Problem.* New York: Scribner's, 1904.

Parker, William Alderman. *Aldermans in America.* Raleigh: Edwards & Broughton, 1957.

Parsons, Karyn. *How High the Moon*. New York: Hachette, 2019.

Paulk, Earl P. *Execution of Six Men*. Fifth Edition. N.p.: N.p., 1952.

Pierrepoint, Albert. *Executioner: Pierrepoint*. Great Britain: George G. Harrap, 1974.

Plowden, Jesse Samuels. *History of Descendants of Edward Plowden I in America*. N.p.: N.p., 1937.

Quint, Howard H. *Profile in Black and White: A Frank Portrait of South Carolina*. Washington: Public Affairs, 1958.

Rankin, Hugh F. *Francis Marion: The Swamp Fox*. New York: Crowell, 1973.

Raper, Arthur F. *The Tragedy of Lynching*. Chapel Hill: University of North Carolina Press, 1933.

Reed, Linda. *Simple Decency and Common Sense: The Southern Conference Movement, 1938–1963*. Published by Author, 1952. Reprint: Bloomington: Indiana University Press, 1994.

Richards, Miles E. *Osceola McKaine and the Struggle for Black Civil Rights, 1917–1946*. Columbia: University of South Carolina Press, 1994.

Robbins, William G. *Lumberjacks and Legislators: Political Economy of the US Lumber Industry, 1890–1941*. College Station: Texas A&M University Press, 1982.

Robertson, Ben. *Red Hills and Cotton: An Upcountry Memory*. New York: Knopf, 1942.

Roefs, William. "Leading the Civil Rights Vanguard in South Carolina: John McCray and the Lighthouse and Informer, 1939–1954." In *Time Longer than Rope: A Century of African American Activism, 1850–1950*, edited by Charles M. Payne and Adam Green, np. New York: New York University Press, 2003.

Roper, Herbert, ed. *C. Vann Woodward: A Southern Historian and His Critics*. Athens: University of Georgia Press, 1997.

Rosengarten, Theodore. *All God's Dangers: The Life of Nate Shaw*. New York: Knopf, 1974.

Rowan, Carl T. *South of Freedom*. New York: Knopf, 1952.

Scranton, Philip, ed. *The Second Wave: Southern Industrialization from the 1940s to the 1970s*. Athens: University of Georgia Press, 2001.

Sharfstein, Daniel J. "Saving the Race." *Legal Affairs* (March–April 2005): N.p.

Shay, Frank. *Judge Lynch: His First Hundred Years*. New York: Ives Washburn, 1938.

Shuler, Rita Y. *Carolina Crimes: Case Files of a Forensic Photographer*. Charleston. SC: History Press, 2006.

Simon, Bryant. *A Fabric of Defeat: The Politics of South Carolina Millhands, 1910–1948*. Chapel Hill: University of North Carolina Press, 1998.

Smith, Lillian. *Strange Fruit*. New York: Reynal & Hitchcock, 1944.

Sokol, Jason. *There Goes My Everything: White Southerners in the Age of Civil Rights, 1945–1975*. New York: Vintage, 2007.

Sosna, Morton. *In Search of the Silent Souths: Southern Liberals and Race Issue*. New York: Columbia University Press, 1977.

South Carolina in 1884. A View of the Industrial Life of the State. A Brilliant Showing 1880–84. Charleston: News and Courier, 1884.

Stockley, Grif. *Blood in Their Eyes: The Elaine Race Massacres of 1919*. Fayetteville: University of Arkansas Press, 2001.

Stout, David. "A Life for a Life, Even at Age 14." *The Sunday Record* (March 28, 1982): N.p.

———. *Carolina Skeletons*. New York: Mysterious Press, 1988.

Sullivan, Patricia. *Lift Every Voice: The NAACP and the Making of the Civil Rights Movement*. New York: New Press, 2010.

Theoharis, Jeanne. *The Rebellious Life of Mrs. Rosa Parks*. Boston: Beacon, 2013.

Tindall, George. *The Emergence of the New South, 1913–1945*. Baton Rouge: Louisiana State University Press, 1967.

Tippett, Thomas. *When Southern Labor Stirs*. New York: Jonathan Cape & Harrison Smith, 1931.

Tolnay, Stewart E. *The Bottom Rung: African American Family Life on Southern Farms*. Urbana: University of Illinois Press, 1999.

Tushnet, Mark V. *Making Civil Rights Law: Thurgood Marshall and the Supreme Court, 1936–1961*. Oxford: Oxford University Press, 1994.

Waddell, Gene, and Rhodri Windsor Liscombe. *Robert Mills's Courthouses and Jails*. Easley: Southern Historical, 1981.

Waldrep, G. C. *Southern Workers and the Search for Community: Spartanburg County, South Carolina*. Urbana: University of Illinois Press, 2000.

Ward, Jason Morgan. *Hanging Bridge: Racial Violence and America's Civil Rights Century*. New York: Oxford University Press, 2016.

Wells, Ida. B. *A Red Record: Tabulated Statistics and Alleged Causes of Lynchings in the United States, 1892–1893–1894*. Chicago: Donohue & Hennesberry, 1894.

———. *Southern Horrors. Lynch Law In All Its Phases*. New York: New York Age Print, 1892.

White, Walter. *Rope and Faggot: A Biography of Judge Lynch*. New York: Knopf, 1929.

Wilkins, Roy, with Tom Mathews. *Standing Fast: The Autobiography of Roy Wilkins*. New York: Viking, 1982.

Williams, Juan. *Thurgood Marshall: American Revolutionary*. New York: Times Books, 1998.

Williamson, Joel R. "C. Vann Woodward and the Origins of a New Wisdom." In *C. Vann Woodward: A Southern Historian and His Critics*, edited by John Herbert Roper, 203. Athens: University of Georgia Press, 1997.

Wood, Amy Louise. *Lynching and Spectacle: Witnessing Racial Violence in America, 1890 1940*. Chapel Hill: University of North Carolina Press, 2009.

Woods, Barbara A. "Modjeska Simkins and the SC Conference of the NAACP, 1939–1957." In *Women in the Civil Rights Movement: Trailblazers and Torchbeareres, 1941–1965*, edited by Vicki L. Crawford et al., np. Bloomington: Indiana University Press, 1993.

Woodson, Carter G. *The Rural Negro*. Chicago: Association for the Study of Negro Life & History, 1930.

Woodward, C. Vann. *Origins of the New South: 1877–1913.* Baton Rouge: Louisiana State University Press, 1957.

———. *Tom Watson: Agrarian Rebel.* New York: Rinehart, 1938.

Woodward, Kenneth L. *Getting Religion: Faith Culture and Politics, from the Age of Eisenhower to the Era of Obama.* New York: Convergent, 2016.

Wright, Gavin. *Old South, New South: Revolutions in the Southern Economy since the Civil War.* Baton Rouge: Louisiana State University Press, 1985.

Wright, Richard. *Black Boy (American Hunger).* New York: Library of America, 1991.

Yarbrough, Tinsley E. *A Passion for Justice: J. Waties Waring and Civil Rights.* New York, Oxford: Oxford University Press, 1987.

Zieger, Robert H., ed. *Organized Labor in the Twentieth-Century South.* Knoxville: University of Tennessee Press, 1991.

Index